PERFORMANCE MEASURES FOR GROWING BUSINESSES

A Practical Guide to Small Business Management

PERFORMANCE MEASURES FOR GROWING BUSINESSES

A Practical Guide to Small Business Management

Stahrl W. Edmunds

Dean, Graduate School of Administration
University of California, Riverside

VNR VAN NOSTRAND REINHOLD COMPANY
NEW YORK   CINCINNATI   TORONTO   LONDON   MELBOURNE

Van Nostrand Reinhold Company Regional Offices:
New York   Cincinnati

Van Nostrand Reinhold Company International Offices:
London   Toronto   Melbourne

Copyright © 1982 by Van Nostrand Reinhold Company

Library of Congress Catalog Card Number: 81-7575
ISBN: 0-442-22605-5

Manufactured in the United States of America

Published by Van Nostrand Reinhold Company
135 West 50th Street, New York, N.Y. 10020

Published simultaneously in Canada by Van Nostrand Reinhold Ltd.

15 14 13 12 11 10 9 8 7 6 5 4 3 2 1

Library of Congress Cataloging in Publication Data

Edmunds, Stahrl.
  Performance measures for growing businesses.

  Includes index.
  1. Small business—Management.   2.   Small business
—Evaluation.   I.   Title.
HD62.7.E34   658′.022   81-7575
ISBN   0-442-22605-5   AACR2

Preface

Small business is more dynamic than large business in terms of earnings on assets, innovation, new job creation, and generating economic growth. Yet small business's share of the economy is slipping. Two types of actions are needed to re-invigorate small business to the role it deserves. The first is *political*—to remove the barriers that exist for small business in the form of tax discrimination, access to capital, and unfair competition. The second is *managerial*—to strengthen further the considerable management capability of small business by providing a feedback mechanism to give small companies the same control mechanisms as larger companies.

Performance Measures for Growing Businesses is addressed to the second task, to provide performance measures that help all small businessmen to improve their feedback control loop, so they know early what corrective actions to take for successful operations. The performance measures in this book are fairly simple to understand and use, although, as with everything, a little practice and effort are needed to do well. With patience, however, performance measurement becomes a habit and the results are better profits. By raising profits and earnings differentials still higher for small over large business, incentives are created to remove the other barriers and to establish for small business the expanded economic role in American life it deserves.

Stahrl W. Edmunds
Riverside, California

Contents

1

Total Performance Measures—The Survival Index

Most small businessmen learn to be better managers than large business executives. They have to be. Small businessmen have all the problems of a larger business—marketing, finance, product improvement, staffing, personnel development, etc.—which they have to do themselves without a staff and with fewer resources. So small businessmen have to be good; it pays off because the earnings on assets for small business are higher than for large businesses in every industry and every size-class.

But how does a small businessman learn to manage and get so good? That is the problem. People can learn something about management in business schools or by working for someone else, but in the last analysis they learn to manage by themselves through trial and error. In this trial-and-error process, some small businessmen fail and never make it. They do not survive because they cannot learn quickly enough where their errors are and how to correct them.

Suppose we are building a brick wall for the first time in the backyard for the patio, and we want to learn to do it right. What would we do? We would string a straight line across the base of the wall to measure its horizontal accuracy, hang a plumb line from above to measure its verticle accuracy, and use a level or bubble gauge to be sure each row was even.

Yes, we would measure our performance and correct for errors as we go. That way we could learn or teach ourselves to build a straight brick wall.

The management of a small business can be learned in the same way, by measuring your performance and making corrections. Good management requires feedback. Learning anything requires feedback, whether it is by biorhythms, tests in school, or on-the-job training.

Okay, so the toughest job of a small businessman is getting his whole act together, that is, making all the parts work in harmony—purchasing, marketing, locating, promoting, advertising, budgeting, accounting, financing, hiring, training, organizing, and so forth. To learn that difficult art of management coordination, the small businessman must have feedback measures to check and correct his performance. Otherwise he can make a mistake and not even know it until failure looms and it is too late. Some of the causes of failure among small businesses are: the lack of easily usable performance measures, feedback, and correction and not learning quickly enough to do the management job right the first time, or at least the second, because there are usually not enough resources in a small business for many mistakes or much of a margin of error.

What this book provides are some simple-to-use performance measures which will enable the small businessman to measure his own performance, make corrections, survive, and succeed. Moreover, this measurement and feedback approach to management success is developed by easy-to-follow methods which are structured in a way to test logically every part of the business, from total performance to cash flow, marketing, budgeting, costs, finances, and all the rest. To keep the feedback process simple, sometimes these measures are rather rough; expert managers in the field from large corporations or academia may say that they are not precise enough and need to be improved. But these measures can be improved upon only after they have been learned and used. Fine houses (often built better than they are today) were built a century ago with crude tools and crude gauges. Craftsmanship is what is to be learned, the craft of managing, and not to be measurement technicians.

All right, then, what are we trying to do? We are trying to learn the difficult art of managing a small business quickly enough to survive by means of measurement and feedback. We learn it by doing, managing, measuring, and correcting. This approach will take some effort to collect a few numbers from your business and occasionally to look up figures in a reference on the performance of other companies. That is part of learning to manage by doing. Most of the reference measures are contained within the book. If not, a reference to a source is given. So it is not hard to do. You merely accustom yourself to the discipline of checking upon how you are doing and making corrections as you go. You are learning the art of management by exception for the entire range of your enterprise. That is, when performance gets out of line (the exception), you correct it.

The approach of this book (i.e., performance measurement, feedback, and management by exception) is fairly unique in the small business literature. There are many good books on small business management, including academic texts on concepts and methods of management, how-to-do-it books on starting or financing a small business, or the excellent books by the Small Business Administration (SBA) on functions of management such as marketing and finance by fields of business such as retailing or service firms. These are all excellent references for the small businessman.

However, the unique aspect of this book is that it provides you with an operational means to check and improve your own performance as you go; this all-important, self-correction feature is not something you will find in other books.

We will start with measures to gauge the overall health of your business. If there are problems, they will generally show up early in overall sales or earnings performance, and we can begin diagnosing the difficulties by more specific measures from there.

STRATEGIC PLANNING MEASURES FOR YOUR BUSINESS

Most firms, large and small, try to develop a strategy or plan which gives them an increasing market share of a profitable product. That is a measure of success, increasing market share and high profits. A first look at your performance, then, might be in these strategic planning terms; you can make a first appraisal subjectively with better measurement later. For example, take the market share and earnings (or impressions of them) and plot them in the appropriate square of Table 1-1.

The purpose of Table 1-1 is to give an overall feeling of the kind of game and in which ballpark you are playing. You can tell where your small business belongs on the earnings scale by looking up your earnings in Tables 1-5 and 1-6. You can find your market share by

Table 1-1. Measures of a Strategic Plan.

	EARNINGS ON ASSETS	
	HIGH	LOW
Market Share		
High	I Winner	II Contender
Low	III Milk Cow	IV Loser

dividing your own sales by the total for your industry class (known as SIC or standard industrial classification code) in *County Business Patterns,* a publication of the Census Bureau, which you will find in most libraries.

For the time being, however, do it the simple way. Merely mark down your impression of where your business belongs on the scale of earnings from high to low, and on market share from high to low. For example, among big businesses, IBM's computer business would clearly go into quadrant I as a winner with high earnings and high market share, Texas Instrument's hand-held electronic calculators would go in quadrant II where they are contending for higher market shares against a flood of competition which keeps earnings low, the U.S. steel industry would go in quadrant III where their market share is falling due to foreign competition but the "trigger price" mechanism (which holds up the domestic price against foreign price cutting) helps provide reasonable profits, and the large U.S. automobiles would go into section IV because they are losing both market share and profitability due to gasoline shortages and foreign competition of small cars with high gas mileage.

Your management strategy is, then, determined in part by where your firm or products stand in Table 1-1. What you do as a manager is dependent upon what you can do to influence the interactions of your market share with earnings. The strategy for each case in Table 1-1 should be examined.

Case I. High earnings and high market share.

This combination is a winner, what every businessman is looking for. If you are already in this position, you already are an outstanding manager and your only problem is to stay there. Your strategy would be to reinvest a portion of your high earnings constantly to improve your product and promotion while keeping your customers well served and satisfied at profitable prices. In other words, your strategy would be to keep ahead of competition and keep profits high.

Case II. High market share with low earnings.

This combination reflects a highly competitive field in which you have to be a contender to win a stronger place with higher earnings. This condition usually exists in the growth stage of a new product cycle. That means you must have satisfied and repeat customers who stay with you during competitive price cuts and promotion blitzes by other contenders in the field. Your strategy is to create such loyal customers that they stay with you as buyers at fair prices despite discounts or marketing campaigns by others to woo them away. That kind of brand or product loyalty usually is the result of superior quality, better service, or advertising recognition. Your strategy then is to out-compete the field by better quality, service, product performance, or consumer recognition, which means you have to spend money on product or market development. After doing that successfully, you would then try to maintain a fair price, increase sales volume, and improve your earnings. This strategy is one of an effective competitor.

Case III. High earnings with low market share.

This condition usually exists with mature products at the end of a product cycle, in which there are few innovations and the product is fairly well standardized and open to competition. In such conditions, as in the steel industry, the entrenched companies in the field with large investments will continue to make profits, even with declining market shares because of foreign competition, because there is a demand in the market for their existing capacity. But profits may be too low to make new investments attractive to build new production capacity, because foreign or other competitors can already handle the incremental demand more cheaply. The strategy in this case is to milk the existing investment for what you can get out of it (which is why the strategy is called the milk cow), and then reinvest the earnings in some other, more reward-ing product lines. This is exactly what the steel industry in the U.S. has been doing in recent years.

Case IV. Low market share and low earnings.

This situation is a real loser because the market is not there and there are no earnings to develop it. The strategy in this case is to get out in time and find some other product line. This is what the U.S. automakers are doing with large gas-guzzling auto-mobiles. They are shifting to the production of smaller, gas-efficient automobiles to compete with the foreign imports. The conditions leading to Case IV problems usually occur with an old and mature product line facing changing conditions, or they occur in new enterprises when the market is very small, nonexistent, or has poor growth characteristics. Measurement can help you recognize the problem and develop a strategy to get out as quickly and with as little loss as possible.

USING A STRATEGIC SENSE TO SURVIVE AND SUCCEED

The previous section has shown us that a successful small business manager has to have some measure of his market performance and earnings to develop a workable strategy for dealing with his external environment and focusing his internal efforts. Indeed, Table 1-1 gives us some good guidance as to what we are looking for in small business, what our goals and strategy should be. For example:

Avoid the Case IV type of businesses with low market share and low earnings. Stay away from the losers.

Enter the Case III type of business of mature product lines with high earnings but low market shares only under two conditions: (1) if you have a much more efficient and low-cost production facility to undercut market prices and still make money, or (2) if you have a product improvement which would give you a better market share. Otherwise stay out of this kind of business.

Enter the Case II type of business with low earnings and high market shares if you are an outstanding marketer and a strong com-petitor who can build up customer loyalty through product quality, service, or better selling.

We all want to be in the Case I type of business with high market shares and high earnings, but these situations are hard to find, except by invention and innovation—which is, after all, the forte of small business entrepreneurs.

Now let us take all these different strategic cases and turn them around positively to see what we are looking for and what a good manager has to do to find the Case I businesses or the strong aspects of Cases II and III (while avoiding Case IV like the plague). Following are five steps which can build your business into a money-making enterprise.

1. Search for growing markets.

Keep looking for new, growing markets where you can get an increasing market share. How? Be sensitive to consumers needs and give people what they want. Spot new buying trends early in pacesetter places like California, New York, London, and Paris. Example: the American manager of the Beatles brought them to Carnegie Hall after spotting a London newspaper telling of their success in Liverpool. Result: Beatlemania swept America.

2. Think creatively about market innovations.

Consumers want something new. Think creatively about why things are done as they are. Keep asking "Why?" until you get a new concept of what will sell. Then keep asking "Why not?"—why not this way rather than that—until you solve the problem of how you can put your product on the market.

3. Compete promotionally for an increasing market share.

Out-do your competitors with a better marketing job. Give the customers something extra: extra value, extra quality, extra courtesy, a little gift, more than their money's worth. And above all, put your money where it grabs attention—in location, where there is traffic, in advertising, publicity, and promotion. Spend your own time getting customers in the door, and delegate much of the rest to others.

4. Select a high return on investment.

Look for low investment situations with high profits, because a small business is going to have to pay its own way fast. Don't try to develop an expensive new technology or reeducate the world, unless you have lots of money to invest and lose.

5. Create a strategy and work your plan.

Trust your hunches and intuition for testing out markets, but measure your markets and profit margins before you plunge. Develop your strategy for a high market share and high profit return into a plan of work to implement it, and then make the plan work by following it.

Notice in this approach that the first three major steps in a business are marketing efforts, the fourth provides a financial target, and in the fifth you develop a strategic plan. These five steps are the key success in small business.

You will also note that the five steps are intensely personal; they are something you must do yourself: search, think, compete, select, and create. These steps represent your thought processes, your individuality, and what you put into the new business, and they are geared to what you can do as an individual. Most small businesses start and survive by the drive and conception of an entrepreneur.

CONTRAST: THE BIG BUSINESS APPROACH

The personal approach to starting and surviving in business is in sharp contrast to the textbook approach, which is drawn from the experience of large businesses on how they maintain and expand their operations. The textbook approach to strategic planning in large business considers the marketing needs of consumers as well, but concentrates much more upon the technology of new product development to create new needs. The strategic planning approach of large businesses is to extrapolate or extend existing markets or technologies into new fields. For example, Minnesota Mining and Manufacturing might extend its market for adhesive tapes from the wrapping market into the soft book cover market, with changes in application and customer and no change in technology. Conversely, Timex might seek to change its product from a spring-wound watch to a microchip digital watch with no changes in customer or market, but a change in the technology of the product. Thus, strategic planning in big companies is usually a matrix or cross-analysis of new markets against technical innovation. For this reason, the typical textbook approach (Table 1-2) ends up with a master planning form which asks the manager or entrepreneur to estimate the change in accomplishment, sales and costs of items.[1]

In this illustration, the company is considering developing a new television tape recorder, which will take five years of research and development (R & D) at $1 million per year, four years to establish in the market—a total front-end investment of $16 million for the research, space, and equipment, another $7 million later for the marketing and advertising campaign, and still another $18 million bank loan to carry the inventory. If the product is successful, it will earn $3 million per year in new profit, against which the marketing expenses can be written off to break even in two years after market introduction (i.e., by year 11). Then, the return on investment will be 19% ($3,000,000 ÷ $16,000,000). If the new product fails, the loss

Table 1-2. Illustrative Long-Range Strategy Summary.

ACTIVITY	CHANGE IN		COMMENTS
	Sales	Costs	
Research and development	0	$ 1,000,000	Potential for 5-yr TV tape recorder development
Products	$10,000,000	7,000,000	
Product mix	30,000,000	21,000,000	Expand all product lines
Services	1,000,000	3,000,000	Warranty and product liability
Inventory	25,000,000	18,000,000	Stock all regions
Subcontracts	4,000,000	4,000,000	Assemble in Japan
Space		3,000,000	Factory floor space 7000 sq. ft.
Equipment		8,000,000	Tooling bill
Employees		4,000,000	Payroll
Customers (no.)	10,000		Double present customers
Sales outlets (no.)	1,000	3,000,000	Need for new sales outlets
Transportation		1,000,000	Truck and rail carriers
Advertising		4,000,000	New ad campaign
Market research		500,000	Design ad and market campaign
Financing		20,000,000	New loan (60%) stock issue
Investments		16,000,000	Research, space, equipment
Management organization		1,000,000	New product division
Government regulation		500,000	Patents and environmental
Economic environment			Favorable consumer income
Industry competition			Four strong competitors
Market share	12%		Take 4 yrs to establish

will be $41 million or the sum of the physical investment, marketing costs, and bank loan on the inventory. So this is a very high-risk example of new product development. If successful, the return on investment is fair; if unsuccessful, the losses are large. This product line is somewhere in between Cases II and IV in Table 1-1 of management strategies, that is, between a contender and a loser. The market share is low, and the return on investment is fairly good (if successful) to questionable (in case of loss). Only a very strong contender in the marketing and product development field would care to take a risk like this.

This illustration was, of course, deliberately designed to show the high front-end costs and high risks of technological product development. As such, it is not the kind of investment that a small business entrepreneur could take. The product takes too much money over too long a time period at too high a risk for the small businessman. Only large, firmly established corporations with strong technical and marketing staffs and ample resources could even consider such a strategy; even they could lose money on it, which is indeed often the case. Only about 5% of the product developments of large corporations pay out in the end. So technical innovation is a high-risk field.

The reason why this book starts out recommending new service and merchandising concepts as the innovative field for the small businessman is because their development costs are small—mainly the time of the entrepreneur—and their payoffs are large.

Therefore, the five-step strategy for small businessmen is in sharp contrast to the textbook method (Table 1-2) for large manufacturing corporations with technological product lines. In the list of 24 planning items in Table 1-2, for example, there are only five marketing items in the whole list and the first one does not appear until item 13. However, market share—the last item on the list—is the payoff and pretty much determines what kind of margin and profit the firm will get. Still, the plan is basically very product-oriented. The plan starts with new R & D possibilities which might be projected from its existing technologies, and then it goes through a product innovation and development cycle which ends up being screened in the marketplace by test marketing and market research.

In summary, the textbook approach to strategic planning is expensive because it requires a large amount of money up front to finance the product innovation-market testing cycle. Most small businessmen cannot afford that approach because they do not have that kind of front-end money. Besides, most small businesses are in retailing, contracting, services, and finance where that kind of technical product innovation is less frequent because the innovation is more often in improved personal service. The technical approach to product-market innovation is all right for the big fellows in manufacturing who have large organizations and oligopoly profits to back them. But, the small businessman will start and survive by a more personal and individual approach to fitting himself into a market that no one else has found or can serve as well as he can.

WHERE ARE THE SMALL BUSINESSES?

The personal and individual nature of success and survival in small business is indicated by the kinds of markets they are in. Small business thrives in the personal markets. The big businesses are where product characteristics are more important. To appreciate where small businessmen survive and succeed, we need some idea where small businesses are. The statistics on small businesses are very poor, even though one-half of the labor is employed by small businesses. There are an estimated 10 million small business firms in the United States, of which about two-thirds are single-person units without any employees. Many of these no-employee firms are part-time avocations of individuals or businesses set up for tax purposes. In any case, the business firms with employees, which number 3.5 million, are basically those engaged in serious, profit-making activity of an organizational nature. Alan D. Star has estimated the distribution of these firms with employees by business sector, distinguishing between small and large firms (See Table 1–3). A small firm is one with less than 100 employees.

Table 1–3 shows where small businesses have survived and succeeded, which is largely in retail trade and services, followed by finance, wholesale trade, and contract construction. These are all areas in which the personal factor counts because the entrepreneur is able to provide the extra touch and individual treatment which customers want. These are the areas of personal service where the businessman can give the customer something extra, something personal, and can keep asking the creative questions of "Why?" and "Why not?" to adapt to new customer needs and solutions.

Table 1-3. Distribution of Business Population
by Size of Firm, 1972.
(number of firms in thousands)

	SMALL	LARGE
Agriculture	32	*
Mining	21	1
Contract construction	309	3
Manufacturing	227	18
Transportation	124	5
Wholesale trade	289	3
Retail trade	1026	5
Finance, insurance, real estate	325	5
Services	987	14
All industries	3440	54

* Less than 1000.
Source: Alvin D. Star, "Estimates of the Number of Quasi and Small Businesses, 1948 to 1972," *American Journal of Small Business,* Vol. IV, No. 2, October, 1979, pp. 44–52.

MANAGEMENT AS PERFORMANCE AND VICE VERSA

So you are in the personalized marketplace as small businessmen adapting to new customer needs. That is your mission. The performance of your mission, to personalize the adaption to new consumer wants, is measurable by (1) a steady increase in new customers (as word of mouth gets around that yours is a highly personalized service) and (2) a high ratio of repeat customers who keep coming back for more.

Good location, advertising, and promotion are essential to start and run a business, but nothing is quite as successful as word-of-mouth recommendations. Friends, and friends of friends, start coming in and there is a steady increase in new customers by referral from old customers.

Equally important is repeat business, or keeping customers satisfied and returning. Successful insurance salesmen typically do about one-half of their business with repeat customers who have new insurance needs. Management consulting firms often get about two-thirds of their assignments from customers who are satisfied and keep coming back. General Motors sells about three-fourths of its new cars to automobile owners who have bought GM cars before.

Cherish the repeat customers; they are the backbone of every business.

Keeping track of new and repeat business is a simple matter of internal record keeping, which many businesses too often neglect. With every sale, note whether this is a new customer or a repeat customer. How do you know? Ask, of course. The very act of asking can be an act of courtesy which helps personalize your service. Someone normally has to talk to every customer in the course of a sale. You train yourself and your staff to ask the person's name; try to remember it and whether the customer has bought before. If you cannot remember, ask the customer: Have you been in before? Were you satisfied? How did you happen to come to this business in the first place? The last question will give you some idea how well your promotion or word of mouth is working for you. Besides, you have shown interest in the customer, who he is, and his degree of satisfaction with your service. It makes you personally interested in your customers, and it gives you a good record for yourself. You can tally up the results of your customer survey by month or year, as shown in Table 1-4.

Suppose your tally of customer responses to your interest in them

Table 1-4. Number of Customers by Time Period.

	1	2	3	4	5	6	7
Average Performance							
New customers	100	104	108	112	117	121	126
Repeat customers	0	60	62	65	67	70	73
Total customers	100	164	170	177	184	191	199
Poor New Sales							
New customers	100	100	80	90	70	80	60
Repeat customers	0	60	60	48	54	42	48
Total customers	100	160	140	138	124	122	108
Poor Repeat Sales							
New customers	100	104	108	112	117	121	126
Repeat customers	0	60	52	43	34	23	12
Total customers	100	164	160	155	151	144	138

reveals the first case, labeled "Average Performance" in Table 1–4. An average performance reveals a slow but steady increase in the number of new customers each month or each year (the economy grows at a rate of about 4% per year and you should do as well), plus a 60% repeat buying or customer loyalty rate. Notice how rapidly sales pile up if you have both good new sales and repeat sales working for you. By the end of the seventh time period, this business has twice the sales it did at first. Moreover, these are rather modest sales increases and customer loyalty rates. Imagine the dynamite in your enterprise if you had a 20 to 30% per year increase in new sales coupled with 75% repeat sales of old customers!

The second case, labeled "Poor New Sales," still has the 60% repeat sales loyalty of the first case, but the new customer sales are erratic and going downward. This case illustrates poor promotion, poor location, or poor word-of-mouth recognition. In fact, this firm is going out of business.

The third case, labeled "Poor Repeat Sales," has the same growth in new sales as the first case, but the buyer loyalty on repeat sales is falling from 60% in the second period, to 50% in the third, to 40% in the fourth, and so forth, down to 10% in the seventh period. This firm is not quite going out of business, but it is not growing. The third case is typical of a high-pressure operation which has to paw over new customers in order to keep going because buyers will not come back a second time.

Management is the ability to coordinate and organize the many interrelated parts of a business. You can be a high-pressure salesman and a poor manager and end up as a case three example of poor service to your old customers. You can provide delightful service to your old customers and be a poor manager of new sales; you will then end up like case two with new sales falling and thus driving you out of business.

But to be like the first case with average performance in both new and repeat sales, you have to be a good manager who pays simultaneous attention to such tasks as good advertising, good promotion, good location, good merchandise and fashion buying, good inventory control, courteous service, personal attention to customers, repair or exchange of unsatisfactory merchandise, delivery, installation, and a little extra besides. Devoting your time and that of your employees to a balance of satisfactions to your customers takes management skill. You need to plan the use of time to see that all these tasks are done, and you have to listen solicitously to what customers have to say.

The planning part of management is to take into account the organization of the many tasks which need to be performed to satisfy your customers. Then you will anticipate in advance the performance specifications which have to be met to be successful in serving both new and repeat customers. That is, management is the organization of the tasks which are needed to meet the performance requirements of your mission: to provide a personalized service to adapt to new customer needs.

EARNINGS ON ASSETS BY SIZE CATEGORY—ITS MEANING

How do you know that you are doing these good marketing things as well as you should? Well, there are two ways. The first is by keeping a record of your new and repeat sales, discussed in the prior section, to see that you have some steady, however small, increase in new sales, and that you are able to hold your own in buyer loyalty at least in the 50% area of repeat sales. This first measure, on new and repeat customers, gives you some idea of whether you are serving your own market adequately.

The second performance measure is to see how you are doing financially compared to other businessmen who face the same kinds of problems that you do. You can compare your earnings on assets by size category to other businesses to see if your overall management performance in the use of your resources is equal to theirs. The second measure, of earnings on assets, gives you some idea of your management performance, whether you are able to organize and balance all the tasks of your business in a way that yields at least an average level of earnings on assets which is as good as anyone else's. Your ability to earn money on assets you employ, and to earn a profit on your new worth, are the ultimate survival measures because these earnings determine whether you can pay your bills and survive.

If your earnings on assets are a key measure of your management performance, how do you go about making the test? There are two main measures of profitability: earnings on total assets, and earnings on owner's net worth. The first measures your management performance in terms of the efficiency or economy with which you use all your resources and is probably the best general management measure. The second measure, of earnings on net worth, shows how much gain in wealth or equity you have made. As such, it is the best measure of personal financial success; it is the preferred measure by most businessmen and investors of their personal achievement.

If you are not an accountant and don't really known how to put together all the numbers to make these comparisons, we can do it together. Assume we are in the retail hardware business. First make a list of all the assets in the business from the bookkeeper's records of the balance sheet:

LIST OF ASSETS	DOLLARS
Cash and equivalents	$ 10,000
Accounts and notes receivable (net)*	20,000
Inventory	30,000
Other current assets	2,000
Fixed assets (net)	40,000
Intangible assets (net)	0
Other assets	8,000
Total assets	$110,000

* "Net" means less depreciation or reserves against losses.

Next, make up a list of items to arrive at earnings from the income statement of the firm:

Total Sales and Receipts	$150,000
Minus	
Cost of goods sold	100,000
All business expenses	45,000
Net Profit (before taxes)	$ 5,000
Plus	
Interest	5,000
Charitable contributions	1,000
Earnings, Excluding Compensation of officers	$ 11,000
Plus	
Compensation of officers	15,400
Earnings, Before Taxes, Including Compensation of Officers	$ 26,400

Now figure the two measures on management performance, as follows:

1. Earnings on assets, excluding compensation of officers, is $11,000 ÷ $110,000 = 10%.
2. Earnings on assets, including the compensation of officers, is $26,400 ÷ $110,000 = 24%.
3. Given also a figure from the balance sheet, showing that the owner's net worth or equity is $39,000, then we can also figure the percentage of profit (before taxes) for the business as: $5,000 ÷ 39,000 = 12.8%.

Now we can see how these figures compare with what other businesses do. Turn to Table 1-5 which shows the earnings on assets by size, including compensation of officers, for all corporations in the United States by type of business. The reason for paying principal attention to earnings on assets, including the compensation of officers, is that small businessmen have considerable discretion as to whether they take their income as profit of the firm or as officer compensation. Executive compensation, earnings, and taxes are discussed more fully in Chapter 12.

Since we are in the retail hardware business, look on the bottom line of Table 1-5 ("Wholesale and Retail Trade") and go across to the third column to asset class $100,000 to $250,000 (our total assets, recall, are $110,000); we then find that the earnings for all corporations in the U.S. in that class are .27¢ per dollar of assets, or 27%—about the same as in our example. The hardware business in our illustration is doing nearly as well as average in this measure.

Now turn to another source, called *Expenses in Retail Business* and you will find that the average profit on investment for hardware stores of this size is 12.8%, the same as in our illustration.[4]

Of course, the illustration was made up to represent an average hardware store, but it does exemplify the method for comparing earnings performance of your company against others in your field. Suppose, for example, the earnings on assets for the hardware store in our illustration had been 16% including executive compensation. These measures of performance would have been only 60% of the average of other companies, and we would know that our performance was down by 40% from what he might expect to do. As an example from Table 1-5, 16% ÷ 27% = about 60%).

Table 1-5. Earnings Including Compensation of Officers for Profit and Loss Corporations, 1976 (earnings per dollar of assets).

ASSET CLASS (THOUSANDS)	UNDER $25	$25–$50	$50–$100	$100–$250	$250–$500	$500–$1,000	$1,000–$2,500	$2,500–$10,000	$10,000–$25,000	$25,000–$100,000	OVER $100,000
Manufacturing	.51	.44	.42	.33	.30	.27	.24	.20	.18	.16	.13
Services	2.49	1.25	.75	.39	.24	.17	.14	.12	.12	.10	.10
Construction	.72	.43	.43	.28	.24	.20	.17	.12	.10	.10	.09
Transportation	.52	.32	.27	.26	.19	.21	.15	.14	.13	.11	.06
Wholesale and Retail trade	.54	.40	.34	.27	.23	.21	.19	.16	.14	.14	.11

Source: Office of the Secretary of the Treasury, Office of Tax Analysis, from income tax data.

October 4, 1979

Similarly, if our earnings including executive compensation were 35%, we would be performing 30% better than the average company in our field.

A TOTAL PERFORMANCE INDEX

Now we are ready to combine the sales index (Table 1-4) with the financial performance index (Table 1-5) to provide an overall measure of business performance. As we shall see, this will give us the basis for some preliminary diagnosis of typical small business problems.

We assume that a business should be able to do as well as the average performance in sales (Table 1-4) or in earnings on assets (Table 1-5). If the business is average in both, we can rate it as 100% of the sales index, and 100% of the earnings index, resulting in a total performance ratio or index of 1.00 x 1.00 = 1.00 or 100%.

That is, the total performance index of a business is the product of its sales and earnings indices. The step-by-step way to calculate your own total performance index, then, is:

1. Take your sales performance and divide it by the third line from Table 1-4 labeled "Average Performance" for the correct year or period.

Your own sales should be increasing at a rate of 4% per year for new sales with a 60% repeat customer rate. Suppose you are in your second year and your total customer purchases (in real dollars adjusted for inflation) are 150% of last year. In Table 1-4 the number of customers had increased to 164 from 100 in the first year (164 ÷ 100 = 164%). Then your sales performance measure is 150% ÷ 164% = 91%.

2. Take your earnings on assets and divide them by the appropriate figure from Table 1-5.

Suppose you run a hardware store with $110,000 in assets and your earnings before taxes including compensation of officers is $34,000. Your earnings on assets would be 31% ($34,000 ÷ $110,000). Then your index of earnings performance is .31 ÷ .27 (from Table 1-5, line 5 column 4) = 115%.

3. Now multiply the sale performance index 91% times the earnings index of 115%, and you get a total performance (.91 x 1.15) of 105%.

The diagnosis of your performance as a small business manager is that you are slightly above average overall with a superior financial performance on earnings but with a substandard marketing performance. You need to put more effort and money into improving your marketing.

Let us take a look at some more possible combinations of the total performance index together with the feedback diagnosis which it provides. There are seven types of cases (Table 1-6).

Any small businessman who has a total performance like type A or better is to be congratulated on being an outstanding manager. Those similar to types B, C, and D might like to do a little better in either earnings or marketing, but they are generally good managers compared to the average.

The managers of business types E, F, and G have real problems: E needs to work hard on improving his budgetary accounting and control to bring up his earnings (see especially Chapters 6, 7, 8, 9), F needs to improve his sales and marketing effort (see especially Chapters 4 and 5), and G needs to improve his whole management performance to stay in business.

Note also that the sales index is really made up of two elements, the new customers and the repeat customers. So really there are fourteen, rather than seven, cases in Table 1-6. If your marketing index is low, be sure to check whether it is due to new sales or repeat sales, because your management response would be somewhat different.

In summary, the total performance index is a feedback measure which enables you to judge your overall managerial ability against other small businesses, and it gives you a diagnosis as to where to

Table 1-6. Total Performance Cases and Diagnosis.

TYPE	TOTAL PERFORMANCE INDEX	EARNINGS INDEX	SALES INDEX	DIAGNOSIS OF PERFORMANCE
A	121	110	110	Superior overall performance
B	110	110	100	Good earnings and average sales
C	110	100	110	Good sales and average earnings
D	100	100	100	Average overall
E	90	90	100	Poor earnings and average sales
F	90	100	90	Poor sales and average earnings
G	81	90	90	Poor earnings and poor sales

check further into the nature of your problems in order to correct them. The following chapters will provide more detailed performance measures to enable you to follow up on the diagnosis, so you can check out and compare the inner workings of your operations for the purpose of making improvements.

SUMMARY

A small businessman needs to measure his own performance and make corrections as he goes along in order to survive; the most difficult problem is making management efficient in all aspects of business operations. Management's proficiency shows up in a total performance measure of earnings on assets and sales progress. These two elements constitute the key measures of business strategy, in which the manager is trying to place his business in the position of a winner with high earnings on assets and a high market share.

A five-step method for moving toward a position of high earnings and high market share is:

1. Search for growing markets.
2. Think creatively about market innovations.
3. Compete promotionally for an increasing market share.
4. Select a high return on investment.
5. Create a strategy and work your plan.

This personal approach to survival and success in small business management stresses the innovative role of the entrepreneur in creating marketable ideas and services which provide customers with something new and extra. The personal, small business approach is in contrast to the technological product development approach of large manufacturers which requires huge sums of front-end investment at high risk.

Small businesses are generally not found as frequently in the manufacturing sector as they are in services, finance, contracting, wholesale and retail trade, unless they have a special technical capability of their own. Small business excels in the more personalized services.

A small business can measure its sales performance by keeping track of its new customer and repeat customer sales. Normally, a business should be able to increase its new sales as fast as the average growth in the economy, about 4% per year, and achieve a 60% repeat customer sales record.

Earnings on assets are perhaps the best overall measure of performance; data from tax returns of all corporations in the U.S. enable a business to compare its own earnings with other companies by general industry and size classes.

The total performance measure, which is a product of the earnings and sales index, provides a feedback measure which allows the small businessman to diagnose for himself the strengths and weaknesses of his own performance. Having identified these strengths and weaknesses, the small business manager may then investigate the causes of these problems (described in following chapters), which provide detailed measures for the operational aspects of running a small business.

The optimistic side of this chapter has been that most small businessmen learn to be better managers than do people in large businesses (Table 1-5). They have to be in order to manage all the aspects of any business with small staffs and few resources. The problem is to learn to be a good manager fast enough to survive, because small businesses do not have enough of a margin of resources for very many errors. The way to learn fast enough and to avoid errors, or at least to avoid repeating them, is to measure your performance against other companies and make corrections as fast as you can. This chapter has shown you how to do just that. The following chapters will enable you to check out every aspect of your business. By the time you get done, you will be what most small businessmen eventually become: a superior manager compared to any executive in the economy.

REFERENCES

1. Golde, R.A. "Practical Planning for Small Business." *Harvard Business Review,* Vol. 42, No. 5, September-October, 1964, pp. 147–161.
2. Star, A.D. "Estimates of the Number of Quasi and Small Businesses, 1948 to 1972." *American Journal of Small Business,* Vol. IV, No. 2, October, 1979, pp. 44–52.
3. U.S. Senate Select Committee on Small Business. *The Role of Small Business*

in the Economy—Tax and Financial Problems. 94th Congress: 1st Session (Washington, D.C., Superintendent of Documents, November 21, 1975), pp. 18–19.

4. *Expenses in Retail Business* is available on request from the National Cash Register Co., Dayton, Ohio, 45479.

2

Short-Term Survival Measures—Control of Cash Flow

Never, NEVER, try to build sales faster than you can generate cash to pay your bills! Sound ovbious? Of course it is. But it is also the single most common cause of business failure. If you want to survive, never build the business faster than you can generate cash.

The odd part is that the smarter you are at mastering the skills of Chapter 1, the more danger you are in of going broke by running out of cash. Yes! Once you have figured out how to increase your earnings and increase your sales (which is what Chapter 1 was all about), you get so excited and motivated that you want to go for broke—which is exactly what many small businessmen do at this stage. How is it possible?

You become impressed with how fast your sales and earnings are going up. Then you spend money faster (to take care of the new volume) than you can collect in cash receipts from sales or customer payments on their accounts. Your expenses run up faster than the cash comes in. You are making a profit all the way, but going broke in the process because you cannot pay your current bills. Still sounds implausible? There is an example later on in the chapter, but unfortunately the example gets a little complicated because it requires some knowledge of accounting. At this point, a simple explanation will suffice.

Sales and earnings both appear on the income statement, and neither appear on the balance sheet where cash is recorded. If you concentrate on building up sales and earnings (which is the total performance measure in Chapter 1), then your attention is focused solely on the income statement. The cash on the balance sheet may decline to zero because you are running up expenses to expand the business faster than you are collecting cash from customers. This is a common malady of small business.

How do you avoid running out of cash to pay your bills? The cash flow statement is a means of connecting your sales and earnings efforts with their effects on the cash account on the balance sheet. Knowing how to make a cash flow statement is perhaps the single most important tool to survival in a small business!

SOME ACCOUNTING PRELIMINARIES

The balance sheet is intended to show how well you are doing financially at any moment of time. It is a financial snapshot of your firm. A simplified balance sheet looks like Table 2–1.

In this new business, the owner put in $20,000 of his own capital in the form of cash, which appears in both the cash account as an asset and in the capital account as his equity. He then buys $40,000 in inventory in order to have something to sell, and the bank lends him $20,000 against the inventory. He buys $20,000 of the inventory on credit from suppliers (i.e., $40,000 total inventory minus $20,000 paid from the bank loan). He also buys $5,000 in equipment on

Table 2–1. Simplified Balance Sheet of a New Business.

ASSETS (THE SUM OF WHAT YOU HAVE)		LIABILITIES (MINUS WHAT YOU OWE)	
Cash	$20,000	Accounts payable	$25,000
Accounts receivable	0	Bank loan	20,000
Inventory	40,000		
Equipment and blgs.	5,000	Total liabilities	$45,000
Total assets	$65,000		
		EQUITY (EQUALS WHAT IS LEFT THAT IS YOURS)	
		Capital	$20,000
		Retained earnings	0
		Total equity	$20,000
		Total equity and liabilities	$65,000

credit from suppliers. Thus he has $25,000 owed in accounts payable to suppliers ($20,000 plus $5,000). When all these transactions are recorded, the statement balances, i.e., the assets equal the equity plus liabilities—the reason why it is called a *balance sheet*.

Where are sales and earnings, which preoccupied our attention as total performance measures in Chapter 1? They are not on the balance sheet and appear instead on the income statement, which is tied into the balance sheet under the title of "Retained earnings." So the income statement is really a detailed accounting of what is happening to retained earnings. As such, the income statement is not a snapshot of a moment in time; it is a detailed record of the process of the business during a whole period, like a month or year, between two moments in time. To understand what is happening in a business, then, you need two balance sheets, one at the beginning of a period (year) and one at the end of a period, plus an income statement as to what happened in between. The income statement looks like Table 2-2.

The $10,000 in net profit can now be transferred to the balance sheet as "Retained earnings". Then the owner's equity becomes $30,000 for the balance sheet at the end of the period; the income statement is the detailed accounting as to why the retained earnings changed during the year.

Other changes would have also occurred in the income statement, which affects the balance sheet. For example, some of the sales (say $25,000) were for cash and the rest ($75,000) were credit or charge accounts, which the business must either carry itself, charge to credit cards, or borrow from the bank. In any case, there is a lag in customer payments which requires the business to have more cash or working capital. Moreover, the higher volume of sales would require

Table 2-2. Simplified Income State for the First Year of a New Business.

Sales	$100,000
Minus cost of goods sold	60,000
Gross profit	40,000
Minus expenses	30,000
Equals net profit (to retained earnings)	$ 10,000

more inventory, perhaps $10,000 more, and the owner has to either pay for that or borrow the needed funds. Increased operating expenses (to handle the higher volume of sales) would include payroll, rent, utility bills, taxes, and office supplies—all of which may not be paid for but owed to persons providing the service. Let us assume those expenses still owed to others to be $30,000. Then the balance sheet at the end of the period reflecting all these changes would be something like Table 2–3.

Table 2–3 is a bit absurd for the sake of illustration because this small businessman has let all his bills and cash pile up, but the bills are piling up faster than the cash. He had $20,000 in cash at the beginning of the period and took in $25,000 in cash sales, for a total of $45,000. But to restock his inventory to replace his sales, he had to spend $60,000 to buy more goods from his suppliers to stay in business and let his accounts payable pile up from $25,000 to $85,000. In effect, his suppliers are lending him credit to finance his customers who are buying on charge accounts. This is unrealistic, of course, since suppliers would not do that; but it illustrates the point that this owner needs more working capital to finance his sales volume. Also, he has borrowed another $10,000 from the bank to increase his inventory, and he has failed to pay $30,000 in expenses for payroll, taxes, utilities, and rent.

Table 2–3. Simplified Balance Sheet of New Business at End of First Period.

ASSETS		LIABILITIES	
Cash	$ 45,000	Accounts payable	$ 85,000
Accounts receivable	75,000	Bank loan	30,000
Inventory	50,000	Other debts	30,000
Equipment and blgs.	5,000		
		Total liabilities	$145,000
Total assets	$175,000		
		EQUITY	
		Capital	$20,000
		Retained earnings	10,000
		Total equity	$30,000
		Total equity and liabilities	$175,000

All of his creditors would want him to settle up quickly. But he has only $45,000 in cash to settle $145,000 in debts. What are his options? They are: (1) put more cash into the business in the form of his own capital, (2) borrow more from the bank, (3) speed up the collection of accounts receivable from his charge account customers, (4) sell off some of his inventory, and (5) plead for more time from his creditors. He has to arrange some combination of these five options, or go bankrupt—even though his sales and earnings are increasing satisfactorily by the total performance measures of Chapter 1. If he goes bankrupt, the owner is out of business, and a court-appointed receiver sells off the assets for the purpose of paying off the creditors. Not a happy ending to what, from the income statement alone, appeared to be a successful business. The poor fellow is going bankrupt while making money. If he had a cash flow statement, he might have been able to stay in business.

THE CASH FLOW STATEMENT

The purpose of the cash flow statement is to trace the impact of operations, as shown in the income statement, upon the cash account in order to try to maintain an adequate cash balance for paying bills at all times. In effect, the cash flow statement shows the changes in all of the sales and expense accounts on the income statement as they affect cash needs. Simply put: cash receipts — cash expenses = cash flow.

The cash receipts and cash expenses have to be projected into the future to be useful for making decisions and avoiding bankruptcy, because you need to estimate the cash balances and cash requirements month-by-month in the future as bills and payroll become due. When the cash flow becomes so low that you are unable to pay bills, your creditors may force you into bankruptcy. You need a measure of your cash needs, then, because that enables you to take corrective action in time to avoid bankruptcy. When you see the cash flow falling below cash needs, your management actions to remedy the situation would be: (1) cut back on your volume of business and your expenses to reduce cash needs, (2) speed up collections of accounts receivable due to you to bring in more cash, (3) sell some assets to raise cash, (4) borrow more from the bank, or (5) put in more cash yourself if you can.

Now let us see where cash receipts and cash expenditures normally come from, so we can begin to make up a cash flow schedule, which is going to save your business from going bust. Table 2-4 shows where cash receipts come from and where cash outlays go.

Table 2-4 is an example of the cash flow management which might have been used in our hardware store illustration in Tables 2-1 and 2-2. If the small business manager had collected $50,000 in accounts receivables from customers, and paid all his current expenses as well as $60,000 for merchandise on his accounts payable, his cash flow statement would look like Table 2-4. Had he used his cash in this manner, his balance sheet would now look like Table 2-5 below, rather than like Table 2-3.

Our small businessman has paid up most of his bills. At least he has paid current expenses for payroll, rent, utilities, and so forth. He is also keeping his account current with suppliers by paying regularly his accounts payable for his merchandise purchases. The creditors will not be pursuing him for lack of paying his bills. True, he owes the bank $10,000 more but the bank is not likely to press him for payment as long as his sales and earnings are up, and as long as he has a $50,000 inventory as security for the loan. So his only real trouble now is that he is short of cash. The sum of $6,000 is a pretty small cash balance upon which to operate. What can he do? He will

Table 2-4. Elements of a Cash Flow Schedule.

Cash Balance, Beginning of Period		$20,000
Plus Cash Receipts (or inflow)		
Cash sales	25,000	
Cash payments by customers on accounts receivables	50,000	
Sales of other assets	1,000	
Total cash receipts	$76,000	
Equals Total Cash Flow		
		$96,000
Minus Cash Expenditures (or outlays)		
Merchandise or accounts payable	$60,000	
Payroll	20,000	
Rent, utilities and other expenses	10,000	
	$90,000	
Cash balance, End of Period		$ 6,000

Table 2-5. Balance Sheet of New Business at End of First Period with Cash Management.

ASSETS		LIABILITIES	
Cash	$ 6,000	Accounts payable	$25,000
Accounts receivable	25,000	Bank loan	30,000
Inventory	50,000	Other debts	0
Equipment and blgs.	4,000		
Total assets	$85,000	Total liabilities	$55,000
		EQUITY	
		Capital	$20,000
		Retained earnings	10,000
		Total equity	$30,000
		Total equity and liabilities	$85,000

probably have to maintain his operations at their present volume until his cash sales and collections from accounts receivable generate more cash. In another period, or month, for example, he should be able to build up another $10,000 in cash, if he keeps his sales, accounts receivable and inventory at their present levels. Why $10,000? Because that is the amount of earnings per period or month.

However, earnings are not cash. Do not be tricked by the idea that earnings come in as cash. Earnings are just a bookkeeping entry, which shows the difference between sales and expenses. Earnings do not become converted to cash, except as they are realized by cash sales, collections on accounts, or sales of assets.

But we have posed the idea that our hardware dealer is going to keep his level of sales, inventory, and accounts receivable the same, in order to get himself out of the slim cash bind that he is in. By doing so, he chooses to keep the cash flow out of his cash sales, rather than expand sales or inventory further. His cash sales are $25,000 per period, of which 60% or $15,000 is the cost of goods sold which we must replace by buying more stock from suppliers, leaving him $10,000 in net cash flow to build up his cash account. By this prudent move, then, at the end of the third period, or month, his cash account will be built up by $10,000, raising it from the precariously low figure of $6,000 to a more adequate working level of $16,000.

Our hardware dealer bailed himself out. How did he do it? He looked ahead, that is, he planned, and he saw that he had to raise cash by keeping the gross margin from his cash sales in the till, rather than spending it. He made up an informal cash flow schedule in his mind, which showed him that if he did not increase any of his expenditures and collected his cash and credit sales on time, he would net another $10,000 to add to his cash balance.

If we recorded what he did in a cash flow schedule (similar to Table 2-4) we would come up with a new schedule for the period shown below as Table 2-6.

Table 2-6 tells us something very useful. The hardware dealer got himself out of trouble by promptly collecting his accounts receivable, so that none of his customers' charge accounts became very old. If his charge account customers had dragged their feet in paying him, say by waiting for 60 or 90 days before settling up, he would have been in big trouble. He was able to pull himself out of the cash bind he was in and build up his cash balance only because his customers paid their bills promptly.

That shows another thing to watch out for as managers: the age distribution of accounts receivable. Accountants call this, "aging the accounts receivable," that is, to show the normal payment schedule

Table 2-6. Cash Flow Schedule of Hardware Store for Second Period.

Cash Balance, at Beginning of Period		$ 6,000
Plus Cash Receipts		
Cash sales	$ 25,000	
Cash payments on accounts receivable ($25,000 collected from past due accounts in the last period, plus $50,000 normal collection from sales in this period)	75,000	
	$100,000	
Equals Total Cash Flow		$106,000
Minus Cash Expenditures		
Merchandise or accounts payable	$ 60,000	
Payroll, rent, utilities, etc.	30,000	
	$ 90,000	
Cash Balance, End of Period		$ 16,000

of customers. In fact, you need an age distribution of customer payments in order to make an accurate cash flow estimate. The next steps then are:

1. Make an age distribution of accounts receivable.
2. Project a cash flow schedule.

When you have learned to do that, you are not going to go bankrupt (at least not without knowing it).

AGING THE ACCOUNTS RECEIVABLE

The aging of accounts receivable is a good way for the small business manager to remind his slow-paying customers to pay their bills promptly, as well as a means for the small businessman to estimate his cash flow.

Make a list of all your charge account customers who have accounts receivable. Then show in the number of days the account is on the books before it is paid. The example in Table 2–7 illustrates how you may check on your collection process.

In this example, out of six customers, four let their accounts go unpaid over 60 days, three over 90 days, and two over 120 days. This is a very poor payment record, and the consequence is to tie up a lot of the small businessman's funds. Make sure to bill promptly and remind customers that payment is due within 30 days. Try hard to get collections on a schedule where most of the payments come in within

Table 2-7. Aging of Accounts Receivable.

NAME OF CUSTOMER	CURRENT BALANCE	NUMBER OF DAYS ON BOOKS				
		0–30	31–60	61–90	91–120	OVER 120
H. Abel	$ 100	$ 60	$ 40			
P. Benson	350	50	100	$ 100	$ 100	
S. Cable	200	50			50	$ 100
T. Denton	150	50	100			
V. Ernst	400	100	100	100	100	
B. Fable	275	75		100		100
Etc.						
Total	$10,000	$2,000	$3,500	$2,000	$1,500	$1,000
Percent	100	20	35	20	15	10

60 days. As it is now, only 55% of the receivables are collected within 60 days, and the rest become long overdue. The longer an account is overdue, the more chance there is for a complete loss due to nonpayment. Besides, this slow-payment schedule, as shown by the percentage distribution at the bottom of Table 2-7, is bad for the cash flow.

The percentage distribution of age of accounts in Table 2-6 can be used to help make a cash flow estimate. Indeed, that is the principal reason for the exercise. If Table 2-6 represents a common pattern in the business month after month, take whatever is the total of accounts receivable and assume that 20% will be paid in 30 days, 35% within 31 to 60 days, and so forth. Therefore, multiply these percentages by the total accounts receivable and that gives the expected cash inflow from customer payments on their accounts. For example, going back to the hardware store illustration in Tables 2-4 and 2-5, we find that the business has $25,000 of accounts receivables on the books and $75,000 in new charge sales per month, or a total of $100,000 of accounts receivable at the end of each month. Given an aging of accounts receivable as in Table 2-7, the cash inflow can be estimated as: $20,000 within 30 days, $35,000 within 31 to 60 days, $20,000 in 61 to 90 days, $15,000 in 91 to 120 days, and $1,000 after 120 days. These estimates can now be put directly into the cash flow schedule to estimate the cash receipts for the future.

THE CASH FLOW SCHEDULE—A MEASURE OF CONTROL

We can now do what we set out to accomplish in the beginning of this chapter: to set up an estimate of cash receipts and expenditures which will assure that we can always pay our bills. That is, we are looking for a control measure which will guarantee that we will not go broke by building up the business faster than we can generate cash. That measure is the cash flow schedule. To make up a cash flow schedule, do the following:

1. Estimate your cash sales per month.
2. Estimate your credit sales, the amount of accounts receivable, and the customer payments on account by aging the receivables as we did in the last section.
3. Estimate other cash receipts from sales of assets or loans.

4. Add items 1 to 3 and you have a total of the cash inflow expected into the business.
5. Next estimate your cash outflow, beginning with the payments you expect to make to buy merchandise each month.
6. Estimate your payroll expenses monthly.
7. Estimate your other operating expenses monthly, such as rent, utilities, repairs, supplies, and so forth.
8. Add items 5 to 7 to get a total of your cash outlay requirements.
9. Subtract the cash outgo (item 8) from the cash inflow (item 4) and you get your remaining cash.

This estimate of your cash flow can be used to compare month by month with what you actually experience; there is your control. You must take care not to spend more than your cash flow schedule allows, or you take the risk of running out of cash. An example of a cash flow schedule projected monthly into the future is shown in Table 2–8.

Our friendly neighborhood hardware man in Table 2–8 is taking another run at trying to get out of trouble with his cash flow problems. He has aged his accounts receivable, as illustrated in the previous section, and has estimated he could collect $20,000 the first month, $35,000 plus $20,000 the second month, and $20,000 plus $35,000 plus $20,000 the third month, and so on, if his sales volume held constant. The cash receipts from accounts payable are entered into the estimated column of Table 2–8 for each month. In addition, we show his cash sales each month, and the one-time increase in the bank loan to carry his inventory. His cash expenditures during January total an estimated $90,000, leaving him a skimpy cash balance of $5,000 at the end of the month.

The *actual* cash flow for January is also shown in comparison with the estimate, and the manager was able to stick close to his targets. His cash sales were a little less, and collections on accounts a little more than estimated. He spent a little more for merchandise and on operating expenses than planned, but he ended up with a $5,000 cash balance as expected.

Our hardware manager's strategy for getting out of trouble in February is interesting. He is selling off his merchandise and running down in inventory in February by $10,000 to avoid running out of

Table 2-8. Cash Flow Schedule.

ITEM	JANUARY ESTIMATE	JANUARY ACTUAL	FEBRUARY ESTIMATE	FEBRUARY ACTUAL	MARCH ESTIMATE	MARCH ACTUAL	YEARLY TOTAL ESTIMATE	YEARLY TOTAL ACTUAL
Cash on Hand, 1st of Month	$20,000	$20,000	$ 5,000		$ 5,000			
Cash Receipts								
Cash sales	25,000	24,000	25,000		25,000		$ 300,000	
Accounts receivable	20,000	24,000	55,000		75,000		825,000	
Sale of assets	0		0		0		0	
Loans	10,000	10,000	0		0		10,000	
Total	75,000	78,000	80,000		105,000		1,135,000	
Cash Expenses								
Merchandise	60,000	62,000	50,000		70,000		720,000	
Payroll	20,000	20,000	20,000		20,000		240,000	
Operating expenses	10,000	11,000	10,000		10,000		120,000	
Purchase of assets	0		0		0		0	
Total	90,000	93,000	80,000		100,000		1,080,000	
Cash, End of Month	5,000	5,000	5,000		10,000		75,000	

cash. That is, his purchases are only $50,000 when they should be $60,000 to maintain a constant inventory level. He has run down his stock to get cash.

The third month collections on accounts receivable pick up to $75,000. With those receipts he is able to pay all his monthly expenses and rebuild his inventory (by $10,000) back up to normal (by purchases of $70,000). Still he can add $5,000 to his cash balance. The hardware business is now out of trouble because the accounts receivable will now come in at least at a rate of $75,000 per month. By keeping merchandising purchases at $60,000 each month and other expenses constant, he can build up his cash balance by $10,000 per month from April onward.

In summary, the cash management strategy used in Table 2–8 to beat the cash crisis was:

1. Draw down cash on hand by $15,000 during the first month to carry the business while accounts receivable payments were low.

2. Convert $10,000 of inventory into cash during February, by keeping merchandise purchases low and running down the stock levels, in order to keep at least a minimum $5,000 cash balance and not go broke.

3. Collect a normal level of accounts receivable in March and each month thereafter keeping expenses constant, and build the inventory up $10,000 to normal.

4. Build up the cash balances by $5,000 in March, and $10,000 in subsequent months, by continuing to collect receivables on schedule and keeping cash outflow constant.

In short, the cash flow schedule has proved to be a measurement and control tool which enabled our hardware owner, in this example, to get out of trouble and become a very solid and solvent business. By the end of the year, his cash balance can be built up to $75,000 according to the cash flow schedule in Table 2–8.

HOW MUCH CASH? MEASURES OF LIQUIDITY.

Is $75,000 in cash enough for this business, or too much?

A business owner wants to have enough cash so that he is sure that he will not go broke by being unable to pay his bills. On the other hand, he does not want so much cash around that it is idle and not earning a profit. The trade-off, then, is between security and profitability. Security is provided by liquidity, i.e., an adequate supply of cash and other quickly salable assets to meet all payments due. What we need, then, is some measure of what has been found to be "adequate" in normal business experience. Such measures can be found in financial ratios. Two ratios in particular are used to measure the degree of liquidity, or cash assets, which a firm needs. These two measures are called the *quick ratio* and the *current ratio*.

The *quick ratio* consists of the cash in a business plus accounts receivable, which can quickly be converted into cash, in relation to the current debts of a business. The quick assets should at least equal the current debt on a 1 to 1 basis. That is, the ratio should be 1.0 or better to meet the acid test of paying all creditors. Let us see how adequate a cash balance of $75,000 is for the hardware store by figuring the quick ratio from the assets and liabilities on the store's balance sheet (Table 2-4). The current liabilities in Table 2-4 are the accounts payable of $25,000 and the bank loan of $30,000 for a total of $55,000. Then

$$\text{Quick ratio} = \frac{\text{cash plus receivables}}{\text{current liabilities}} = \frac{\$75,000 + \$25,000}{\$55,000} = 1.8$$

The quick ratio of 1.8 means that cash and receivables are 1.8 times the current liabilities. A 1.8 ratio is very conservative and is higher than it needs to be to meet the acid test of liquidity of paying off all creditors. The cash balance could, by this measure, be reduced to $30,000 and still have a quick ratio of 1.0. This tells us that nearly $45,000 in excess cash is being carried in the account, which could be put to better use in terms of making a profit.

The *current ratio* is the relationship of all current assets, including inventory, to the current liabilities. Conservatively, this ratio should be at least 2 to 1. In our example, then, from the hardware store:

$$\text{Current ratio} = \frac{\text{current assets}}{\text{current liabilities}} = \frac{\$150,000}{55,000} = 2.7$$

The current ratio in this example is also higher than it needs to be. About $40,000 in excess cash in the business could be used for profitable investment, and still leave a current ratio of 2 to 1.

A cash balance of about $30,000 to $35,000 is probably enough, in the hardware example, to meet conservative financial ratio requirements. Therefore, the business by year end (Table 2–8) would have about $40,000 in excess cash which could be used to expand the business in some profitable way.

MEASURES OF TOTAL CASH FLOW

Now let us take a different look at the cash management problem, from a longer point of view. We have looked at cash flow so far from a very short-term viewpoint, because businesses go broke in the short term. We have spent a lot of time on the monthly interaction between cash receipts and cash payments, which has involved us heavily in looking at collecting accounts receivable in relation to current debts, such as accounts payable and bank loans. The reason we spent so much time on that problem is that it is the most important one to control on a day-to-day basis, and failure to control cash flow results in bankruptcy.

However, let us assume that we know how to make a cash flow schedule and to always be sure that we generate enough cash to cover the daily costs of the business. That is, we always collect our accounts receivable fast enough to cover our cash outlays. We have seen how to do that in previous sections.

If we always collect our receivables as fast as outlays, then the amount of additional cash flow in the long run is equal to the earnings of the business plus its depreciation on assets. Now that statement is sort of a quantum leap ahead. Let me explain. If we look back at the discussion of the cash flow schedule in Table 2–8 again, we see that after March (when the business got through the erratic changes in accounts receivable and inventory), the net new cash flow of $10,000 per month was equal to its monthly earnings.

Earnings are not necessarily cash; they are just the accounting difference between income and expenses and can end up anywhere—in inventory, in repaying bank loans, and in adding to other assets. But they also can end up as cash, if you manage the cash flow schedule to turn them into cash. That is what we did by year end in Table 2–8. We collected the profit off both the cash and credit sales and accumulated it as more cash; we increased the cash during the year by $55,000 and ended up with a $75,000 cash balance on hand.

The second item which can potentially be converted as a net addition to cash is the depreciation on assets. Depreciation is a capital charge, which is allowed by the Internal Revenue Service (IRS) as a deduction against income, to pay a business back for the capital investment such as building and equipment which is being used up, worn out, or has to be replaced. Depreciation, like earnings, are a net addition to the funds of the company; depreciation also can be converted to cash through careful control of the cash flow schedule.

Chapter 3, as well as containing a more detailed explanation of depreciation and its uses, will teach us more about using the total funds of a business. For the time being, take it as a matter of faith that earnings and depreciation can be converted into cash; in the long run, they are a measure of the amount of net new cash flow which is available to the business. Maybe that is not altogether clear yet, because the mysteries of accounting are not easily dispelled in one short chapter. Yet it is true that earnings and depreciation are, in the long run, net additions to the cash flow of a business.

Another way to project cash flow, then, is to take the present cash balances of a business and add to them the earnings and depreciation of a future period. This method is roughly correct as a means of judging the future flow of cash over a full period, like a year, but it tells you nothing of the cash crunch which may occur on a weekly or monthly basis if immediate cash outlays outrun cash receipts. We started first with the monthly cash flow schedule as a measure and means for short-term control so you would not go broke in the short run while looking ahead over a longer period. Now, however, we are ready to look further ahead, because we have the measure and means to control short-term cash problems through the cash flow schedule.

The cash position of a business can be built by adding its earnings and depreciation to present cash balances. The future cash flow and future cash balances are our main source of new investment money. We want to keep reinvesting our excess cash profitably so that we get the greatest possible return on investment. We saw in the previous section how to measure the adequacy of cash through the quick ratio and the current ratio. To the extent that these two measures help determine that the business is carrying excess cash, the business manager will want to consider additional investments, either to expand the sales of the present business or to branch off into new products or lines of business.

However, building up a business or making a prudent new investment takes time, thought, planning, and care. You need to know when the cash balances in your business will build up to the point at which they can be reinvested. That is, your reinvestment or expansion plans must go on in parallel with your cash management plans, so that the two will come together at a point in time when you can act upon them. Timing is the essence of good business management. One of the critical timing problems is to have the cash when you need to invest. By "invest" we mean either expand the present business or invest in something new. Either way, the cash must be on hand when the opportunity comes.

There are two ways to estimate what your future cash balances will be over the next year or two. The first way is to project your own cash flow and earnings, just as we did in Table 2-8. This is probably the best way.

A second way is to compare your own projection of cash flow with the cash flow of other businesses. This measure of total cash flow can be made from Table 2-9, which shows the cash flow of all corporations by asset size and general industry type. Table 2-9 is figured by adding depreciation to earnings, including executive compensation, as a percentage of assets as shown in Table 1-5. To these earnings have been added the average depreciation on total assets by all corporations, by size and industry, from the Federal Trade Commission reports. Table 2-9 shows the average depreciation and average earnings including executive compensation for all corporations in the United States. These averages may be a little low, because they include all corporations with and without earnings (that is, they include corporations losing money). As an overall guide, they are a useful, general measure of the total cash flow which you might expect. You should do at least as well as these averages, and most likely you can do better. You can grade yourself as good, fair, or poor by comparing your own cash flow with these averages. If you do better than the averages in Table 2-9, you are doing a good job. If your performance is the same as in Table 2-9, you are doing a fair job because there are some losers averaged into the results. If your cash flow is running less than the averages in Table 2-9, you are headed for trouble; and you need to go back to the earlier sections of this chapter, as well as to Chapter 1, in order to tighten up your control by better cash flow scheduling as by beefing up your earnings so you get high net additions to cash balances.

Table 2-9. Cash Flow of Corporations, Per Dollar of Assets, by Asset Class.

ASSET CLASS (IN THOUSANDS OF DOLLARS)	MANUFACTURING	SERVICES	CONSTRUCTION	TRANSPORTATION	WHOLESALE AND RETAIL TRADE
Under $25	$.60	$2.51	$.75	$.57	$.58
$25–$49	.53	1.05	.46	.35	.42
$50–$99	.51	.77	.46	.30	.36
$100–$249	.42	.41	.31	.29	.29
$250–$499	.39	.25	.26	.21	.25
$500–$999	.36	.19	.22	.23	.21
$1,000–$2,499	.27	.15	.19	.17	.21
$2,500–$9,999	.22	.13	.14	.16	.17
$10,000–$24,999	.20	.13	.12	.15	.15
$25,000–$99,999	.18	.11	.12	.13	.13
$100,000 and over	.17	.11	.11	.07	.12

Source: The Office of the Secretary of the Treasury and the Federal Trade Commission.

Let us see how our example, the hardware store, compares with the average cash flow performance in Table 2-9. The hardware store started out with total assets of $65,000 (Table 2-1). Looking at asset size $50,000 to $99,000 and across to the column headed "Wholesale and Retail Trade," we find an average cash flow of 36¢ per dollar of assets for all corporations in this group. Average performance for the hardware store, then, would have been to generate $23,000 in new cash flow (.36 x 65,000). In fact, the store did better than that; it generated $55,000 new cash during the first year (Table 2-8, the difference between cash receipts of $1,135,000 and cash expenses of $1,080,000). Hence the performance of the store was good. Moreover, we also discovered by comparing its ending cash balance of $75,000 with the quick and current ratios, that it already had nearly $40,000 in surplus cash at the end of the period which could be invested.

Let us look ahead to next year and see how much more its cash balances might build up. The earnings per year are $120,000 and the store has little or no depreciation on its $5,000 of equipment. The cash balances at the end of the second year, then, could be as much as $195,000 if the owner maintained the same kind of cash flow control which was outlined earlier.

Again, let us compare the actual performance of the hardware store against the average for all corporations in Table 2-9. At the end of the first year, the store has total assets of $205,000 (i.e., $75,000 cash, $75,000 accounts receivable, $50,000 inventory, and $5,000 equipment). From Table 2-9 we find that the average cash flow is 29¢ per dollar of assets, which would make $59,500. The hardware store's performance is good and doing more than twice as much as the average.

These comparisons, then, suggest that the hardware store's performance is good. Its owner should be considering expanding the business or reinvesting a sum up to $100,000 by the end of the second year; this would leave him with $50,000 in cash in the business plus average living expenses.

In practice, of course, the hardware owner would probably reinvest gradually in building up the business from the end of the first year into the second by expanding his inventory, promotion, sales, and accounts receivable. However, he would do so under the carefull control of a cash flow schedule, such as Table 2-8, to be sure that he is able to generate cash as fast as he builds up the business. This owner got the message: never, NEVER, try to build up sales faster than you can generate cash to pay your bills!

SUMMARY

The most common way that small businesses fail is by running out of cash, usually the result of the owner concentrating on expanding sales and profit too rapidly without regard to what is happening to his balance sheet.

A balance sheet records the amount of financial resources available to the small businessman at any point in time.

The income statement shows how sales, expenses, and profit are progressing over time.

The cash flow schedule is the linchpin which ties the income statement and the balance sheet together by showing the changes in cash that are occurring. As such, it is the single most powerful tool of the small businessman to avoid bankruptcy and to stay solvent.

The aging of accounts receivable, done by figuring the time taken by customers to pay their accounts, provides the basis for estimating future cash receipts from credit sales.

A cash flow schedule can be made by showing the sum of monthly cash receipts from cash sales, payments on accounts receivable, bank loans, or sale of assets in relation to the cash outlays for operating expenses.

Cash balances can be built up by keeping cash outlays below cash receipts, in effect, by converting earnings into cash.

The amount of cash balances that a business should carry may be determined by the quick ratio and the current ratio. These measures indicate that, conservatively, cash and receivables should at least equal current liabilities, and current assets should at least be double current debts.

Any surplus cash, beyond the needs of the business or beyond that indicated by the quick and current ratio measures or beyond the obvious needs of the business, should be considered for expansion of the business or reinvestment in order to maximize the profitable use of cash resources.

A small businessman should plan ahead in using his cash resources profitably by estimating the timing when surplus cash will become available for reinvestment opportunities. This can be done with the cash flow schedule used in conjunction with profit planning of new investments.

In the long run, earnings and depreciation are major sources of additions to cash. Thus, for future years, cash flow can be estimated by adding estimated future earnings and depreciation to existing cash balances.

Small businessmen can compare their own cash flow performance with a measure of earnings and depreciation for all corporations (Table 2-9) from Treasury Department and Federal Trade Commission data on earnings and depreciation by size and major industries.

By careful attention to the several internal and external measures of cash flow management in this chapter, small businessmen can avoid the common cash crisis which many businesses experience. Instead, they can devote their attention to building cash balances, expanding their business, and going on to profit planning—the topic of the next chapter.

3

Profit Planning—Measures of the Total Flow of Funds

The primary strategy of business is to search for product lines with a high profit margin and a high market share (Chapter 1). Having selected a product line and market, the small businessman must quickly learn how to manage cash in order to survive the cash crisis—the most common cause of business failure—as well as to learn how to build up cash balances for expansion or reinvestment (Chapter 2).

Next the small businessman needs to learn to make sound and profitable investment decisions in the use of the cash balances he has built up. That is what this chapter is about. In other words, we are returning to the primary strategy of the small businessman in Chapter 1 and asking the question: How can you increase your profit margins by reinvesting your cash balances?

In Chapter 4 we ask the second half of the strategy question from Chapter 1: How can you increase your market share by careful use of your cash balance?

By the time you finish the first four chapters, then, you will have a rounded set of tools to succeed in business. From there on we go into finishing touches of how you trace out your future or track down your problems.

Within this framework, let us turn our attention to profit planning, or how you increase your profit margins by shrewd and prudent use of your cash balances, which you have learned to manage so well.

SOME EASY ACCOUNTING PRELIMINARIES AGAIN

To do prudent profit planning, we need to make use of accounting information about the workings of the business again. You are not an accountant, and perhaps could care less. But take it easy, you learned the hard part in the last chapter. All we need to do now is to add on a bit to what you know about cash flow.

Remember, the cash flow statement shows all the changes in cash receipts and cash expenses during a period. As such, the cash flow schedule accounts for the net change in the cash balances from the beginning to the end of the period. The reason we concentrated so much of our attention on the cash account is because running out of cash can put you out of business.

But what of all the other changes in the total financial resources of the business? What happened to them? That is a question we have to answer to get at the total profitability of the business, because cash does not represent all the resources which the owner has. His total resources are all his assets less his debts. Unless we understand how all these assets are being used, we cannot diagnose all the alternative choices open to the manager.

The change in the total funds of the business, all its assets and debts, can be measured exactly the same way that we handled the cash flow schedule—except now we analyze the change in all the accounts, not just the cash receipts and cash outlays. That is how this chapter builds upon the hard stuff that you have already learned from Chapter 2.

The analysis of the changes in all the accounts is known as the *sources and uses of funds,* or the *flow of funds statement,* and like the cash flow statement, it is simple. The cash flow schedule accounted for changes in cash. The flow of funds statement accounts for the changes in all your funds. That is important, because all your funds are what we want to maximize in terms of profit.

THE FLOW OF FUNDS STATEMENT

The flow of funds statement is the basic tool necessary for the profit planning. What does it look like? How can you make it up?

Perhaps the simplest thing would be to have your bookkeeper or accountant make it up for you, not that it is difficult to do yourself. You merely take the balance sheet of the ending period and subtract from each account listed in it the amount in the same account found in the balance sheet at the beginning of the period. For example, simply subtract the cash balances of the two balance sheets, the beginning cash balance from the ending cash balance, and go on making subtractions, item by item, through all the accounts on the balance sheet. That gives you the net change which occurred during the period. You then arrange each item, whether plus or minus, as to whether it was a source of funds or a use of funds—the reason why the statement is also called the sources and uses of funds, or simply the fund statement.

The reason I suggested that you let your accountant do it for you is that he can do it quite easily and quickly, whereas you may puzzle over it a bit. Also, the fund statement is not commonly published in annual reports, and it does not appear in basic accounting courses. That is, unlike the terms "balance sheet," "income statement," and "cash flow schedule," the fund statement is not something a businessman may come across in common parlance. The fund statement is commonly in use in large corporations by chief executives (prepared for them by their accountants) as a means of examining their investment options and decisions. But the fund statement is not commonly found in books about small business. Perhaps it is thought to be too esoteric for small businessmen, belonging more to the special skills of accountants. I disagree. I think that if big businessmen find it a useful tool for profit planning that small businessmen should do the same, if for no other reason than to be competitive. Besides, the fund statement is a useful tool for investment decision making. More than that, it is easy to prepare for anyone who can subtract, and it is a useful measure of investment decisions.

So let us assume that you have subtracted the account balances at the beginning of the year from those at the end of the year. What do you do then? How do you interpret the result?

A fund statement looks like Table 3-1.

Here we see an example of a business, let us say our friendly hardware store which we encountered in the last chapter, using several sources of funds to expand its business by building up inventory, adding new fixtures and equipment, and expanding its building space. The business has also paid down its bank loan and tax liability.

To obtain the funds for this expansion, the business used sources of funds from earnings and depreciation, used up some of its cash balances, collected accounts receivable, and borrowed more from creditors on accounts payable.

Table 3-1. Illustrative Fund Statement for a Small Business

SOURCES OF FUNDS		USES OF FUNDS	
Earnings	$10,000	New Equipment	$15,000
Depreciation	12,000	Building Expansion	20,000
Decreases in		Increases in	
Cash	18,000	Inventory	10,000
Accounts receivable	5,000	Cash	0
Increases in		Decreases in	
Accounts Payable	10,000	Bank loans	5,000
		Tax liability	5,000
Total Sources of Funds	$55,000	Total Uses of Funds	$55,000

You can apply the same kind of fund statement to your own business, merely by subtracting the beginning balance sheet from the ending one, and by remembering the following rules:

1. Any decrease in assets is a source of funds.
2. Any increase in assets is a use of funds.
3. Any increase in liabilities is a source of funds.
4. Any decrease in liabilities is a use of funds.
5. Positive earnings and depreciation are sources of funds.

According to these rules, then, you can see that any account can appear on either side of the fund statement, depending upon whether it is plus or minus for the period. In Table 3-1, for instance, cash is shown as a source of funds because the cash balance was decreased, or drawn down, during the period. That is, the cash balance at the end of the period minus the beginning of the period was minus $18,000. Had the subtraction shown the difference to be plus $18,000, that is, a build up of cash balances, then cash would have appeared on the other side of the fund statement (along with inventory in Table 3-1) as a use of funds, under the subheading "Increases in Cash."

What does the fund statement tell you? It tells you where all your money came from and where it went. That is, it tells you how you raised and invested all your funds. The hardware store in Table 3-1 raised its funds mainly from cash, earnings, and depreciation, and used the funds mainly to expand the business in inventory, equipment, and floor space.

Was that a good investment decision? Now we are getting into profit planning. We can only answer the question of whether Table 3-1 represents a good investment decision if we understand the profit implications of what was done.

There are several measures which we can apply to analyze the prudence of this investment decision.

1. The rate of return on investment—which deals with the issue of how much profit will be earned on the investment compared to other alternatives.
2. The break-even point—which deals with how soon the investment will begin to earn a profit.
3. The financial ratios—which deals with whether an optimum mix of assets was utilized by the investment to achieve the best rate of return.

We will deal with each of these measures in turn as a means of doing our profit planning.

The Rate of Return on Investment

The rate of return on investment (often referred to as *return on investment* or *ROI*) is perhaps the most common and pervasive measure of investment performance used in business decision-making; naturally a good deal of writing has appeared on the subject. In this literature, several methods—from simple to complex—of figuring ROI appear. The simplest form of calculation is merely to divide the annual expected profit by the investment. The more complicated forms of figuring ROI recognize that a dollar in the future is not as valuable as a dollar today, and therefore profits in the future are discounted to represent the present value of money to an investor. These methods are called the *discounted rate of return*.

Let us start with the simplest rate-of-return calculation. Our hardware store, in Table 3-1, has invested $45,000 in inventory, equipment, and space to try to expand its volume of sales. What return can be expected on the $45,000 investment?

To estimate the future profit, we have to make the same sorts of assumptions as those made by the hardware store owner. Let us assume, as he did, that by expanding his inventory by 20% (i.e., by $10,000 from $50,000 to $60,000) he could increase his sales volume by 20%. That is, the business manager assumes that his sales are limited by the amount and variety of stock he is carrying, so he increases the variety of his offerings to the customer.

Also, let us assume that his store was rather crowded, so he felt a need to expand his fixtures, showcases, equipment and space, in order to accommodate the added inventory and to make a better showing or display of his present stock. The store owner believes that by improving traffic and display in the store, and generally making it more attractive, he can increase his total sales by another 25%. What basis does he have for this subjective judgment? He may have checked around his area among competitors and looked at industry statistics on hardware sales per square foot of floor space that makes him feel this is a reasonable estimate.

All right, then his estimated increase in sales is expected to be 50% from $100,000 to $150,000 (i.e., 120% or 1.20 for stock increased multiplied by 125% or 1.25 for space and display improvement equals 1.50 or 150% in sales volume). If he maintains his same expense and net profit margin as before, he will earn 10% on the added sales of $50,000, or a profit of $5,000. The net profit of $5,000 divided by the investment which he made of $45,000 yields a simple rate of return of 11.1%.

A return of 11.1% is all right, compared to industry averages, but he should be able to do better. One way to have done better might have been to increase the inventory more and the facilities less. The hardware owner put $35,000 in fixtures and space expansion in order to achieve a 25% increase in sales, and he put $10,000 in inventory to get a 20% sales increase. He is getting a 2% increase in sales per $1000 of inventory investment, but only a 0.7% increase in sales per $1000 of facilities investment. If it had been practical for him to make a smaller facilities expansion and a larger inventory expansion, his mix of investment would have yielded a higher return.

Discounted Return on Investment

The annual net profit divided by the investment—for example the 11.1% shown above—is a simple and rough way to figure return on investment (ROI), and it is known as the simple rate of ROI. But it ignores the time value of money, that is, money in hand today is worth more than the same amount expected 5 or 10 years from now.

Everyone expects to earn a rate of interest on their savings in the bank; indeed, the bank charges a prime interest rate on loans to its customers which varies from 8 to 20% depending upon business conditions, inflation, and whether money is tight or easy. Let us assume on average that the cost of capital (i.e., the expected interest rate) is 10% per year. How much would the hardware store investment be worth over a 10-year period if it produced $5,000 per year at the end of each year for 10 years, assuming a 10% cost of capital?

You can figure that out on your hand calculator by putting in the $5,000 as the dividend and then divide by 1.10%, record the answer, and keep punching the "equals" button ten times (i.e., to divide the result each time for 10 years). The answer you would get will be what is shown in Table 3-2.

Table 3-2. Present Value of $5,000 per Year for 10 Years at 10%.

END OF YEAR	DISCOUNTED VALUE OF $5,000 AT YEAR END
1	$ 4,545
2	4,132
3	3,757
4	3,415
5	3,105
6	2,822
7	2,566
8	2,333
9	2,120
10	1,928
Total	$30,723

The present discounted value of a stream of income, or profit, of $5,000 per year for 10 years, at a 10% return, is $30,723. However, the hardware owner invested $45,000 hard dollars now in order to obtain a stream of discounted profits worth $30,723. In other words, he paid or invested nearly $15,000 too much for this profit return. He should have invested only $30,723 for the discounted value of a stream of profit of $5,000 per year for 10 years at a cost of capital of 10%.

How much profit per year should he receive for 10 years at a capital cost of 10% to warrant an investment of $45,000? The simplest way to figure that out is to get a book on investment finance out of the library and look up the present value tables which show the amount of discounted cash flow per year at 10% for 10 years produced by a principal sum of $45,000. We can approximate that amount on a hand calculator by assuming that at 10%, the mid-value discounted profit in the fifth year of the ten years should be about $4,500 (or 10% of 45,000). And because we are discounting cumulatively at 10% during the year, we should consider the value during the fifth year to be somewhat higher, which turns out by trial and error to be 4,545. Now put the number 4,545 in your calculator and multiply it by 1.10 (the interest rate) cumulatively five times. The result is $7,320. Now if you were to take $7,320 and discount it for ten years at 10%, the same as we did in Table 3–2 above, you will find that the total discounted value of the income stream of $7,320 per year is approximately $45,000. That tells you that you should receive a profit of $7,320 per year for 10 years at a 10% cost of capital to warrant your investing $45,000.

Is there any way our hardware owner could have invested his $45,000 to produce an annual profit of $7,320 per year? You may recall that he makes a 10% profit on sales. That means he would have to invest his funds to produce another $73,200 per year in sales (which would yield a profit of $7,320 at .10 x $73,200). As it was, he invested his funds to yield a $50,000 increase in sales volume, and a $5,000 profit, which he did by putting $10,000 in inventory and $35,000 in facilities. He got a 2% increase in sales for each $1,000 put into inventory and a .7% increase in sales per $1,000 put into facilities. Suppose we change the mix. How much more would we have to put into inventory, and how much less into facilities, out of the $45,000 to produce $73,200 in sales and $7,320 in profit?

We can figure this out (cursing algebra all the way, perhaps) by the expression: $2x + .7 (45,000 - x) = 73,200$ where x is the amount to be invested in inventory. The expression says that if x is the amount put into inventory, we will get 2 times that amount in sales, plus .7 times the remainder of the $45,000 (which is $45,000 - x$) by investing in facilities. Solving that formula, we find that and inventory investment of $32,000 and a facilities investment of $12,900 would produce sales of $73,200 and profits of $7,320 per year. In other words, the hardware owner got his investments backwards. He should have put $32,100 in inventory instead of $10,000 and he should have put $12,900 in facilities instead of $35,000. By reversing his investment strategy and putting his funds into inventory at a ratio of about 3 to 1 versus facilities, he could make his $45,000 produce a 10% ROI on a discounted cash flow basis, i.e., $7,3200 per year.

In other words, investment strategy is a matter of seeking the most appropriate mix of investments out of the total funds available from the flow of fund statement to produce a discounted ROI in keeping with the cost of capital or the profit targets of the owner. To do that, you need to identify all the sources and uses of funds, to identify the available capital and the potential investments. Then the investment results should be tested by a discounted rate of return to find the optimum mix of investments to produce the greatest profit.

Break-Even Analysis

The ROI analysis shows your projected profit rate from which you would decide to invest or not to invest. But there is another little problem in the back of the minds of every small businessman, especially those who are conscious of the importance of cash flow: How much activity will it take for the investment to break even? We can look at this problem through a measure called *break-even analysis.*

A break-even analysis is based on the idea that some expenses are fixed and do not change with sales volume, while other expenses vary directly with sales activity. Examples of *fixed expenses* are rent, utility costs, depreciation on fixtures or equipment, interest, taxes, and so forth. *Variable expenses* would include cost of goods sold, materials, supplies, direct labor costs, packaging, and so forth. Expenses from the income statement based upon a sales volume of, say, $100,000 can be broken down into two groups, variable and fixed, as in Table 3–3.

Now suppose there are 260 working days in a year, with about 50 customers per day. That makes 13,000 customers served per year, at an average sales of around $8 each. We can also see that the cost of serving each customer is about $5.75 each ($76,000 divided by 13,000). While the variable cost of $5.75 is directly related to the number of customers served, the fixed costs will be $16,000 per year regardless of the number of customers.

However, we know that the number of customers fluctuates from

Table 3-3. Fixed and Variable Expenses for Break-Even Analysis.

VARIABLE EXPENSES		FIXED EXPENSES	
Supplies	$ 2,000	Rent	$ 6,000
Direct labor	20,000	Depreciation	3,000
Packaging	1,000	Interest	2,000
Advertising	2,000	Taxes	2,000
		Utilities	3,000
Expenses	25,000		
Cost of goods sold	50,000	Total fixed expenses	$16,000
Total variable expenses	$75,000		

time to time, depending upon prosperity, weather, season, and so forth. How many customer sales on average does it take to break even? Even more important: What is our profit at different volumes of activity? This is a crucial question in terms of investment, as to whether or not we need more capacity. In terms of our hardware store example, does it really pay to invest in facilities at all? At what volume of activity will we break even with such an expansion (which is reflected in the higher rent and depreciation shown in Table 3–3)?

The break-even chart plots the expenses on the vertical scale and the volume of activity on the horizontal scale, in this case the number of customers served. The $16,000 fixed cost is plotted as a horizontal line across the base of the chart, because it does not vary with the volume of activity. The variable cost is added to the fixed cost at a rate of about $5.75 of cost per customer sale. This gives the ascending line of total costs per unit, as seen in Figure 3-1.

Next on Figure 3-1 we plot the sales revenue to be received from increased volume of activity as a diagonal line from the left bottom corner to the top right corner. Notice where the revenue line crosses the expense line. That is the break-even point.

Anything below the break-even point, between the revenue and expense line, is a loss. Anything above the break-even point, between the revenue and expense line, is a profit. Notice how the losses widen at the low end of the chart, and how the profits become wider at the high end of the scale! The higher the fixed costs are, as a proportion of variable costs, the wider is the spread between the revenue and cost lines at the ends of the scale. That is, high fixed costs tend to

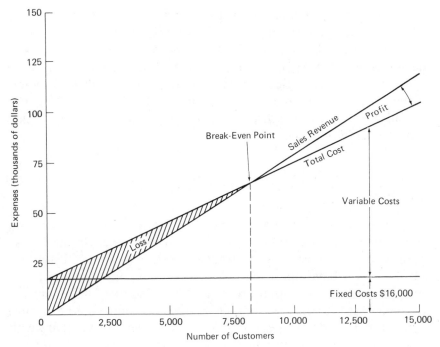

Figure 3–1.   Break-Even Chart.

produce large losses and large profits around the break-even point. In this particular example, the fixed costs are small relative to variable costs, and so the profit and loss spreads are rather narrow.

The break-even point in this example is at about 8,200 customers and $62,000 in sales volume. What does this measure tell us about the decision to expand the facilities of the hardware store?

First, a decision to expand should never be made if it raises the break-even point above the minimum experience in sales volume. In other words, this hardware store should not undertake the additional facilities investment if its sales volume, in past experience, ever drops below the $62,000 annual rate, because we know that will produce a loss.

Secondly, the owner of this business might give thought to cutting his variable costs or raising prices, if competition permits, in order to widen his profit spread on the break-even chart. Raising prices, if he can maintain the same competitive volume, will raise the sales revenue line upward on the chart. Cutting variable or fixed costs will lower the total cost line. Either or both actions on the part of the manager will widen the profit spread on the chart.

Thus, the break-even chart is an important measure in investment decisions in two ways: first, to determine whether losses are likely to occur by increasing fixed costs, and thus the break-even point, higher than minimum sales levels, and second, by pointing out graphically whether profit spreads need to be improved by raising prices or cutting costs.

Financial Ratios

We have now examined two aspects of the investment decision in profit planning, first its ROI, and second its impact on the break-even point. The next issue we want to explore is what effect an investment will have upon the balanced uses of our resources, i.e., does it produce an appropriate mix of resources? The mix of resources used can be seen, of course, by the accounts on the balance sheet. But how do the proportions in these accounts compare with other successful businesses?

Financial ratios provide a measure of the balanced use of assets and resources. Dun & Bradstreet, Inc. publishes annually a compendium of *Key Business Ratios* for 125 lines of retailing, wholesaling, and manufacturing.[1] These business ratios are a valuable measure in financial management. Table 3-4 shows the median ratio for 14 key business ratios for hardware stores in comparison with the hardware store illustration we have been following.

The financial ratios for our illustrative hardware store are derived from updating the balance sheet in Table 2-5, with the cash flow statement in Table 2-7, and by then assuming a sources and uses of funds statement as in Table 3-1 with the additional investment going $32,000 into inventory and $13,000 into facilities. We also assume that the hardware store is now earning $50,000 net profit per year. These assumptions yield the last column labeled "Illustrative Hardware Store."[2]

The illustrative hardware store, compared to the Dun and Bradstreet (D & B) ratios, is low on capitalization, low on debt, and low on inventory. This is perhaps what you might expect of a new

Table 3-4. Key Business Ratios for Hardware Stores (Median), 1977.

BUSINESS RATIO	DUN AND BRADSTREET: HARDWARE STORES	ILLUSTRATIVE HARDWARE STORE
Current assets to current debt (times)	3.79	3.28
Net profits on net sales (%)	3.56	4.20
Net profits on tangible net worth (%)	8.63	28.00
Net profits on net working capital (%)	14.18	21.7
Net sales to tangible net worth (times)	2.97	6.7
Net sales to net working capital (times)	3.30	5.2
Collection period (days)	n.a.*	n.a.
Net sales to inventory (times)	3.9	14.6
Fixed assets to tangible net worth (%)	14.3	10.0
Current debt to tangible net worth (%)	35.0	39.5
Total debt to tangible net worth (%)	98.6	20.0
Inventory to net working capital (%)	89.3	35.6
Current debt to inventory (%)	46.3	85.3
Funded debts to net working capital (%)	38.2	0

* n.a. = not available.
Reprinted with permission of Dun & Bradstreet.   (D & B)

small business that was bootstrapping its way to survival and success. The illustrative hardware store is close to the D & B averages on the first two ratios. On the next four ratios, the illustrative store is high because it is undercapitalized in net worth and working capital. The sales to inventory ratio is also high compared to the average because the illustrative store has low inventories. The fixed assets and current debt to tangible net worth are close to the norms. The total debt to net worth is low, which suggests that the hardware store could borrow more from the bank as a loan to purchase more inventory; this is also indicated by the current debt to inventory ratio. The inventory to working capital ratio indicates that the inventory is probably one-half the size of what it should be. The lack of funded debt also indicates another source of borrowing open to this business in order to bring its inventory into better balance.

While the financial ratios of the illustrative store are perhaps extreme as an example of an undercapitalized new business, the use of the business ratios as measures of financial management indicates the decision means by which managers can seek to measure their use of resources in order to bring them into better balance. This is not to say that a small businessman should follow the business ratios blindly. To some extent, it is a competitive advantage to have a new business like a hardware store run a good profit on a low inventory, compared to the industry averages. However, too much deviation, as in this case, may indicate loss of sales and profits due to underinvestment in inventory and undercapitalization of the business.

The investment strategy which our hardware store owner should now follow in his profit planning, based upon this analysis, is to cultivate his relations with a bank where he can establish his credit-worthiness through his good profit performance and good cash flow management, as indicated by his liquid asset ratios. His business merits additional bank loans to build up his inventory, sales, and profit. As he accomplishes this buildup of his business (including his cash balance by the cash flow management tools of Chapter 2), he should then seek to get part of his short-term bank loans funded into longer term debt. All this while, of course, he should be building up his own net worth in the business through retained earnings. By following this strategy, he will be able in perhaps two or three years to amass adequate capitalization for his firm.

SUMMARY

The primary objective of a business is to build its profit margins and market share. The flow of funds statement is a basic tool for profit planning.

You can construct a sources and uses of funds statement by subtracting the items in the beginning balance sheet from the end of the period balance sheets.

You then classify each item as to source or use by the following procedures:

1. Any decrease in assets is a source of funds.
2. Any increase in assets is a use of funds.
3. Any increase in liabilities is a source of funds.
4. Any decrease in liabilities is a use of funds.
5. Positive earnings and depreciation are sources of funds.

The fund statement tells you where your investments went during the year. Projections of future uses of funds can help you analyze estimated future profits.

The measure of an investment decision is return on investment. This can be figured as a simple return, i.e., estimated annual earnings divided by the amount of the investment. Or it can be figured more precisely to take into account the time value of money by the discounted rate of return, which is figured by dividing future payments by the cumulative cost of capital over the expected years.

The rate of return earned by different investments within the firm, such as inventory versus facilities, can be looked upon as alternative mixes of investment to see which yields the highest profit.

Once the rate of return is determined, the businessman will next want to know what the break-even point will be under the new investment, which will presumably increase fixed costs.

The break-even point can be measured by adding the variable costs per unit of activity to the fixed cost to see at what point the total costs are covered by sales revenues.

An investment should never be made if it raises the fixed costs and break-even point above the minimum sales level from recent experience. To do so would be to ensure losses whenever sales dropped to their minimums.

The break-even chart also helps the businessman decide, by examining the spread between costs and revenues, whether he should consider cutting costs or raising prices, if he can do so competitively.

After investment plans have been made, but before they are implemented, their projected effect on the balance sheet and income statement should be measured through the use of financial ratios.

Financial ratios enable a businessman to compare his financial performance with other firms in his field, specifically to see whether he has a balanced use of resources.

The appropriate mix of resources is crucial to profit planning; financial ratios provide guidance as to an exceptional or unusual use of resources for the businessman to examine.

The 14 business ratios compiled by Dun and Bradstreet are useful measures of industry performance, with which the small businessman may compare himself. The ratios are of sufficient variety to measure the appropriate balance of inventory, cash, working capital, current debt, long-term debt, fixed assets relative to net worth, and the profitability of the firm in relation to working capital, sales, fixed assets and equity. In some cases, deviations from the ratios may indicate unusually good financial performance, such as high profit on sales, or a high current asset ratio to current debt. In other cases, the ratios can be used to diagnose undercapitalization, inadequate inventory, poor collections, or poor return on fixed assets.

Profit planning, then, proceeds by using the fund statement to identify investments which have or will occur, measuring the rate of return on investment, seeing that the investment does not raise the break-even point beyond minimum sales experience, and testing through financial ratios whether the balance and mix of investments is appropriate and optimum.

The strategy of building profits through investment planning can become a part of the everyday operations of a business by the practice of following this sequence of measurements. If you do that regularly, you can build your profits and your business to be competitive with anyone in your industry. When you have accomplished that, you are well on the way to financial success.

REFERENCES

1. Dun & Bradstreet's address is 99 Church Street, New York, New York, 10007.
2. For an excellent guidebook on how to figure business ratios, see *Ratio Analysis for Small Business,* published by the SBA, Small Business Management Series. This book is sold by the Superintendent of Documents, U.S. Government Printing Office, Washington, D.C. 20402.

4

Measures of the Future: The Product-Market Plan

Marketing is the heart of a successful small business. For that reason, this chapter should, perhaps, have been the first in the book. So far, what you have done is to learn how to survive financially.

Still you want to *do* something with your business, to build it up and make it a success. In the first chapter we discussed general strategies of building a successful business. One such strategy is to find a product that could have a high market share. The problem is to find this product.

A high market share implies two things: (1) having a product or concept that sells and meets consumers needs and (2) securing a superior competitive position as compared to others. So we want two things when we start out thinking about marketing: to meet consumers needs and to get a superior position. For the most part, we can accomplish both of these goals by assuring the quality of what we sell. Consumers want something a little better than the run-of-the-mill stuff on the market. "Something better" means quality in the product or service—something extra, something different, something special.

The "special" quality of our product helps us to sell. Marketing is the management of the whole sales process. Just as it is easier to row downstream, it is easier to sell something special. You are giving customers what they want, and consumers' attitudes are flowing with you. If you have to sell something consumers don't particularly want, selling is tough, like rowing upstream. You can only do it by a high-pressure hard sell, while rowing as hard as you can all the time to find some new prospects. That kind of selling is not much fun. But selling something people want can be fun. You are pleasing them, helping them, serving them. They like it. You will enjoy it, too.

Marketing can be a fun thing to do, then, if you start off right, with the right concept. The concept is to know what people want and give them something special.

There are two ways to know what people want. One is to have selling or market experience in the field so that you get a "feel" for what people want by your previous sales and conversations with customers. That is why prior experience, and learning the game on someone else's money, is the way to go if you can.

The second way to find out what people want is to investigate or explore their needs yourself by inquiry, conversation, interviews, or formal market research. I have learned that a good way to start is to ask wholesalers and retail dealers. That may seem like giving the competitive game away, right in the beginning, but it need not be. You ask the question about a quality feature, not about how you are going to put it on the market. I worked for an electronics company that thought it could develop a brighter TV picture tube, because the existing tubes only generated about 15% of the light that they could theoretically produce. I talked to a lot of wholesalers and dealers and asked: "How much difference would a brighter tube make in sales?" Within three days and a dozen interviews I had a good idea of the substantial market demand for the tube. Unfortunately, the tube was tricky to produce in quantity with high-performance quality. This was a market success and a product failure, fortunately discovered before spending much money on it.

A happier ending occurred when a merchant had the concept that children deserved a shopping outlet of their own that dealt in kids' stuff, with all the furniture, fixtures, displays, services, and even afternoon tea, geared to kids' taste and stature. He had some experience, but he went around to other stores and browsed the children's departments and asked: "What do kids really like that you have here?" Sure you can get answers. Why shouldn't the salesperson tell you what kids are buying and what they like? You may be a customer wanting to corroborate your own choice of a present. The merchant set up a children's specialty store that was a success.

In short, the fastest and most reliable way to check out quickly whether a marketing idea will work is to ask the people who are in the market, the salespeople first because they are easiest to locate and interview. Next, you would check out the customers themselves, but that is more time-consuming and expensive. We will deal with that in the next chapter on marketing research.

At the start we are trying to verify a marketing concept or image, to locate a position for ourselves in the market. Marketers speak of "positioning" their product in the market. What do they mean by "market position?"

MARKET POSITIONING AS A MEASURE

Market position is a place you occupy in the market, your private space which has distance from other people's space and position. "Position" is just another word for your image, but it is more useful in the sense that position can be measured.

A beer or tire manufacturer can show you graphically exactly where their brand lies in a position relative to other brands in terms of key attributes: for beer attributes like lightness, dryness, maltiness, heartiness, or price; for tires attributes like wearability, traction, puncture-resistance, softness of ride, and price. Among brand manufacturers these types of attributes are measured by consumer attitude surveys, the market researchers then calculate the strength of each consumer preference by a statistical technique called *discriminate analysis* or *multidimensional scaling*. These are rather elegant terms and techniques which mean simply to determine the importance or priority which the customer places upon that quality or attribute relative to others. The relative importance of these qualities can then be put upon a graph to occupy a space, and that space is the brand's product-market "position." In a sense, then, the market position is a measure of what consumers want and what "image" they have of competitive products.

We can do the same thing as small businessmen in a less formal way to test out market ideas on a small scale. For example, suppose you are a manufacturer's representative selling furniture and you get the idea that there may be a market for waterbeds which you can enter with a small business of your own. Your experience and inquiries tell you that the key qualitites or attributes which customers want in a waterbed are its fluid-softness, distinctiveness, informality, sexiness, and leakproof safety. You realize you are appealing to a narrow market segment—the youthful, laid-back generation—but that is okay because there are enough of them around to support several small businesses.

Now you realize to some extent that being leakproof and soft are opposite attributes, because to be leakproof the material needs to be thicker, stronger, and stiffer. Hence you need to know which of these attributes is the most important. In the meantime, of course, you scout around for a supplier of materials who can give you the strongest, most durable, burst-resistant plastic available with good flexibility. Then you test the market concept by talking to wholesalers and retailers in the trade as to which of these qualities is the most important, and you talk to friends and customers as well. You begin to realize that sexiness is perceived as fluid-softness, and distinctiveness is synonymous with informality. So you have three important attributes: fluid-softness, informality, and leakproof safety. But you have a fourth important attribute—price—because you must always consider the price of your product to the consumer.

You then realize that informality is a furniture design quality, which you can accomplish with a low, hardwood frame, lined with a metal tank, to hold the water mattress. The bed frame lies flat on the floor, and that is its distinction and informality. The metal liner provides safety against leaks and water damage. Now you have a product concept. You do some more interviewing, and you arrive at your own rating of the market position of your product, which is shown below as product A in Figure 4–1, compared to competitive products B, C, and D.

Figure 4–1 could be shown in a variety of other ways, such as softness versus leakproof safety, or informality versus softness. Moreover, more elegant charts can be made with the space depicted in three dimensions. But Figure 4–1 is simple and tells us what we want to know. That is, our product A occupies a unique position and

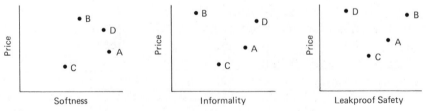

Figure 4–1.   Product-Market Position of a Water Bed.

space in the market. Product A has a good quality with respect to all three attributes at a moderate price. That is what we have to sell from this position—good quality at a fair price. Not terribly exciting perhaps, but a solid sales appeal.

Product D is probably our toughest competitor, because he has achieved a greater softness and a higher degree of style in informality. D is a furniture designing company and has outdone us by a beautiful bed frame with the informal look to appeal to the laid-back generation. So D's style will be hard to compete with, but we will compete favorably in price. D's price is higher, and D also has poor quality as to leak-resistance.

Producer B is going to compete on leak-resistance all the way, because he has the best product on that score, but at the expense of softness. Besides B is not a furniture maker and has no sense of design. He simply has put a box on the floor.

Producer C is going to be a hard price competitor. C's quality is not as good as ours on any of the three attributes, but he can beat us on price all the way. Against C we will have to sell quality.

Does product A have a viable market-product position? Well, yes, it is fairly good—as good as, and perhaps slightly better then, any competitor in the field—but product A is not going to run away with the market. Product A should get a slightly higher share than the rest, followed perhaps by D and C if they do their marketing well.

If we are going to go into business with product A, we have to sell good quality at a moderate price. We need to create the image of ourselves and product A as the quality product of the masses—the Chevrolet of the waterbed business. A few style buffs will go off to D, price-cutters to C, and safety fiends to B, but we will get the rest if we do our market jobs.

What is the marketing job?

AWARENESS AS A MEASURE
OF MARKETING PERFORMANCE

The first marketing job is to create awareness of our product attributes. We want customers to recognize that product A has the best overall quality in softness, informality, and leakproof safety at a fair price. That awareness means we have to communicate information to them.

The best place to start with awareness is with yourself and your staff. Unless *you* have a sharp image of your product's attributes, you will not be able to communicate it to others. The reason we went through the product attribute interviews and graphing the market position of the product is to create a clear image in our own minds of what we are selling, and to train the staff to sell those qualitites. Our own awareness as salespeople must be sharp to convey awareness to a customer.

Beyond that we have to bring customers into our store to communicate the attributes to them and make them aware of the special quality of what is offered. That brings into play the whole array of marketing activity, what we will call the *marketing mix.* Everything you do in marketing management is aimed first at awareness and then at closing the sale, but the special qualities of the marketing mix which apply to communicating awareness are: (1) traffic and location, (2) personal selling, (3) advertising, and (4) sales promotion.

Location requires care in selecting a site where people can easily find you. For some types of products, particularly convenience goods where time is the essence of a sale or shopping goods where comparison is the essence, you want to be in a high-traffic zone with other shops, which also means high rent. Therefore, you have to bring people into your store once they are in the vicinity.

Bringing people in is done by advertising to create the first awareness of your presence, general quality, and location. Advertising can be a waste of money unless you appeal to a specific segment of the market that is your clientele in the sense of consumer attitudes and needs. So your advertising must go into a media with a message that is directed toward your market segment.

Bringing people into your store is also done by sales promotions, special sales, and special features which will appeal to your market segment. In waterbeds, a demonstration day could be a sales promotion in which people and prospective customers are invited in to slosh unabashedly on a waterbed. Other sales promotions might emphasize other attributes—softness by allowing customers to compare your waterbed with samples of product C and B, leakproof safety by a special guarantee and warranty, and style and informality by placing your bed in a fully furnished model room.

Once you have used location, advertising, and sales promotions to bring in prospective customers, the rest is up to you by personal selling. You have to convey your image of your product's attributes and qualities to the customer in a way that encourages their trial and then purchase.

We will say more about awareness in the context of the total marketing mix later, but now we want to turn attention to measuring awareness. Measuring awareness can be done by market research surveys which ask questions about the customer's degree of knowledge about waterbeds. Does he or she even know they exist, and if so, can he or she recognize the different qualities of various brands? Market surveys can be quite elaborate and precise. We will show you how to do a market survey in the next chapter. Even without a market survey, you can sample opinion by inquiry in conversations, among people you meet, and by asking drop-in customers where they heard about your product. Your early samplings may be incomplete, but they are the beginning of a measurement.

You want to have the measurement firmly in mind, that is the proportion of the customers in your market segment who are aware of your product. The measurement is this: percentage of awareness has to be higher than your market share, or you are not making it. If you are starting out in the waterbed business for the first time, your market share is zero; awareness of your product has to higher than zero if you are going to bring in any customers. As a rough rule of thumb, awareness should be half again as high as your market share. If your market share is 20%, the awareness of your product or store should be at least 30% of the customers in your market segment. The reason you want to keep raising awareness higher than your market share is that everyone is not going to be a customer, at least right away, and besides you want to keep your business and sales moving.

Well, you know roughly what your market share is. You can interview enough people by conversation to get an idea of awareness, and your measure of performance will be to keep that awareness half again as high as your market share.

THE TEST OF MARKETING EXPERIENCE

Well, you may say, this marketing business is more effort than I bargained for. Is it worth it? What I had in mind was hanging out my shingle and letting people beat a path to my door—like building a better mousetrap. What is wrong with that?

There is nothing wrong with that if you can stand the risk of losing your investment. Maybe you will get lucky and people *will* beat a path to your door. But how are they going to know you are there, or that what you offer is special, unless you tell them?

The SBA gives six methods for success in a small store.[1] They are:

1. Cater to customers—know their needs, give them a bit extra.
2. Build an image—use steady solid promotion to create a favorable recognition of your merchandise.
3. Encourage teamwork—work with your employees, don't keep secrets from them, give them the facts about your merchandise.
4. Plan ahead—use teamwork to plan special sales and promotions.
5. Look for profit volume—determine your break-even point and control sales and expenses to balance out at a high profit.
6. Pay your civic rent—help build your community and the people in it will help build you, because you will know them and they will know you—awareness again.

The SBA's "Marketing Checklist" (Small Marketers Aids No. 156) stresses many of the same points from the experience of small business. Some of the questions in the checklist include:

Have you estimated the total market you share with competition?
Should you appeal to this entire market rather than a segment?
Do you stress a special area of appeal, such as lower prices, better quality, wider selection, convenient location, or convenient hours?
Do you visit market shows and conventions to help anticipate customer needs?
Do you ask your customers for suggestions?
Do you know which media (radio, television, yellow pages, newspapers, handbills) can most effectively reach your target customers?
Are your promotional efforts fairly regular?

These are only a few of the 200 or so questions in the checklist, but they give you some sense of the importance of pointing your marketing toward a target clientele with a clearly defined market-product position from which to sell.

Okay, you say, that is just good advice from the SBA. What do they know? Well, they know what has made thousands of small businesses, to whom they have made loans, succeed or fail. But perhaps there is even more convincing evidence.

About 120 of the major corporations in the United States support a computer data-base project called the Profit Impact of Marketing Strategies (PIMS), which is operated by the Strategic Planning Institute associated with Harvard University.[2] The project grew out of the experience of General Electric Corporation beginning about 1960, in their attempt to find better answers to the causes of GE's successes and failures with various products. In 1972, some Harvard marketing professors convinced GE that the data base would be even more valuable if the experience of more companies was included. This was done by adding companies like Exxon, duPont, Mead, J.P. Stevens, and others who contributed their product-financial-market experience on new lines of business. The data was sanitized or made confidential by multiplying it by an arbitrary factor. A subscribing company has access only to its own data and the general sanitized data of all companies, but not to any information about another company.

Considerable secrecy still surrounds the findings, but some general results are of interest to all businessmen, large and small. The PIMS project measures 37 factors—including technology, R&D, and market activity—that account for the success or failure of products. Suppose a firm has a low market share (say 10 to 15%), and is making small expenditure on R&D (2%) as well as on marketing (4 to 5%); what can it do to strengthen its product-market position relative to competition? Should it make some large new R&D commitments, or large new marketing commitments, to try to make a product innovation or make a major marketing push? The PMS data base says, no.

✓1. High marketing expenditures for low-quality products usually end up hurting profitability.

2. Low market share competitors who spend money on R&D to out-innovate competitors usually do not come up with a significant

technical advance, and if they do, stronger competitors usually seize the opportunity away from the weaker company by bringing in a close substitute and beating them at the marketing game.

3. The attempt to compete by bringing costs down through large-scale mechanization and automation will usually not work for a weak company because it will not have enough capital or competitive strength to succeed and ends up instead in a cash-flow crisis.

4. Heavy R&D, marketing, or investment are even more dangerous for weak companies with labor unions, because the drain of the expenditure plus the union is more than the financial resources can bear.

What is there left for the small or weak competitor to do? The PIMS Study says the best remedy for a weak market share is to have high product quality, to be a good follower, tighten cost controls, concentrate on a more sharply defined market segment, and strengthen services to customers in some important respect.

What does all that amount to? It means understanding the marketing concept and running a good marketing mix.

THE MARKETING CONCEPT AND MARKETING MIX

The marketing concept assumes that every aspect of a business, whether finance, production, legal, accounting, personnel, or marketing, has the purpose of identifying, anticipating, and satisfying customer needs. "Identifying" means having an image of the product-market position and how the firm's qualities satisfy consumer needs. "Anticipating" means looking ahead to find the new markets of the future. "Satisfying" means assuring that the customer gets good use from the product or service, that it is reliable, repairable, and usable, and that the firm stands behind its products.

The marketing concept grew up out of the tendency for business to be too product- and production-oriented, as most businesses were from 1870 to 1950. That is, business thought of itself as putting a product on the market, and it was up to the sales department to sell it. This is the hang-out-your-shingle syndrome again. But sales departments cannot sell poor products for very long unless the customer is happy with it, and the sales department cannot by itself remedy the problems of dissatisfied customers unless the designers, researchers, manufacturers, financiers, lawyers, staff, and chief executives recognize that they have a responsibility to see that the product does what it claims to do. In other words, the whole organization has to understand, believe in, and fulfill the image, attributes, qualities, or product-market position of the company—or else it will not work. That is the marketing concept.

The marketing concept means that all of management, all management functions, are concerned with selling and satisfying customers—not just the sales department. Therefore, the *marketing mix* is what it takes to have satisfied customers and it encompasses the whole range of business activities which impact the customers. In practice, the marketing mix is usually narrowed down to those services which are more immediate in their effects on customers, and these services or departments are:

1. Product development (R&D, engineering, production, and marketing).
2. Market segmentations and merchandising (marketing).
3. Distribution channels (marketing, shipping, and logistics).
4. Pricing (marketing, accounting, and finance).
5. Advertising (advertising and marketing).
6. Personal selling (marketing).
7. Sales promotion (marketing and advertising).
8. Packaging (production, logistics, shipping, advertising, and marketing).
9. Product assurance (engineering, quality control, and legal).
10. Servicing (engineering, field service, legal, and marketing).

In a very real sense, then, the marketing concept indicates that the whole business organization is involved in the marketing mix. Let us see how the marketing mix works in more detail.

Product Development and Technological Innovation

Product development may be simply the creation of a new market concept, like the waterbed illustration, in which the innovator is adapting existing products to new consumer needs. Any good idea man with a feel for the market can do this kind of innovation; such new product concepts are the most feasible approaches to start a small business because they require little capital.

A second kind of product development is by the lone inventor, who comes up with an idea which advances the technological state of the art in a unique way that gives him an exclusive and proprietary position which can be patented. The invention of xerography or the valves for aerosol cans were of this nature and resulted in new businesses that made fortunes. Inventions usually require that the inventor raise large funds privately to develop the product to marketable form, otherwise he is likely to lose the benefits of the innovation to other investors.

Once established, small firms may have an owner-inventor or a small R&D staff which carries on its new development work out of the earnings of the ongoing sales and products. In fact, such innovation by small firms is rather widespread and has yielded remarkable results in new products.

A study done for the U.S. Office of Management and Budget indicates that small firms have compiled a striking record of innovation compared with larger firms.[3] The findings show that:

1. Firms with less than 1,000 employees accounted for almost one-half of the major U.S. innovations during 1953–1973.
2. The ratio of innovations to sales is about one-third greater for small firms with less than 1,000 employees than in larger firms.
3. The ratio of innovation to R&D employment is four times greater in smaller firms (less than 1,000 employees) than in larger businesses.
4. The cost per R&D scientist is one-half as great in the small firms as it is in the large ones.
5. Nevertheless, only 8% of Federal government R&D awards went to small firms, although we saw in Table 1–3 that small businesses constitute 98% of the firms.

According to this study, the number of innovations in manufacturing per $10 billion in sales was roughly 3 per $10 billion in sales for small firms during the period 1953–1966, and it fell to 2 per $10 billion in sales in 1967–1973. As a measure of probability for the small businessman with annual sales of $1 million per year, his chances of making a major technological innovation are about 1 in 50,000. Those are long odds, of course, but they are not discouraging. The odds are better than most lotteries and mean more than anything that, although innovation is not a matter of chance, you really have to know your field and work at it. Large companies whose odds are less than small businesses at only 1.5 per $10 billion in sales, try to develop superior knowledge through concentrated effort, and they narrow their odds of success in a new product innovation to perhaps 1 in 100, and after market screening to about 1 in 20.

If you really have superior technical knowledge of your field and work extensively on product innovation, your performance measure of likely success is perhaps 1 in 100 to come up with a technically feasible product idea, and 1 in 20 that a technically feasible idea will test out as being marketable.

Market Segmentation and Merchandising

The way to determine whether a product concept is marketable is by market test and interview, which was covered briefly earlier in this chapter in Market Positioning. A more detailed description of how to do market research as a way to test the saleability of products will be covered in the next chapter.

Assume now that we have a product-market innovation, developed by any of the several means discussed in the previous section, and let us assume also we have a clear idea of its market position. What do we do next in formulating the marketing mix?

Our next step is to study the market in enough detail to identify the segments or the market, or types of consumers, to whom our product will appeal. This process of analyzing our clientele—who they are, where they are, what their attributes, tastes, needs, and income are—is known as market segmentation. We are trying to pinpoint where our market segment or clientele is and how we can reach them.

You reach your clientele largely through distribution channels, locations, and merchandising. Merchandising is having the right product in the right place at the right time and includes determining distribution channels and locations, which are discussed separately in the next section. But merchandising is especially having the right stock of goods to sell at the right time. Department store and fashion goods marketing are predominantly merchandising operations. The buyers have to select the right new styles for each season, order them in advance so they will be in stock and on display at the right time, and order them in the right quantity and in the right mix. Merchandising is foremost a selection process, based upon deep knowledge of consumer attitudes and the logistics problem of seeing that goods are in the right place at the right time.

How can you tell if you are doing a good merchandising job? The best measure is whether you sell your stock briskly or promptly, which is indicated by the sale-to-inventory ratio. Example:

$$\text{Sales-inventory ratio} = \frac{\text{sales}}{\text{inventory}} = \frac{\$200,000}{\$\ 50,000} = 4.0$$

If the annual sales are $200,000 and the average inventory is $50,000, then a 4.0 ratio means that the inventory is turning over, or being sold, four times a year. An inventory turnover of four times a year is more or less average. The Dun and Bradstreet business ratios show that most retailers have sales-inventory ratios from 3.0 to 7.0, depending upon the type of business. Wholesalers' and manufacturers' ratios are slightly higher (about 5.0 to 12.0).

A sales-inventory ratio of 4.0 is a performance measure that you should be able to meet. Such a ratio can also be expressed as the number of days supply you have on hand. An inventory turnover of four times per year means that you are carrying, on average, a 90-day supply of stock on hand in relation to your sales. To have more than a 90-day supply ties up a good deal of working capital. With high-priced items in the inventory, like automobiles or appliances, dealers usually prefer to keep a 30- to 60-day supply, which is ample for customer selection and not too costly in working capital. A 90-day supply among new automobile dealers is a cause for concern and special merchandising and promotion efforts. A 120-day supply is near-panic.

At the other end of the spectrum, of course, are perishables, perhaps of low value per unit, but the loss is complete if kept too long. Baked goods, fresh fruits and vegetables, fish, and other perishables are managed in terms of almost daily turnover rates. A 4-day supply may be a disaster unless the retailers merchandise and promote their sales.

The measure of merchandising performance, then, varies by product, but for most small businesses a 90-day supply with a 4.0 sales-inventory ratio is satisfactory.

Distribution Channels and Location

Marketing management is concerned next, along with market position, product innovation, and merchandising strategy, with distribution channels—or what kinds of outlets to use, and where they are located. A small businessman considering a single store will obviously only concern himself with one retail outlet, but still the locational decision is important. Other small businesses, particularly manufacturers or franchisers, will be considering multiple outlets, and they will have to decide what kind of sales outlet—company store, independent franchise store, independent dealer, general merchandise stores, manufacturer's agents, etc.—is best for their needs.

The temptation to any manager is to have as many sales outlets as possible, in the hope that more outlets mean more sales. This is not a good idea, because too many outlets will spread your marketing costs too thin and will make the profit to the outlets too small.

The measure of how many sales outlets a business should have is as many as make a reasonable profit. Unless the outlet or dealer is making a profit on sales on your goods, he will not give them the attention and promotion they need. The strength of General Motors is not so much that its cars are better than anyone else's; it is that their dealers are stronger and make more money. The dealers can afford to give service and provide sales promotion in good times, and ride out bad times. Many other automobile dealers make only a marginal profit in good times, and thus cannot afford heavy sales promotion; they lose money and fold in bad times. That has been the history of the automobile business, and the downfall of the small manufacturers. There is something to be learned from that experience. The rule and the measure is: have only as many outlets as you can afford to service well and which can make a reasonable profit on their own.

As to location, whether one outlet or many, the site depends upon where the customers are and what kind of service they need. Their service requirements are related in turn to the kinds of goods being offered, for example:

1. Convenience goods are generally low in price, similar in performance, often have a brand name, and are bought on the spur of the moment at the convenience of the customer. Such articles as toiletries, housewares, and home supplies are convenience goods and best located where there is a high traffic pattern of customers, such as in shopping centers or near office centers.

2. Shopping goods are higher in price and have a different performance than other products, such as appliances, or they are style items, such as women's fashion clothes. People want to shop and compare before spending the higher price for these goods, and they want to compare the styles and performance among products before buying. Shopping goods are best located near each other, in shopping malls, high-fashion streets for clothes and boutiques, or low-price discount centers for appliances.

3. Specialty goods appeal to special buyers for special uses, such as sporting goods, high-fidelity equipment, or health care and convalescence items. These items are likely to be high enough in price, and special enough in attributes or performance, that buyers will travel some distance to buy them. The main marketing factors, then, are advertising and promotion to make the specialty goods known, plus a location on transportation corridors so that people can easily get to the outlet.

4. Industrial goods are usually sold in person by a salesman who calls on the purchasing agent in the buyer's offices. Performance and price are the most important factors, sometimes along with speed of service or installation. The seller of industrial goods would want to locate in a low-rent district, to keep his price down, but at a site with major transportation links to urban centers so that service and installation can be swift.

If you are engaged in the sale of convenience or shopping goods, you may wish to make a traffic count. To do so, select several possible sites and pick the times of day when you might expect very little traffic and a lot of traffic. Then appear at that site at the appointed times and count the number of people going into stores of your type, and interview a few customers who are passing by. You will soon get a measure of the relative traffic for your business at one location compared to others.[4]

If you are more concerned about the merits of one locality versus another for your type of merchandise, you may wish to make a study of the consumer characteristics in one neighborhood versus others. For this purpose, the SBA has available Small Marketers Aid 154, *Using Census Data to Select a Store Site*. Briefly, the guide tells you how to make a market analysis of different localities from census data. The census data is broken down into tracts, or small geographical areas varying in size, usually two to four square miles. For each of these areas, the census has sets of tabulations called the Population Series (known as P-1, P-2, etc.) which describe particular characteristics of the population in the census tract. For example:

P-1, General characteristics of the population, covers race, age by sex and by age distribution.

P-2, Social characteristics of the population, covers nativity, parentage, country of origin and year of school completed.

P-3, Labor force characteristics of the population, shows the occupational distribution of the area, such as professionals, managers, self-employed, sales, clerical, operatives, laborers, farm workers, service workers, etc.

P-4, Income distribution of the population, shows the family income by income classes, median income of families, and median income of unrelated individuals.

The most important characteristics among these, to describe the market segments you are trying to reach, are likely to be age distribution, education, occupations, and income distribution. These characteristics are most likely to influence buyer behavior in terms of taste, needs, or ability to pay. For example, we might compare two illustrative census tracts (as in Table 4-1) to try to decide upon a store location.

Tract A is smaller in population than Tract B. Tract A also has older population distribution, higher education, higher income, and more managerial, professional and self-employed workers than Tract B. Tract B has more minorities, a younger population, more unemployment (or less employment) among youth, lower educa-

Table 4-1. Illustrative Use of Census Tract Data To Select a Store Site.

CHARACTERISTICS	TRACT A	TRACT B
Total Population	3,300	4,000
Race		
White	2,900	3,100
Black	200	400
Hispanic	200	500
Age By Sex		
Male, all ages	1,600	2,300
Under 14 years	150	400
15–19	150	400
20–24	200	500
25–34	200	300
35–64	550	450
65 and over	350	250
Years Of School Completed		
Persons 25 years and older	2,300	2,300
Elementary school	300	800
High school	1,000	1,500
College	1,000	500
Occupation		
Total employed, 16 yr and over	1,000	950
Professional	100	50
Managerial	150	20
Self-employed	150	20
Sales and clerical	200	110
Operators	250	200
Laborers	50	300
Service workers	100	200
Income		
All Families	1,200	1,100
Under $10,000	300	450
$10,000–$14,999	200	300
$15,000–$19,999	200	200
$20,000–$29,999	250	100
$30,000–$39,999	200	50
Over $40,000	150	—

tional attainment, lower incomes, and more blue collar workers than Tract A.

Tract B might be a possible location site for a food store, convenience goods, or every-day clothing because of the large young population with a need for staple goods. Tract A would be a better location site for specialty or shopping goods stores because of its higher income and higher educational attainment.

In short, the census tract data and traffic surveys can be important measures for determining location and for identifying the market segment you are serving.

Pricing

Pricing is your opportunity to reflect your marketing strategy as you perceive it in your market-product position. If you have a product with superior performance and quality that is clearly perceived by customers, you will want to maintain a prestige price somewhat above the market. Otherwise, you may lose customers who associate price with quality; that is, they think that the more expensive an item is, the better quality the item has. Prestige pricing, however, is only practical if there is an apparent difference in quality between your product and the competition, i.e., everyone knows that your product is better.

Otherwise your pricing strategy is likely to be: (1) to meet the market price of competitors, (2) to meet market prices but discount them for special promotions, or (3) to discount market prices and try to be the low-cost seller in your field.

The last strategy of being the discounter and low-cost seller is practical only if you are a large-volume seller who can get huge discounts from suppliers, or if you have special suppliers who can sell to you at low cost. These situations are rare.

Most retailers end up, then, either trying to meet competitive prices in the market, or else discounting a few items for special promotion.

The discounting of special items for sales promotions is often referred to as offering *loss-leaders*. Loss-leaders are effective only when they are widely publicized or advertised. The purpose of a loss-leader is, of course, to bring customers into the store in the hope that the loss-leaders will cause the customer to buy other items upon which to make up the profit.

If you are engaged, for the most part then, in meeting the competitive prices in the market, your main measure of pricing is to shop around and see that you are in line with your competitors. You can keep track of market prices in your area by watching competitive advertisements or by actually doing comparison shopping in other stores.

Prices are usually set by a markup. A percentage markup is arrived at by multiplying some customary markup percentage times the cost, for example 40% times a cost of $6.00 = $2.40 or a retail price of $8.40 ($6.00 + $2.40). However, you should recognize that a 40% markup on cost does not yield you a gross margin in gross profit of 40%, rather the gross margin is 28.5% ($2.40 divided by $8.40 = 28.5%).

When we were dealing with cash-flow, break-even points, and investment decisions, we were concerned with finding a gross margin which would cover our expenses and yield a profit. If your expenses are usually running 30% of sales and you want a 10% profit on sales, for a total margin of 40%, then you should divide the cost by 60% (or 100% − 40%) to get the selling price. In other words, you want a dollar markup of $4.00 over cost, not $2.40. The relationship between the pecentage markup over cost and the gross margin is shown in Table 4–2.

Most fashion goods, shopping goods, and specialty goods are sold

Table 4–2. Percentage Markups on Cost in Relation to Gross Margins on the Sales Price.

PERCENTAGE MARKUP ON COST	=	PERCENTAGE GROSS MARGIN ON SALES PRICE
100		50
66.7		40
50		33.3
42.8		30
30		23
25		20

at the higher markups in Table 4–2, while convenience goods and staples are at the lower end of the scale.

Advertising and Public Relations

Public relations is the use of personal as well as communication media to carry your message about your image or product position to your customers. Public relations includes the use of newspaper stories, television, radio, direct mail, speeches, demonstrations, community involvement, and special events to make yourself and your business known.[5]

Advertising is that aspect of public relations in which you use paid space in a media to carry out message about your product-market position. Most business firms spend 1 to 2% of sales on advertising, and sometimes more, to try to launch a new store, new product, or establish a brand name. While staying within your advertising budget, you should select that media which is most likely to yield a return in sales (and eventually a profit). In this sense, advertising planning is like profit planning discussed in Chapter 3. You want a return on your advertising dollars.

Advertising expenditures are often wasted. If you have a store with a local clientele, you will not get much benefit out of advertising in a countywide newspaper, because most of the readers will not be in your shopping area. You might better have spent the money on direct mail sent to your neighborhood. Some common-sense rules of good advertising are:

1. Pinpoint your audience or customers and try to find the media that gets directly to them.
2. Keep your advertising message simple. People do not retain more than one or two ideas (or product attributes) at one time from a message.
3. Use some attention-getting design, headline, or picture so the person reads your ad.
4. Select a readable type, format, and logogram and then stick with them for repeated advertisements, so that customers begin to recognize your message and products.
5. Measure the results of advertising, to see that you are getting an adequate return from your expenditure. The measure should

be that the added cost of advertising should at least equal the added profit from sales over a period of time.

How do you measure advertising effectiveness? There are two main ways. The first is to run special promotions on individual products among your merchandise, or to use coupons to give the customers a special price. Then you can measure the increase in the sale of the advertised product, or count the coupons, to get a direct impact measure of advertising effectiveness.

Sometimes, however, you may wish to advertise your special image or product-position. This is image-, or institution-, or attitude-building. You are trying to build awareness, which we noted earlier is so important to success. To measure the effectiveness of attitude advertising, you can do periodic surveys among customers of their attitude and awareness. However, this may be expensive or time-consuming. A simpler way is simply to measure the change in sales volume over a period of several months as you run the advertising campaign.

Personal selling

Personal selling is one of the more underrated and ignored aspects of marketing. High-pressure selling gave salesmanship a bad name. Now no one wants to admit they are selling, but we are all selling something all of the time—our ideas, our hopes, our personalities, ourselves. Personal selling is not bad, it is the way we communicate with people. What *is* bad is imposing our own wishes or a fraud upon someone else.

If you fulfill the wishes of the customer (rather than imposing your own), personal selling is a service and an act of friendship. So the first rule of selling is to find out what the customer wants, needs, likes, and is interested in. The second rule is to give the customer what he wants.

Or somewhat more formally, personal selling is usually a series of steps.

1. Get the person's attention—a pleasant word, a smile, and an inquiry as to their interests.

Without the customer's attention, communication cannot begin.

2. Find out their needs, not just what they say they want but

what they like: what features, performance, qualities, or attributes appeal to them.

3. Tell them in terms of their own interests as to qualities about your product.

4. Illustrate the use of your product, by demonstration or just telling them about your experience and the experience of others.

5. Tell them a little about yourself, what you know of the field, the product, or its use, why you like it.

Your own enthusiasm and knowledge are the most convincing evidence to the customer.

6. Get the customer to try the product, or to try it on, if you can.

7. Verbally get the customer to agree that the product meets the needs that they want (step 2 above).

8. Prompt the customer to close the purchase by offering to wrap the item, send it, or have them sign an order.

Most customers will make the decision and close the purchase at this point.

9. If the customer demurs, review again what the customer said they wanted and how the product meets all those qualities.

10. Try to prompt a purchase decision again by suggesting that the item is just what the person needs, or it looks well on them.

11. If the customer still refuses to decide, thank them for coming in, suggest they think about it a bit or look around, and give them your name or card.

Chances are they will be back if you did a good personal selling job.

12. Be sure not to talk too much.

The higher the price of the item, or the higher its style or performance distinction, the more time the customer needs to consider its comparison with other products or other needs.

13. Be sensitive to when a customer wants to close by their general attitude of consent, and do not ask for an overt declaration of purchase.

Make buying easy by preparing an order for them to sign, or beginning to wrap the item for them.

The crucial steps are 3, 4, and 5 above in which you convey your own personal knowledge, enthusiasm, and authenticity which conveys your product image as clearly meeting their stated need.

The more knowledgeable and natural you are, the more convincing you will be, and the more fun you will have at personal selling.

Do not be dismayed by turn-downs. You cannot win them all. Often the customer does not have the money or really did not have a clear idea of what he or she wanted in the first place. If you sell one-fourth to one-half of your prospects, you are doing fairly well.

Sales Promotion

A sales promotion is an attention-getting event intended to arouse buyer interest and bring them into a store. The events must be fresh and new to capture attention, and the occasion must suit the environment and needs of the customer. Many such events are seasonal, such as for new models, new styles, back-to-school, and summer-wear. Some are topical, such as King Tut specials, Hawaiian prints, Italian imports, Western Days, Boy Scout week, and Founder's day. Others involve contests, give-aways, price reductions, clearances, two for the price of one, one cent sales, and so forth.

The importance of promotions is that they build customer contacts; as such they should be regularly planned and not just one-shot or occasional events. The other feature of promotions is that they should tie in with the image or market-position of the store, so that they reinforce a message. Skillful promotion takes ingenuity and attention by the manager, and no one can really tell him how to do it. The creative part of merchandising is for the owner to conceive a sense of surprise and interest on the part of a customer by a promotion which reinforces the image of the business. Good promotion can make the sales of a good product better through building awareness and creating opportunities for personal selling.

Packaging, Product Assurance, and Servicing

Packaging, product assurance, and servicing are all important parts of the marketing mix which deserve the attention of the manager. In some ways, however, their role is self-explanatory. Packaging is a way of making the product more appealing, by attractive design, by brightly colored wrapping, or by utilitarian means. The styrofoam containers for McDonald hamburgers, for example, are a utilitarian and attractive way to preserve the temperature and flavor of take-out orders.

Product assurance is a means of standing behind the performance of a product and guaranteeing that it does what is claimed. This may be done through warranty, refund, repair, or service policies.

Servicing a product is the means of repairing a product in the field to maintain its usability. This may be done by having mobile repair units, or by having convenience service centers throughout the areas of consumer use.

PLANNING THE MARKET MIX

All of these ingredients of the marketing mix need to be combined and coordinated for successful consumer satisfaction; the means of coordinating is the marketing plan. The marketing plan assigns tasks and budgets to people to carry out the schedule of activities required in the marketing mix.

Perhaps an example would be useful. In 1971, Isaac Fogel started the Classic Corporation in Bethesda, Maryland to sell waterbeds. He had some experience in the furniture and bedding field. He contracted out manufacture of the waterbeds to suppliers at first. The waterbed sales went fairly well during the first years, but the sale of bean-bag chairs really carried the expenses until the waterbeds caught on with consumers. The original sales territory was confined to the East. From 1973–1977, the company went into its own manufacture, not only of waterbeds, but also for leisure living furniture throughout the United States. In 1978 the business was expanded again to include the manufacture and distribution of furniture and bedding products to consumer, institutional, and health care markets at home and abroad. The company proceeded by expanding its natural markets and product lines. Planning is essential to the success of a small business, in Mr. Fogel's view. Objectives of the plan must be obtainable and communicated to the staff. A good way to assure the objectives are realistic is to review factually: (1) the base of capability and market position from which you are starting, (2) the personnel available to accomplish the objectives and implement the tasks, and (3) the potential cost involved. Planning involves commitment to a specific result on a specific time schedule. That is the way that Mr. Fogel built the Classic Corporation from a new business to a multimillion dollar enterprise within a decade.[6]

SUMMARY

Marketing is the heart of a business, and the product-market position of a firm is the heart of its marketing.

The product-market position, or image, of a firm can be measured graphically by showing the attributes or qualities of a product on a scale in relation to competition. This graphic portrayal indicates the "product space" which you occupy in the market.

The first job of marketing is to create awareness of the image or product position of your firm, and this can be done through advertising, location, personnel selling, and sales promotion.

Consumer awareness can be measured by interview or surveys as to whether customers know the special attributes of your product. Consumer awareness should be half again as high as your market share to make steady sales progress.

Experience of large and small companies is that high product quality is the most essential ingredient to remedy a weak share, and that beyond that the best policy is to strengthen cost controls, concentrate on a special segment of the market, and strengthen costumer services.

The marketing concept assumes that every aspect of a business must have the purpose of satisfying consumer needs, and the whole array of services within the company constitute the marketing mix.

Product development is risky for small firms, but small companies have higher innovation rates than large firms. The key is superior technical knowledge within the firm and testing the market before committing large investments.

Merchandising entails bringing the right products to the right place at the right time. The measure of good performance is in the sales-inventory ratio of about 4.0 (an inventory turnover of 4 times per year or inventory not exceeding a 90-day supply), for most product lines.

The distribution channels and locations of outlets are related to the market segment which is being served, that is, the nature of the customers, where they are, and who they are in terms of characteristics such as age, education, income, occupation, and so forth. Locational studies can pinpoint these characteristics by the use of census tract data.

Pricing strategy depends upon the nature of the product and its market position. Prestige pricing is possible when distinctive quality or performance differences are apparent. Discount pricing is possible when special low-cost suppliers are available. Otherwise, most firms follow the competitive market price, with special promotions to enhance their image and sales.

Advertising needs to use media pinpointed to particular customers; the advertisement should carry a simple, clear, attention-getting message.

Personal selling is the most essential part of marketing, and the most important features are the knowledge and enthusiasm of the seller.

Sales promotion consists of attention-getting events which have a freshness and appeal to bring customers into the store. Promotion should reinforce the product position or image of the firm.

Packaging, product assurance, and service are important ingredients to keep customers satisfied and make them repeat buyers in the future.

All of the elements of the marketing mix are implemented by means of a marketing plan which assigns tasks and budgets to personnel to carry out the objectives of the market activity on time and on schedule.

Marketing is essentially managing tasks to meet consumer needs and satisfactions. When done well, it is the basis of business success, as illustrated by the Classic Corporation which went from being a waterbed dealer to a multimillion dollar corporation in less than a decade.

REFERENCES

1. For details, see SBA Small Marketers Aid No. 127, available from your nearest SBA office.
2. Smith, P. "Unique Tools for Marketers: PIMS." *Dun's Review,* October, 1976.
3. Scheirer, W.K. *Small Firms and Federal R&D.* Office of Management and Budget, Executive Office of the President (undated, released 1979).
4. For details, see SBA Small Marketers Aid No. 152, *Using a Traffic Study to Select a Retail Site.*
5. For details, see SBA Small Marketers Aid No. 163, *Public Relations for Small Business.*
6. Fogel, I. "Importance of Planning in Small Business," Paper no. 20. 24th Annual Conference of the International Council for Small Business, July 23–26 1979, Quebec City, Canada.

5

Marketing Research—
Measures of Market
Performance

Once you have a clear idea of your product-market position and have thought through the tasks to be done in the marketing mix, as we discussed in Chapter 4, the next step is to implement the marketing plan and keep track of how well you are doing. That is, you want to carry out the marketing effort and measure your performance against your marketing goals. Operational marketing means doing the work. Marketing control is seeing that the work gets done. Both of these marketing activities require a set of facts.

The facts about marketing operations, i.e., the work being done, can be collected internally from your own sales statistics. These facts include such information as sales per month, dollar increase in sales, sales trend, sales per sales-employee, sales per account, new accounts opened, new customers, repeat sales to old customers, sales per transaction, costs per transaction, profit per sales transaction. While this seems like quite a list, most of it is calculated from dollar sales, number of customers, and the expense and profit from the income statement. These facts tell you whether you are meeting your sales goals, whether your business is increasing, whether you are building new customers, what your costs per sales are, and whether you are making a profit on sales.

The second set of facts about marketing control has more to do with your customers—who they are, where they are, and what their behavior is. The purpose of these facts is to see that the marketing work is being done in the right way, in the right place, and with the right customers. That is, you want to compare what you are doing (the first set of operational marketing facts) with what you ought to be doing to reach your full market potential (the market control or performance data). Most of the marketing performance data is external data about customers and marketing potential which has to be sought from outside sources. Getting data from outside sources is usually called *marketing research*. Marketing research can cost time and money. You will want to learn as much as you can about your marketing potential with the least cost. The least expensive way to get marketing information is from government or trade publications. The conducting of marketing surveys, to collect information yourself, is sometimes necessary; we will discuss later how to do low-cost market surveys when needed.

The main point, however, is that marketing management requires you to compare what you are actually doing with what you should be doing to reach your market potential. That is the way you can correct and improve your marketing effort. What you should be doing, of course, refers to satisfying customers. This means getting the facts to show what it takes to satisfy them, and how much buying power they have, provided you try to do everything required to meet their needs. Presumably, if you do what is required to meet their needs you will reach your full market potential. What we really are comparing then is your actual market performance against your potential market performance. That gives, as well as new goals and marketing tasks, control and direction to your marketing effort.

MORE ABOUT MARKETING PLANS

Marketing is essentially a matter of directing actual sales performance and comparing it against a marketing plan. The marketing plan is a set of tasks, budgets, assignments, and schedules intended to carry out the marketing mix in order to reach your marketing goals. We discussed marketing plans briefly in the last chapter, except we specified neither how you set your marketing goals nor how to make a marketing plan. Marketing goals are determined by identifying your customers and setting quotas of sales based upon work you do to satisfy them. A marketing plan is made up by organizing the marketing work into sets of tasks, schedules, budgets, and personnel assignments.

Let us assume that we are in the paint business with both a showroom and one outside salesman who calls upon large painting contractors. Last month's sales were $125,000, of which $75,000 were to do-it-yourself customers in the showroom, and $50,000 were to painting contractors. You think that a sales goal of $140,000 for next month is reasonable, because it is a summer month when more homeowners do their painting, you have a new line of colors in a new acrylic paint that is durable with easy clean-up, and your salesperson has a good list of new prospects. You expect to increase your sales promotion to homeowners and the number of sales calls to painting contractors. A very brief outline of a marketing plan might look like Table 5–1.

Table 5–1. Illustrative Marketing Plan for a Paint Store.

FUNCTION AND TASK ACTIVITY	ASSIGNMENT	BUDGET	SCHEDULE
Merchandising			
Restock color lines	Manager	$1,000	Aug 10
Add new acrylics	Manager	1,500	Aug 5
Study school demand	Manager	—	Aug 20
Pricing			
Discount old colors	Manager	—	Aug 2
Special on acrylics	Sales clerk A		Aug 8
Advertising			
Direct mail/homeowners	Sales clerk B	400	Aug 12
Ad/contractor's paper	Manager	400	Aug 9
Personal Selling			
Showroom demonstrations	Sales clerk A	—	Every Saturday
More showroom hours	Clerks A and B	1,200	Fridays 9 A.M.–9 P.M.
Prospect list for	Outside salesman		
contractors		—	Aug. 14
Increase outside calls	Outside salesman		Every day, report weekly
Packaging			
Palletize large orders	Stock boy	200	Begin Aug. 15
New shopping bags	Manager	50	Aug. 20
Product Assurance			
Guarantee color matching	Clerk B	100	Aug. 15
Servicing			
Home demos for beginners	Clerk A	—	Aug. 20

This brief outline of a marketing plan calls for a series of tasks intended to broaden the paint store's product lines to new color offerings plus a new kind of acrylic paint which should appeal to both homeowners and paint contractors for its durability plus ease of application and clean-up. The manager intends to advertise these new qualities by a direct mailing piece to homeowners and an advertisement in a trade paper for contractors, and to explore the paint market for public school maintenance. The manager also plans to hold showroom demonstrations of his new products and increase the showroom hours in order to accomodate response to his promotions. The outside salesperson is to build a larger prospector list through referral and mailing lists among painting contractors, and to increase the average number of sales calls per day from four to five. To speed up service on orders to contracts, larger orders will be palletized for quicker delivery, and new stronger shopping bags are being ordered for homeowner orders. Sales clerk B is going to take special training in color mixing and matching, and the store is going to guarantee satisfaction with the match or redo the order. Sales clerk A is going to hold home demonstrations for the new products for those who are beginners at their own home decoration. The manager expects that these marketing actions will increase sales by $20,000 during the month.

MARKETING CONTROL

Having made up a marketing plan to increase sales, the manager next wants to follow-up to see that sales in fact do increase, and if not, why not. His source of information will be the internal sales statistics. He can keep track of weekly and monthly sales in total, by showroom and by contractors sales. He can record the number of customers at demonstrations, number of shopping customers, and number of purchase transactions and divide such numbers by the sales personnel who handled them. This will give him figures on store traffic and sales transactions per sales person. He can also figure the number of new prospects and number of outside sales calls made by the outside salesman. By attaching his selling costs per transactions to each sale, he can estimate whether the demonstrations, added working hours, added sales call, or new prospecting paid for themselves or lost money. The manager can see if the advertising paid off in terms of new inquiries, more shoppers, or increased sales by comparing the cost of advertising with the returns from inquiries, shoppers, or sales. Perhaps the manager will find that his plan was not entirely on target; the number of sales calls and prospects may increase more (or less) than he planned. In that case, he could adjust his targets for the marketing plan upward or downward for the next month.

All right, so the manager is testing and measuring his performance against a plan. That is the essense of market control. The manager needs to make up reasonable goals and targets for his staff, assign tasks and budgets, and then check up on the results by watching the sales statistics as to performance. Sounds simple enough, doesn't it? Well, it is, with one small problem: we need to know what reasonable marketing goals are. The manager can base these goals upon his past experience, which is a good way to begin. But who is to know whether past experience is close to, or far from, the potential sales that he should be doing? That is our next question. Can we estimate what the market ought to produce in the way of sales? The answer to this question requires market research.

MARKETING RESEARCH—MEASURES OF SALES POTENTIAL

To estimate sales potential for a particular product or store, you need some base-line data on: (1) sales of the product by all stores for a region, such as by state, county, or nationally, plus (2) number of households by income and age distribution for the same area. In the previous chapter we showed how to use census data to get median income and number of people or families in your trading area for locational purposes. Now we want to find out how much buying power or sales potential your particular trading area has. So we shall assume that its buying power is proportionate to its population size and median income within some larger area of which we can get published data.

Suppose you know from your wholesaler or trade association that paint sales nationally are $15 billion per year, or $1.25 billion per month. You also look up the buying power of your county in the trade magazine *Sales and Marketing Management* (usually in the July or August issues) at your local library. You find that the county buying power is .065% of the U.S.A. Then you multiply .00065 times $1.25 billion and you estimate that the paint sales in your county are $812,500 per month.

You might be able to get an actual number for sales of paint stores for your county or city from sales tax data, which would be a short-cut for you and also provide more accurate county data. If sales tax data are available, they will usually be published annually by your state's tax office, and large local banks or chambers of commerce will frequently have the local sales tax data on hand.

In any case, whether you got the facts directly from sales tax data, or estimated it from a buying power index, we shall assume in the illustration that county paint sales are about $812,500 per month.

Next we again consult *Sales and Marketing Management* and find that our county has a population of 140,000 with a median income of $4,200 per year. We also know that the trading area of our store (determined from the census data by the same approach as in the last chapter on locational analysis) is 60,000 people with a median income of $4,000 per year. We can than figure our trading area as a proportion of the county. For example, if $812,500 of paint sales per month are purchased by 140,000 persons, the average purchase per person is $5.80. This may seem high as per capita paint purchases, but by including sales to painting contractors we are also including all industrial, business, and governmental painting. Our trading area of 60,000 persons should, then, purchase about $348,000 in paint monthly ($5.80 x 60,000), except that the median income in our trading area is 4.8% lower than the county. So we revise the market potential downward by 4.8% of $340,000 to $331,000 (95.2% x $340,000). The estimate of the sales potential for our trading area, then, is $331,000 per month based upon average purchase rates based upon income and population.

Our paint store currently sells $125,000 per month out of the $331,000 sales potential, or a market share of 38%. There are two other major paint stores who are our competitors in this trading area, so we have a slightly better than average market share (average would be 33.3%). Raising our sales to $140,000 means we will be competing more vigorously and trying to get a 42% market share. That is perhaps a big order, but we are strong competitors; at least we know where we stand.

Of course, we cannot treat the $331,000 sales potential as static.

We should revise it upward from last year's data (which will be what you will find in *Sales and Marketing Management*) for the increase in population and the increase in income in your trading area. Perhaps the population has grown 3% since last year, and incomes have gone up 7%. The market potential of $331,000 should be revised upward to $365,000 ($331,000 × 1.03 × 1.07). On this basis, our sales goal of $140,000 does not look quite so ambitious, because it is still only a 39% market share ($140,000 ÷ $365,000), which makes the marketing goal more a matter of getting our share of the growth in the trading area.

In summary, you can usually estimate your market potential and market share from published statistics by calculating a buying rate per person, per household, or per dollar of income. This is a common and fairly satisfactory way to arrive at your market potential. The automobile industry, for example, estimates its market potential for automobiles by using auto-buying rates by income class of consumers. Buying rates by income class are usually a more reliable way to estimate than using per capita or on overall income. The Bureau of the Census periodically obtains buying rates for a few high-priced products, like automobiles and appliances, but not for lower priced products like paint or clothing. You can get help from your local Department of Commerce field office as to what are the most specific data available of your products or industrial classification. You can then use the best data available from published sources to estimate your sales potential.

In our illustration of the paint store, the paint industry and the individual store were selling near the national average buying rate or close to their potential for the region. That may not always be the case, of course, and then the market potential estimate is even more important for market planning. Suppose the paint store had found that its market potential was $365,000 a month, its own sales were $125,000 per month, and there were no other paint stores or competitors in the trading area. That would be a most significant finding, because then the store should undertake a vigorous sales expansion program, by getting more outside salespeople to call on contractors, by expanding the existing store, personnel and sales promotion, or else by considering opening new paint stores in additional locations.

The reverse finding is also possible, that the sale potential is dwindling due to loss of population or a population shift from higher to lower income households. Then the store manager might want to consider changing his price line in the store to cheaper goods, or moving out of that trading area to a more prosperous location with a better market potential.

In any case, the marketing potential measure becomes incorporated into the marketing goal and market plan of the manager by examining a reasonable market share and planning a marketing mix and sales promotion plan to get the highest possible share.

MARKETING RESEARCH—MEASURES OF CONSUMER PREFERENCE FOR SPECIFIC GOODS

Well, you may say, this method of estimating market potential is all right, and perhaps it does aid in setting sales goals for a marketing plan, but it only gives you a sales total based upon average buying rates. What I want is something more specific. What do consumers think of my products and of my store, and what are their preferences in buying those products versus something else or someone else's? If these are the questions you are asking yourself, congratulations! These are the most important marketing questions of all. You should be seeking answers to them. Unfortunately, the answers to such questions are going to cost more money to obtain, because you cannot get them from published sources. You have to go out and get the information for yourself; that means conducting a marketing survey.

Unless you have had some experience with marketing surveys, you had better get some help. There are consultants and firms who do marketing surveys. Costs range from $10 to $100 per interview, and the total survey would probably cost from $5,000 to $100,000. That is probably too expensive for many small businesses. Where else can you turn? One likely source is to get in touch with your local university. Call the marketing department of the business school. They sometimes will do marketing survey projects by using student help as a means of training their students in real problems. You may expect to pay for the out-of-pocket costs for the survey, and perhaps a modest hourly rate for the students. Simple mail questionnaires with small samples can sometimes be done for $500 or more. Personal interview surveys could cost a few thousand dollars, but it is still a fraction of the cost of having it done commercially.

You can, of course, do your own market survey. But the things you have to be careful about, and the reason you may want to have help, are to assure the validity of the sample and of the findings. The *sample* means the number of people you contact out of the total market trading area. You cannot afford to contact them all, and if you contact only a small part of them, the question arises as to the representativeness of that group. Similarly, there are problems in the way you ask questions; if they are biased or ambiguous the findings will be biased and ambiguous. Also, the initial temptation is to ask too many questions, things you would like to know but do not *have* to know. If too many questions are asked, the response rate drops as consumers weary of imposition on their time. But, if you do have to do the market survey yourself because you cannot afford to hire a consultant or get university help, here are a few do-it-yourself rules.

1. Make a list of the least number of facts you need to know to make up a marketing plan.

For example, who is buying by age, sex, and income class? What does the buyer prefer among the main attributes of the product—fashion, color, durability, or price? You could ask for such facts in four or five questions. Keep the questions few and keep them simple.

2. Next, make up a table which shows how you would tabulate the answers.

The reason for making up the dummy tabulation is that if you cannot tabulate it, you are not really going to use it, and you had better not ask it. The table might read across the top: the number of purchases per year of your product by income class and might read down the stub or vertical axis: age, sex, and product qualities per-ferred. You will be surprised how many questions you will revise or throw out when you start thinking about tabulating the answers, either because the answers don't make any sense or you realize they do not really affect your decision anyway.

3. For the questions that survive the winnowing process of steps 1 and 2, frame several versions of the same question as simply and straightforwardly as you can.

Test these several versions of each question on your employees, wife, family, friends, etc., and after they have answered ask them what they think the question meant and what they meant by their answer. Again, you will be surprised at the varied interpretation of questions which seemed to you at first to be straightforward and similar. For the several surviving versions of the best questions, try a few out on customers who come into your store or on strangers on the street. Now take the best questions which survive all these tests and arrange them into a questionnaire or survey instrument, with the simplest and most agreeable questions first—the more difficult ones come later.

4. Study the questions yourself and decide whether you think that questions are so obvious and easy to respond to that you can get answers by mail survey, telephone survey, or personal interview.

The longer and harder the questionnaire, the more likely you will have to use personal interviews, which is also more costly, in order to get an adequate response. If in doubt, do a pilot test again by mail, telephone, or interview.

5. Next you have to decide how to sample your trading area, i.e., who you are going to approach for a response.

The most reliable form of sample has been found to be a *random area sample* which means to select the respondents randomly from a geographic area. The other major form of sampling is the *representative sample* in which you try to identify respondents who make up the attributes of your consumers, such as age, sex, and income class, but this form of sampling has not proved to be as reliable as area sampling.

To do a random area sample, get a detailed map of your local trading area which shows blocks and houses or parcels. Such maps can usually be purchased (or reproduced) from your local government planning department or the tax assessor.

Next draw a grid of lines equidistant from each other on the map. Ten horizontal and ten vertical lines will form a grid of 100 squares. The sample of persons or households to be interviewed is to be drawn from the square areas on the grid—the reason why this is called an area sample.

The size of the sample can be calculated statistically, and size depends upon the number of characteristics in the population and in the questionnaire. Figuring an appropriate sample size is where the university help would be useful. In most cases a sample size of at least 100 responses is likely to be necessary for valid results, sometimes more if the variables or characteristics are numerous.

We then need to identify 100 or so respondents on the map by some random means. One means is to number the squares in grid and number slips of paper to correspond to them. Then mix or shake the numbers and draw them by lottery. Another method is to get a table of random numbers from a statistics book from a library and pick the numbers from the table.

Suppose you have randomly picked twenty squares from the grid for interviewing and you are going to make five interviews per square area. Again use lottery or the random numbers table to select five homes or parcels within the square area.

Interviewers should be courteous and well groomed, and they should be trained to use a standard approach for the questioning. If the interviewer finds that there is no one at home, he or she should go to the next adjacent house until an interview is completed.

The same procedure can be used for telephone interviewing except that you will also need a street directory with phone numbers in order to select the sample.

If you use a mail survey, you will have to considerably increase the number of questionnaires sent out in order to get an adequate response rate. While response rates as high as 40 to 50% have been achieved on mail surveys for topics of high interest, the normal commercial market survey is likely to have more like a 5 to 20% response, and that depends upon the simplicity and motivators in the survey. The main motivators are: (1) a simple, easy-to-answer questionnaire, (2) an appealing transmittal letter which relates the results to the respondent's self-interest, and (3) a modest reward, such as enclosed coin or small gift. Response rates can be increased by a prior letter which introduces the survey, so that the questionnaire is expected. Response rates also improve with follow-up letters. With low response rates, in the range of 5 to 10%, a follow-up telephone interview of a sample of the nonrespondents should be made to determine if their answers are similar to those you have received.

When all the questionnaires are received, the tabulation or results begins. Make up tally sheets to record the responses, in the same form as the final tabulation, but leave enough room under each heading to tally the results of each questionnaire. The final tabulation for a simple paint survey might look like Table 5–2 below.

This set of findings gives us important characteristics of paint-buying customers and tells us where our store stands in the market

Table 5-2. Illustrative Tabulation of a Paint Survey.

| | NUMBER OF RESPONSES BY INCOME CLASS | | | |
	UNDER $15,000	$15,000–$30,000	OVER $30,000	TOTAL
All Respondents	35	45	20	100
Male	18	25	11	54
Female	17	20	9	46
Age				
Under 25	9	6	0	15
25–44	10	14	6	30
45–64	7	18	10	35
65 and over	9	7	4	20
Paint Purchased in Past Year				
1 gal. or less	10	10	3	23
2–5 gal.	5	12	8	25
Over 5 gal.	5	8	7	20
None	15	15	2	32
Where Purchased				
Our store	10	11	4	25
Other stores	10	30	14	43
Why Purchased				
Price	12	7	2	21
Colors	3	5	9	21
Durability	3	7	3	13
Ease of application	2	9	1	8
Brand	0	2	3	5

versus others. For example, the survey is right on the nose with respect to our market share, or 37% of the market. That is, our store sold paint to 25 out of the 68 customers who bought paint during the past year. However, our market share of the purchasers below $15,000 in income was 50%, for the $15,000 to $30,000 group it was 37%, and over $30,000 it was 22%. That is, our sales concentration is at the low end of the market in terms of income, and we can see that the determinants of purchase for our group are heavily on price and ease of application. Clearly our store is not doing well in the upper end of the market where the purchase decision is based more upon brand name or the variety and shades of colors. Or, in simple words, our market share is concentrated in the low-profit end of the paint business.

If we want to improve our profit position, we need to develop additional paint lines and sales promotion which will appeal to higher income purchasers on the basis of color variety and brand name. That is a very obvious signal, loud and clear, from this survey. Moreover, it gives us clear new goals for our next marketing plan. Our only dilemma is whether we can hang on to the low-end of the market, where we currently have our concentration of market share, and still add the upper end of the market to our sales. There is kind of a conflict of image involved, for clearly our store is now appealing to the price-conscious do-it-yourselfer, and that image is quite different from that of a high-quality decorator's shop. So we will have to be careful in our market plan and sales promotion. We might be able to augment our image by adding a separate "decorator's color showroom" with brand names in the store and promoting it directly by mail to higher income families.

In any case, the marketing research survey has proved to be a measure of our specific market in terms of: (1) who our customers are in terms of age, sex, and income class, (2) what the buying rates for paint are by quantity and income class, (3) what product characteristics determine the purchase decision by income class, (4) what our image or product-market position is, and (5) what new market plans and product lines we need to add to improve our profits. The expenditure of a few hundred dollars has yielded some very valuable information.

MEASURES OF SALES COSTS

So far we have seen how to estimate sales potential, market share, and specific buying patterns for your product. These are all essential to make up a marketing plan. Next you will want to control performance to realize the sales targets of your marketing plan. You will recall the example of a market plan given earlier in Table 5–1 listed tasks and budget in performance of the marketing activity. One form of control, then, is to monitor the task performance and budgets to see that they are met.

Another form of control is to check your selling expenses against others. Selling expenses vary by type of product and industry, depending upon how much personal selling is entailed. Total selling costs (including those for sales personnel, sales management, travel, and advertising and promotional expenses) usually vary in the range from 7 to 12% of sales. The lower percentages apply to standardized products of recognized performance, the higher percentages to products where quality or performance has to be demonstrated or personally explained. Sales costs for some industrial products sold in large volume are as low as 4 to 6% of sales. To make more specific comparisons with your own industry group, you can turn to sources of information on selling expenses, such as *Expenses in Retail Business* from National Cash Register Company, or the magazine *Sales and Marketing Management*. The latter publication gives specific costs of salesman calls, which usually run from about $15 to $30 per call (and higher for technical products) depending upon the territory and the number of sales interviews can be scheduled per day.

If your total selling costs are 10% of sales, within which the cost of salespeoples' salaries is 6.5% of sales, then you can prepare a table showing how much each salesperson should sell weekly in relation to their salary. For example, in Table 5-3 the weekly sales are compared with weekly salaries and the 6.5% guideline is drawn in to show when you break even on sales salaries.

Table 5-3 gives you a graphic idea of how the weekly sales volume per salesperson must keep in step with his weekly salary in order for

Table 5-3. How Much a Salesperson Should Sell.
(salary cost percentage)

WEEKLY SALES	WEEKLY SALARY				
	$100	$150	$200	$250	$300
$1,000	10.0	15.00	20.0		
1,500	6.7	10.00	13.3		
2,000	5.0	7.5	10.0		
2,500	4.0	6.0	8.0	10.0	
3,000		5.0	6.7	8.3	10.0
3,500			5.7	7.1	8.5
4,000				6.2	7.5
4,500					

the firm to control its sales costs. Perhaps a simpler way for a business with few salespeople is merely to take their weekly salary and divide it by 6.5% (or multiply by 15.4). For example, if you had three salespersons whose salaries are $150, $200, and $275 per week, then you can construct a specific weekly sales quota for each, as follows:

SALESPERSON	WEEKLY SALARY x 15.4 =	WEEKLY SALES QUOTA
A	$150	$2,310
B	200	3,080
C	275	4,325

The control of sales costs and the performance of selling tasks in the marketing plan are important to achieve your sales goals and profit for the firm, but you should never take your own eye as manager off your own task to increase the sales potential and market share of your firm. That means knowledge of the market, good sales performance, and having a current marketing plan.

OTHER MARKETING GUIDES AND MEASURES

In addition to the key marketing measures covered in previous sections, a number of other marketing guides and measures may be helpful from time to time. These include: (1) mailing and prospect lists, (2) correlations of sales with income, and (3) industry and trade association comparisons.

If you see a need to enter a specific market segment which is new to you, you may wish to use mailing lists or prospects lists as the basis for your sales promotion. For example, automobile dealers use lists of registered automobile owners whose cars are two to three years old as prospect lists, because most new car buyers trade in their second or third year. Our paint dealer seeking to penetrate a new upper-income market might get a list of homes five to eight years old from building permits or tax assessor lists. Sometimes a purchased mailing list may serve as a proxy for a target market segment you wish to reach. For example, the mailing list for *The Wall Street Journal* in your trading area, if it were available, would serve as a prospect list for middle- and upper-income business executives. The yellow pages of the telephone book can direct you to firms who sell mailing lists from all kinds of sources, such as magazine subscribers, professional associations, trade associations, clubs, and business groups. You can make your own mailing prospect lists from the Chamber of Commerce, local civic associations, and the yellow pages of the telephone book. Whenever you have a need for a mail sales promotion in your marketing plan, you should explore the best source of prospect or mailing lists to reach your market segment.

If you wish to measure or forecast your sales, you can make a good estimate by relating your sales to a general measure of income or production. Most retail sales correlate highly with the Gross National Product, or with national income, and personal income. All of these statistics can be found in your library monthly in the *Survey of Current Business* of the Department of Commerce, or *Economic Indicators* from the President's Council of Economic Advisors. To use the data, simply take one of the income measures, like personal income, and plot it on a graph with a scale of its own in billions of dollars. Next plot your own sales on the graph on a separate scale in thousands of dollars geared to match the steps in (or proportionate to) the personal income scale. Now you have two lines plotted over several years, personal income and your own scales. Most likely they will move closely together. If so, you can figure a rough ratio of your own sales to personal income, or, if you want more specific information, you can figure a correlation ratio and regression formula (or have a college student do it for you). In any case, you can now (even with a rough ratio) project your own sales expectations as a ratio of the state of the economy and forecasts of personal income into the future. There are many such forecasts available in business sections of newspapers, from banks, or from government publications like the *Survey of Current Business*. These forecasts and correlations of income with your own sales will give you some idea of what to expect in terms of your own sales targets.

Comparisons with industry statistics and trade associations provide valuable specifics as to the performance of your own line of business. Most trade associations are membership groups and you should join one in your own field if its information and services are worth the cost to you. Some industry comparisons, particularly in manufacturing, are available in the industry and trade section of data in the back of the *Survey of Current Business*. Other sources of comparison data are the publications of the National Federation of Independent Business (490 L'Enfant Plaza East, S.W., Suite #206, Washington, D.C. 20024). Its *Quarterly Economic Report for Small Business* gives trends and expectations for prices, earnings, sales volume, inventory levels, credit conditions, and general business conditions. The Federation's *Fact Book on Small Business* gives such data as sales per employee (about $38,000 per employee for retail stores) and gross receipts (sales) by size of firm and by industry group. An interesting fact from the *Fact Book* is that 43% of all small business owners work from 49 to 64 hours per week and only 13% work less than 40 hours. That proves that being a small businessman is not easy. You have to work hard to do a good marketing job.

SUMMARY

Marketing is essentially a matter of directing actual sales performance of a business and comparing it against a marketing plan. The marketing plan, in turn, is based upon factual information as to sales potential, market share, buying rates, and customer preferences; these facts become the bases for marketing goals and the assignment of marketing tasks. Marketing control is then achieved by comparing actual performance against market potential.

A marketing plan can be devised to lay out the sales work or tasks to be performed, with assignments to individuals along with budgets and schedules. These budgets and schedules can be monitored, along with actual sales achieved, to see whether the marketing plan is being effectively carried out.

A measure of total sales potential is important so that a firm can tell how much new growth in sales, or how much competition, exists. Measures of sales potential can be developed by taking average buying rates for a larger region, from published sources, and scaling them down to your trading area. That is, you would multiply the population and median income within your trading area by the buying rates for your product in the county, state, or nation.

Measures of consumer preferences for specific goods in your trading area are not likely to be found in published sources, so you will have to make your own market surveys to determine customer attitudes. To make your own market surveys, you would create a random area sample of persons to be interviewed, predetermine the final tabulations you must have for a decision, test a set of questions which will respond to the tabulation, and make up a questionnaire with as few and as straightforward questions as possible. The findings should be used in revising your marketing plans as to customer buying rates, market share, customer preferences in buying decisions, and your product-market position.

Once your marketing plan is in operation, you can keep track of your sales costs through your marketing budget in the plan, as well as by comparing your marketing expense as a percentage of sales to your industry. Generally, marketing expenses run about 7 to 12% of sales depending upon the volume and the amount of personal selling involved. You can also determine the sales quota for each salesperson by dividing the weekly salary by the percentage of marketing salaries you have budgeted against sales.

Other marketing measures that small businesses can use are prospect and mailing lists for new potential sales, projection of your own sales as a correlation with personal income, and industry comparisons.

We noted in the last chapter that marketing was the heart of a successful small business, and factual market information is the heart of marketing. Such information can be developed by market research. Much of the information is available by comparing your own internal sales statistics with published sources. If you have to go to the expense of your own market survey to understand your customer's buying behavior, you will at least know that you have created a proprietary competitive advantage by knowing more about your market and how to sell in it than do your competitors.

6
Cost Measures of Performance

The careful control of costs is your most direct means to improve profits. We saw in the first chapter that the business strategy of managers is to seek a high profit margin and a growing market share. The last two chapters have been devoted to making your market share grow. That market growth establishes your revenue. Once you have done all you can to influence and improve your market share and revenues, your gross revenue is relatively fixed in the very short term. That is, your sales revenues are determined by external forces, such as economic conditions, competition, and consumer attitudes, and your own marketing actions. Some external forces, like the economy, are beyond your personal control, which means that your revenues may not be influenced by your own actions once you have done the best marketing job you know how.

But internal costs are not beyond your personal control. These costs are, indeed, one of the few factors in your business over which you have almost complete control. Since profit is determined by revenues − costs = profits, you can see that cost control is the principal means by which you can influence your profits. That is, given a level of revenue determined by your marketing plan and partly by external market forces, your best hope of determining your own profits is to manage your cost so that the residual earnings are as high as you can make them.

Cost control to some people means penny-pinching; but if you pinch pennies on the wrong things, such as a well-conceived sales promotion plan, you are counterproductive and can ruin the business. In reality, then, cost control is having a sense of priority as to what is most important to your business success, and seeing that each level of expenditure pays off in sales and profits. To do that you have to know where each type of expenditure goes, and that means having major costs centers where you can identify groups of costs as they relate to their profit contributions. *Cost center* means simply a group of tasks, or an organizational unit, upon which you keep records and accounts. The process of keeping accounting records of major activities or cost centers is called *cost accounting*. Cost accounting is a rather formidable term for keeping track of where your major expenditures go by their purpose. That idea is simple and straightforward enough. You already know enough about accounting in general, from previous chapters, to see that all we have to do is to identify those activities we are interested in keeping track of and giving them a separate accounting title which lets us accumulate all the costs against them as expenditures are made. That, in a nutshell, is cost accounting.

WHAT COSTS ARE WE INTERESTED IN WATCHING?

The first question in control or cost accounting is: What costs do we want to keep track of so we can influence them? Now remember we want to influence these expenditures in a positive way so that they contribute to sales or profits, and not in a penny-pinching way where they hurt sales or profits. That means that the cost centers must be identifiable with sales revenues, which means we want each major product to be a cost center. Why? Because we record sales by product groups. Therefore, we want to keep costs by the same product groups so we can subtract the costs related to those sales and arrive at a profit.

Cost centers are, first of all, product groups. Next, within any product groups, we may want to keep track of costs by major work functions, such as manufacturing, marketing, and so forth.

Also, there are different kinds of costs depending upon how tightly we can identify them with a product or organizational unit. For example, some costs are *direct* which means they go directly and wholly into the product; for example, the cost of steel to make the frame for a car, for a dishwasher, or for a toaster is a direct material cost. The cost of the truck driver who delivered the steel is an *indirect cost* because the driver also delivered a great many other materials, for other products, at the same time. Therefore, we have to estimate what part of their services pertain to a product being produced. Still fuzzier is the cost of the factory itself which produces many products, because its cost has to be spread over time (like 10 or 15 years) as well as over many products. We call these *allocated costs* because management and their accountants decide how much of the cost over time to allocate to each product.

All right, in cost accounting and cost control we have three tiers of expenditures to make up the cost center: (1) the product determines the center because that is the way we record sales, (2) the task group or organization, such as manufacturing or marketing, makes up the second cost control identification because that is the way the major work is done, and thus they are responsible for controlling large groups of expenditures, and (3) the cost elements which make up the expenditures according to the tightness with which they can be identified with the product. The cost elements are:

1. Direct material—costs of materials that enter the product wholly and discretely.
2. Direct labor—costs of work which directly make the product.
3. Indirect materials—costs of materials which go into a process, but not the product, such as lubricants or office supplies.
4. Indirect labor—costs of work which go into a process, but not directly into the product, such as maintenance men, repairmen, and truckers.
5. Manufacturing overhead costs—the allocated costs of the plant over time to the product.
6. Direct marketing expense—the cost of selling a particular product.
7. Selling, general, and administrative expenses—the allocated costs of the general office operation which runs the business.

The reason we classify expenses into these cost elements for monitoring is that the indirect and allocated overhead expenses are the ones most likely to get out of line and become overexpended with bad effects on profits. The direct expenses bear watching, too, but here you have very direct comparisons to make within your own company from the past. You have good measures of performance. That is, you usually know what the material costs of a product are from your past experience. If you run a restaurant you know that raw food costs are usually 40% of sales revenue. If raw food costs get higher than that, you either have to find better suppliers or raise your prices. You usually know what your selling costs are, say 9% of sales, as we saw in the last chapter. If selling costs go higher than that, you have to check over your marketing plan and cut down on the least essential tasks.

With indirect and allocated costs, however, you do not have as tight a measure of performance because in both cases, the cost is an estimate and comes into being as an expense by a decision not directly tied to the product. For example, suppose you expand your plant to build valves as well as pumps; the pumps bear some of the overhead cost of the new plant even though you built it to make valves. The pump business may not benefit directly from the new plant. You wanted to make valves. But the pump business gets stuck with some of the costs, and the pump profit margin shrinks. Or take another example. Suppose you hire a new secretary because your correspondence is behind. But the secretary adds to the general administrative expense and does not really help either the valve or the pump business. So the profit margins on both valves and pumps shrink again because you felt it would be great to have a new secretary.

The point is, indirect and allocated costs have a way of creeping up and eroding profits for reasons not related to the benefit of the cost center (or the consumer). Moreover, the creeping inflation of indirect and allocated costs represents the wishes and decisions of the manager. So let's face it frankly, you—the manager—are the cause of rising indirect costs and the shrinkage of profits.

The problem of cost control, then is largely an internal struggle of the manager, within himself, trying to set priorities. We all yearn for things we want to have but cannot afford: new secretaries, fine offices, new factories, bigger stores, more help, an easier life, more luxury. Yes, that happens in business, too, and the disease is worse there than at home. At home what you cannot have stares you in the face because you run out of money. In business, the lust for luxury is obscured by the fact that the business is making money, and all you need is a rational economic excuse for converting the business's funds to something you desire by calling it a business necessity or part of your business plan. There is a saying that as long as a small business works out of a back room or garage, it thrives; when it builds its first building, it is on the way out. Henry Ford made millions in the automobile business while in his old factory and offices, but when he built his new offices and factory in Dearborn, his business hit the skids. The cause was a poor marketing plan, perhaps, a failure to give customers the colors, styles, and accessories that General Motors did. But were the events unrelated? Only Henry knows for sure. Why did he not invest in new products rather than new buildings? That was a decision from which, in 50 years, the business has not been able to recover.

One problem of small businesses is that personal and business priorities get mixed up. The personal desire for pretense and show becomes cloaked with business justifications. After all, what is all that profit good for if you cannot show it off a bit—that sort of thing, very human, and very dangerous.

How do you guard against letting the overhead costs of the business rise, in preference to more profit-oriented investments? There are two ways. One is to make a well-documented business plan and submit it to outside criticism for objective appraisal, whether by bankers, consultants, colleagues, or an outside board of directors. In short, seek the common sense of other good minds.

The second way to check on your own inevitable tendency to mix personal and business motives is to compare your own cost performance with others. This can be done, in part, through the use of Cost of Doing Business ratios.

Cost of Doing Business Ratios as a Performance Measure

Other businesses have similar problems to your own. Other businesses use standard accounting methods. The accounting by costs centers, product lines, and cost elements is common throughout business. Therefore, you can examine your own cost control and performance by cost standards of other businesses. These are often available through trade associations and, for business in general, through the Cost of Doing Business ratios of Dun & Bradstreet. Table 6-1 below shows the cost of doing business for partnerships in many lines of trade, manufacture, finance, and services. Similar data are available from Dun & Bradstreet for proprietorships and corporations.

The most important ratio in Table 6-1 is the Cost of Goods Sold, which tells you whether you are buying efficiently or not. You can actually tell whether you are getting a competitive price on your purchased goods by looking in the table under the title of "Merchandise Purchased." If your own percentage of Cost of Goods Sold is higher than shown in the table, you need to sharpen up your purchasing activity. You can also tell about how much to spend on merchandising from the column "Labor and Supplies"; generally the labor costs are about two-thirds of this ratio and the balance are supplies.

The reason for checking the competitiveness of your cost of goods sold is that it is crucial in determining your gross margin, which is what you have left for your costs and profit.

The next most important figure in Table 6-1 is the Profit on Business Receipts, because that tells you how well you are doing and what your cost control target is. For example, in our retail hardware store illustration, the cost of goods sold is 74.25%, the gross margin is 25.75% of which the profits should be 7.06%, leaving total costs to be controlled of 18.69% (25.75% − 7.06%). In other words, if you are in the retail hardware business and your cost control target is any higher than 18.69% of receipts, you are not going to make the profit from your business that you should.

The next two most important ratios for you to watch, in terms of cost control, are depreciation and salaries. Depreciation is the charge made to write off and recover your facilities investment. If your facilities investment is too large, that is, you overinvested in facilities, the depreciation and amortization charges would be more than the ratios in this column. That would be a danger sign, because it would mean that your allocated fix costs are getting out of line and perhaps out of control.

Similarly, the columns salaries and wages, plus payments to partners, tell you whether your indirect labor expense is getting out of hand. If so, your general administrative expense will be too high to be competitive or to yield the kind of profit you deserve.

So what do you do if the alarm goes off and you find that your costs are too high? Then you need to pay attention to cost control methods, which we will discuss the following sections in terms of: (1) production scheduling and control, (2) buying and inventory control, (3) control over direct costs and pricing, and (4) allocation decisions regarding overhead costs.

Table 6-1. Cost of Doing Business—Partnerships.

INDUSTRY	Total Number of Returns Filled	SELECTED COSTS				SELECTED OPERATING EXPENSES							Deprecia- tion Amortiza- tion	Profits on Business Receipts
		Cost of Goods Sold	Merchandise Purchased	Labor, Supplies	Gross Margin	Salaries and Wages	Payments to Partners	Rent	Interest	Taxes	Bad Debts	Repairs		
		%	%	%	%	%	%	%	%	%	%	%	%	%
ALL INDUSTRIES	1,062,268	46.73	31.34	5.51	53.27	8.66	1.95	2.57	8.33	3.94	0.20	1.47	6.54	6.62
RETAIL TRADE	167,091	71.60	68.61	2.32	28.40	7.34	1.71	2.11	0.69	1.98	0.20	0.50	1.17	6.80
Bldg Materials, Hardware, Garden Supply, & Mobile Home Dealers	8,719	74.25	70.52	2.84	25.75	6.26	1.94	0.99	1.07	2.10	0.48	0.46	1.25	7.06
General Merchandise Stores	4,871	74.89	73.79	1.51	25.11	7.44	0.99	1.60	0.55	1.62	0.11	0.35	1.00	6.70
Grocery Stores	16,479	81.70	80.52	0.59	18.30	5.13	1.03	1.00	0.33	1.42	0.07	0.39	0.78	4.41
Other Food Stores	7,852	71.52	66.02	4.55	28.48	6.89	1.81	2.04	0.27	1.73	0.04	0.58	1.20	8.14
Motor Vehicle Dealers	6,164	84.71	78.12	2.41	15.29	3.99	1.04	0.64	1.06	0.86	0.34	0.41	0.45	2.89
Gasoline Service Stations	17,190	78.19	75.50	1.74	21.81	4.10	1.15	1.87	0.25	2.05	0.13	0.25	0.75	7.92
Other Automotive Dealers	5,845	71.38	70.54	1.75	28.62	7.27	1.76	2.11	1.04	1.65	0.23	0.41	1.04	6.92
Apparel & Accessory Stores	13,162	63.97	64.93	1.73	36.03	9.03	2.59	3.61	0.53	1.89	0.23	0.37	1.03	9.49
Furniture & Home Furnishings Stores	10,951	67.09	65.19	1.97	32.91	7.50	2.55	2.21	0.73	1.93	0.52	0.37	0.95	8.43
Drinking Places	10,711	48.54	46.07	2.08	51.46	13.54	2.65	3.24	1.69	4.45	0.09	1.28	2.99	9.23
Eating Places	24,039	49.45	43.42	5.27	50.55	16.62	2.45	4.85	1.10	3.79	0.06	1.14	2.45	6.98
Liquor Stores	4,387	77.75	76.85	0.69	22.25	4.54	1.40	1.73	0.74	2.03	0.08	0.49	1.13	7.04
WHOLESALE TRADE	28,103	83.22	78.27	1.74	16.78	3.48	0.88	0.56	0.45	0.92	0.17	0.37	0.67	5.99
RETAIL & WHOLESALE TRADES	195,503	75.86	72.16	2.11	24.14	5.92	1.40	1.54	0.60	1.59	0.19	0.45	0.99	6.51
MANUFACTURING	30,620	66.40	42.22	14.84	33.60	5.81	1.71	1.38	1.32	1.88	0.18	0.99	3.23	7.60
Lumber & Wood Products, except Furniture	5,076	67.42	34.22	17.47	32.58	4.92	1.39	2.12	1.93	2.05	0.10	2.21	4.84	0.16
Printing, Publishing & Allied Industries	6,152	39.77	22.07	13.16	60.23	15.04	3.63	2.49	1.02	2.49	0.55	0.65	2.32	14.37
Machinery, except Electrical	2,493	60.40	33.89	20.87	39.60	5.75	3.65	1.22	0.80	2.20	0.27	0.63	2.54	15.13
Other Manufacturing Industries	16,899	70.32	47.48	13.98	29.68	4.75	1.36	1.08	1.27	1.73	0.14	0.79	3.03	7.75
CONSTRUCTION	63,096	72.72	14.30	24.34	27.28	4.21	2.06	0.64	2.07	1.51	0.12	0.69	1.96	7.49
General Contractors	22,993	80.67	11.00	24.23	19.33	2.48	1.34	0.46	2.72	1.18	0.09	0.59	1.69	3.75
Special Trade Contractors	39,888	55.89	21.33	24.60	44.11	7.90	3.59	1.03	0.69	2.22	0.17	0.92	2.51	15.36
Masonry, Stonework & Plastering	5,919	50.94	11.44	31.50	49.06	9.68	3.60	0.70	0.53	2.35	0.06	0.54	1.83	17.92
Painting, Paperhanging & Decorating	5,208	39.97	6.33	27.68	60.03	8.32	6.73	1.09	0.37	2.36	—	0.65	1.98	26.43

Plumbing, Heating & Air Conditioning	5,332	65.18	32.00	21.04	34.82	6.28	2.15	0.70	0.57	1.93	0.27	0.42	1.55	13.26
SERVICES	191,150	12.91	5.60	3.37	87.09	21.90	3.65	4.80	3.19	2.92	0.15	0.81	5.78	25.89
Total Hotels & Other Lodging Places	14,631	19.83	9.65	4.82	80.17	18.55	1.48	4.93	17.01	7.09	0.31	3.36	13.99	(10.40)
Total Personal Services	25,842	26.34	11.91	10.70	73.66	15.68	4.96	5.91	1.25	3.28	0.30	1.50	5.03	19.00
Barber Shops	3,013	11.50	3.34	1.38	88.50	20.46	13.07	9.48	—	1.99	—	0.57	2.82	29.43
Beauty Shops	8,138	25.20	5.78	18.81	74.80	20.86	6.31	8.08	0.78	3.11	—	1.00	2.88	16.88
Laundries, Dry Cleaning & Garment Services	9,140	23.76	6.35	12.84	76.24	18.67	3.31	6.56	1.86	4.17	0.17	2.25	7.45	11.38
Business Services	26,531	18.89	6.82	5.32	81.11	15.49	4.47	3.21	10.89	2.34	0.42	1.10	28.63	(4.34)
Total Automotive Repair & Services	17,425	47.02	36.22	7.95	52.98	10.01	2.67	4.42	2.67	2.83	0.16	1.07	6.03	12.84
Other Repair Services	11,612	44.03	32.46	9.66	55.97	8.50	5.34	2.33	0.89	2.60	0.21	1.29	2.51	17.95
Amusement & Recreation Services Incl. Motion Pictures	15,047	24.54	8.32	4.12	75.46	16.91	2.61	6.18	4.61	4.10	0.13	1.61	19.58	(11.95)
Total Medical & Health Services	19,546	7.43	1.78	3.31	92.57	21.83	3.33	5.05	1.15	2.48	0.12	0.44	1.39	37.13
Offices of Physicians	9,911	1.86	0.78	0.71	98.14	19.38	3.68	4.62	0.27	1.66	0.02	0.34	0.79	48.34
Total Accounting, Auditing & Bookkeeping Services	12,522	1.75	—	0.97	98.25	37.72	7.07	4.84	0.64	2.70	0.09	0.24	1.31	28.19
Certified Public Accountants	8,090	1.73	—	0.88	98.27	38.04	6.81	4.81	0.65	2.71	0.09	0.24	1.27	28.41
Engineering & Architectural Services	6,161	25.99	1.67	6.92	74.01	23.80	3.26	2.85	0.44	2.15	0.10	0.19	0.85	16.51
Legal Services	27,801	1.23	—	0.13	98.77	22.30	2.86	5.41	0.31	2.12	0.08	0.22	1.24	50.54
TRANSPORTATION, COMMUNICATION & SANITARY SERVICES	14,331	35.65	14.60	5.44	64.35	11.66	2.41	2.98	4.32	3.76	0.51	3.29	13.11	0.35
Trucking & Warehousing	8,746	30.85	16.98	4.90	69.15	14.06	3.24	3.98	1.83	4.02	0.11	5.23	7.08	8.65
Other Transportation	2,997	46.08	14.40	6.22	53.92	5.77	0.63	1.73	6.45	1.99	0.13	1.14	16.78	(1.89)
Communication, Electric, Gas & Sanitary Services	2,588	21.68	6.52	5.08	78.32	20.69	4.76	—	7.00	8.14	3.12	2.69	22.29	(23.22)
FINANCE, INSURANCE & REAL ESTATE	430,326	11.65	2.69	1.03	88.35	5.95	1.59	2.65	34.62	11.66	0.38	3.14	19.01	13.93
Security, Commodity Brokers & Services	2,184	—	—	—	—	20.41	5.88	3.07	12.52	2.36	0.34	0.17	0.54	2.94
Insurance Agents, Brokers & Service	7,876	15.94	—	1.27	84.06	9.71	3.30	1.70	0.33	1.18	0.36	0.17	0.69	15.06
R.E. Agents, Brokers & Managers	15,937	42.39	13.53	3.22	57.61	7.83	3.40	2.38	18.70	4.61	0.24	1.12	4.68	(4.75)
Operators & Lessors of Bldgs.	250,648	0.68	0.26	0.12	99.32	4.13	0.66	2.83	40.86	15.08	0.24	4.28	26.39	(18.08)
Lessors, other than Buildings	30,497	7.37	3.10	0.12	92.63	1.56	0.69	3.34	36.17	13.36	—	2.76	13.61	6.19
MINING	14,053	28.36	7.76	4.60	71.64	3.54	0.76	1.72	2.18	2.96	0.03	1.69	5.73	(1.19)
Oil & Gas Extraction	12,261	20.95	6.97	1.78	79.05	2.73	0.75	1.99	2.74	3.28	0.02	0.79	5.41	(12.14)
AGRICULTURE, FORESTRY & FISHING	122,625	62.87	23.05	8.71	37.13	1.81	1.17	3.77	4.43	2.12	0.03	3.62	7.01	9.46

( ) = Loss

Production Scheduling and Control

Production scheduling and control sounds like factory jargon, but everyone is engaged in production. The production of a retail hardware store is the delivery of the right goods at the right time in the right place to satisfy customer demand. That is a scheduling problem—the scheduling of work.

Work scheduling can be accomplished in a number of ways. The worst way is for the manager to keep it in his head and not tell anyone. This is the worst method because schedules will get fuzzy and mixed up in the manager's head as time changes, and even if they don't, no one will know what they are and so can do nothing about them.

Schedules are meant to be performance goals of work tasks, both for the manager and all the workers. Employees have to agree on that performance, or at least know about it, in order to do it.

The simplest way to think of production scheduling is to think of it as the organization of work. The work has to be identified, put in sequence, and given a time frame. So the three essentials of production control are: (1) a list of work tasks, (2) the sequence and order of tasks, and (3) time schedules when the tasks must be done.

Let us take a simple example of a business that decides to have a "Back-to-School" promotion sale during the period August 15 to September 15. Right away, a deadline stands out in front of you—by August 15th, everything has to be ready.

We start from the deadline, August 15th, and work backwards to take into account the amount of time required to get the work done. That time is the *lead time* for each major set of tasks. In this illustration there are three major sets of tasks: (1) ordering the back-to-school stock, (2) ordering additional shelves on which to show the stock, and (3) creating a sales promotion advertisement to sell the stock. The manager thinks that the lead time on ordering shelving is almost three months, on stock roughly two months, and on the advertising campaign one month. That means he has to start organizing this work by at least May 15th, and possibly earlier if there are any variations or hitches in the ordering process. Let us assume also that this manager wants something a little special, not just a run-of-the-mill back-to-school sale. Hence he has to spend a little extra time in searching and comparison shopping among suppliers to find his special items and advertising theme. He has to include that search time into the schedule as well.

The steps which the manager takes to do his work scheduling are: (1) he lists all of the tasks to be done, (2) he puts them into sequence, and (3) he puts a time schedule on them. The result is portrayed in a graph, called a *Gantt chart,* that helps him visualize the whole work sequence and appears below as Figure 6-1. The chart is shown in weeks, although it could be made up in terms of days instead.

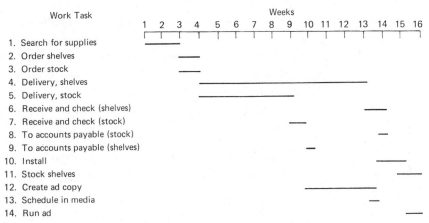

Figure 6-1.   Work Schedule for the Back to School Sale.

In this work schedule, the critical time problems become clear, namely the tasks (1) to search for the right items to buy and (2) to deliver the shelves. Indeed, this 16-week schedule presents the manager with a real crunch in the last three weeks trying to get everything ready on time.

Moreover, if anything in the schedule slips, particularly the delivery of the shelves, the manager is in trouble. He will not be able to run his sales promotion on time, which could be very bad for his sales. What can he do?

He can start earlier and reschedule the work with more slack time in the delivery of shelves from the supplier. By adding three or four weeks to the schedule, the manager can ease up on his critical time schedules, allow for some delays and variation, and have more time at the end to install and stock the shelves. In other words, a slacker schedule can take some of the panic out of his work.

The Gantt chart shown above is the simplest way to organize work by making up task lists and schedules graphically. However, the shortcoming of this type of chart is that it does not show very well the interconnections of one set of tasks with others going on in parallel, particularly if the sequences of work become numerous and complex. A more graphical way to see the impact of one task upon another is called the *network chart*. We can convert the tasks in Figure 6-1 into a network by numbering each task and showing them in a sequence in which a task that must be done first precedes all others which depend upon it. Each numbered task is then drawn as a circle with a line connecting it to all preceding tasks, laying out the chain of events to complete the work. Such a network would show more clearly than a Gantt chart that the stocking of shelves must be preceded by the installation of the shelves, which must by preceded by the delivery of the shelves; so this becomes the longest "critical" path in the schedule. All the other paths going on in parallel, such as ordering the stock and preparing the advertisements, have ample "slack" time in them. In terms of control, then, the manager wants to monitor what happens on the longest or critical path, because this will determine whether or not he gets the job done on time or not. Figure 6-2 illustrates a network chart and uses the same tasks as does Figure 6-1.

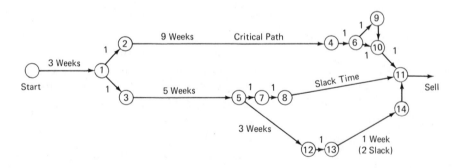

Slack Time = Time Not Needed to Accomplish Tasks.
Critical Path = Path of Tasks with No Slack, and Therefore Critical to Manage on Schedule.

Figure 6-2. Network Chart for the Back to School Sale.

The 14 numbered work tasks are the same as shown in Figure 6-1. The network, showing the necessary preceding events on a time scale, demonstrates clearly that the critical path is the delivery of the shelves.

A production work schedule, such as we have seen above, is probably the single best form of performance measurement which you can devise and use in your business. It is better than comparisons with other companies in that it fits your work situation perfectly. The fact that you as manager devised and designed it is another important plus factor, because in designing the work flow you come to understand it personally and in depth. You know intimately all the critical managerial problems if you think them through and work them out in advance. More than that, you develop a sense of time and costs as to how long each task should take.

Some managers apply time and motion studies to tasks to see what their shortest time should be. I am not recommending that small businesses engage in such time and motion methods, although there is an important place for these methods in large industrial operations. Moreover, there are simplified versions of such studies, for example the Michigan time and motion standards; these standards enable anyone to make a composite of all the separate motions (such as an upward arm flex) that make up a task and then attach standard times to their performance from past experience and studies. However, the small businessman has too many important managerial tasks to coordinate, in most cases, to get into that degree of analysis. Rather, the small businessman should get his sense of time for scheduling by doing most of the major jobs himself, as efficiently as he can, and by observing another capable worker who may do it differently. From his own sense of performance and time, the manager can not only set reasonably good time schedules but he can also train and teach others under his supervision to the tasks well.

Indeed, perhaps the greatest advantage of production scheduling as a performance measure is that it makes the manager do all the tasks, think through the work, and train others. That is to say, production scheduling is perhaps the single best educational tool for a manager to understand his own business, as well as his best performance standard and control method.

Once the production schedules are established, of course, control follows by monitoring performance to see that it is on time and on schedule. If the tasks are not done properly or on time, then the manager uses exception reporting to note those parts of the work that are not going well and studying them further to see why not. Many times the problem will not be the fault of the worker, but rather lack of materials or good layout. Other times, the employees may have fallen inadvertently into ineffective work habits which the manager can correct by retraining on the job. In other words, when the production control schedules slip, this is not an occasion for witch-hunts but rather for solving new problems which were not anticipated clearly beforehand.

Buying and Inventory Control

Inventories are a large investment item for most business. In wholesale and retail trade, inventory normally ranges from 30 to 40% of the total investment in all assets. In manufacturing, inventory is in the range from 15 to 25%, which is smaller of course than in trade because manufacturing has heavy asset investments in facilities. In either case, the size of inventory investment is substantial enough to warrant special attention and control. This is particularly true because the inventory is a composite of stock and materials which vary in usage. Typically the highest usage items may constitute only 10% of the items in stock but account for 70% of the usage. The next most active items may constitute 20% of the stock items and 20% of the usage, which leaves a remaining 70% of the items accounting for 10% of the usage.

Obviously, the little-used items raise questions about whether money should be tied up in keeping them in stock at all. This is not to say that all low-usage items in inventory should be eliminated, because they may be quite crucial to the sales or production of other merchandise. But the typical skewed distribution of inventory usage does make clear the necessity for keeping close control over inventory for two reasons: (1) to see that the active items are always in stock so that sales are not lost for out-of-stock condition, and (2) to see that inactive items are stocked at an essential minimum or eliminated from stock so they do not tie up money and space.

Inventory control consists of two main parts. The first part is keeping records to show the major items in inventory on stock cards so you know what quantities remain in stock; the second part is setting up procedures for timely reordering. As to the first, record-keeping, the active stock items should be recorded upon a stock card which shows the amount on hand, the withdrawal from stock in quantity by dates, the average usage rates, and the minimum reserve on hand at the time of reordering.

The second step in inventory control, timely reordering, may be viewed in two parts—the time of reordering, and the quantity of reorder. The time of reordering is called the *order point* and may be calculated as the lead time in days to get new stock delivered, multiplied by the usage rate in units per day. Suppose you are using or selling a great many gallons of paint per day. The reorder time to get new paint delivery is 16 days. The usage rate is 19 gallons per day. The reorder point is 16 x 19 = 304 gallons. That is, you would want a minimum reserve of 304 gallons of paint on hand so that you would not run out. Any time the stock card showed a withdrawal down to 304 gallons you would reorder.

How much quantity would you reorder? The economic order quantity can be found by determining when holding costs of the item equal the order costs. The *holding costs* are such items as interest on the capital tied up in inventory, insurance, labor costs for stock handling, space costs, and inventory losses. The *ordering costs* are the personnel costs for search for suppliers, preparing purchase orders, checking on purchase placement, receiving and inspection, posting the stock record cards, and paying the invoice.

The economic order quantity (EOQ) can be calculated as:

$$EOQ = \frac{2 \times D \times O}{C \times I}$$

where D is the average demand or usage during the period, O is the ordering cost, C is the cost per unit of the ordered item, and I is the percentage inventory carrying cost. Suppose the gallon of paint costs $5, the carrying costs of inventory are 30%, the order costs $14, and the average demand is 19 gallons per day. Then the economic order quantity (EOQ) is:

$$EOQ = \frac{2 \times 19 \times 14}{5 \times .30} = \frac{532}{1.5} = 355 \text{ gallons}$$

Now the manager knows that his minimum stock and order point should be 304 gallons of paint, and when he gets down to that stock level he should order 355 gallons as the EOQ where he minimized his reorder costs versus holding costs.

In summary the key to inventory control is to anticipate buying needs from demand or usage, and then purchase in economical lot sizes to minimize holding and order costs. The inventory buying should also be done, of course, in light of the marketing plan discussed in Chapters 4 and 5. That is, the manager should study the market, know the competition, and set sales and profit performance goals as a means of judging the balance of stock to be ordered for the inventory.

Control Over Direct Costs and Pricing

Most businesses determine their prices initially as a markup over costs; although if demand is unusually strong, they may temporarily shift to demand pricing in which they ration their available supply over their estimate of total demand at the minimum price that will clear the market. More simply put, charge what the traffic will bear. Demand pricing is very much more difficult and subjective than cost pricing, because most businessmen do not have enough information on the consumers' demand curve for various quantities at various prices to know what prices will clear the market. Some examples of demand pricing do exist when shortages are extreme and the seller can test the market almost daily or weekly to tell whether the supply is being sold. During the 1979 gasoline shortages, both the oil companies and gasoline dealers raised their prices steadily, daily or weekly, until the gasoline lines disappeared (which was evidence of clearing the market). Similarly when the coffee crop froze in Brazil in 1977, coffee companies raised their prices periodically until demand diminished to balance off the supply.

Besides these unusual cases, however, pricing is usually based upon costs because that is the way the seller can try to assure his profit margin. The usual pricing procedure is to add direct material costs plus direct labor costs, multiplied by an overhead rate to cover indirect and overhead facility costs, multiplied by a profit margin. To simplify the calculation, the overhead rate and profit margin are often lumped together to form the gross margin or markup, which may be 40% or more.

The cost plus a markup form of pricing, in itself, necessitates a form of cost control, because the selling price is at least partially determined externally in the marketplace by competition. If all sellers experience about the same increases in costs and raise their selling prices more or less together by the same amount, independently of course and not in collusion (which would be an antitrust violation in restraint of trade), then only a modest reduction in sales is likely to occur as consumers generally buy less in response to higher market prices. But if any one seller raises his prices well above the market, based upon higher costs or profit target, that seller may expect to lose considerable sales to other competitors whose prices remain unchanged and lower.

In other words, an independent and sticky market price forces a business manager to control his costs within a rather narrow range of what his markup and competitive selling price will allow. This fact means that one measure of cost control is the market price itself, less the markup, which equals the necessary range within which costs must be contained. If the control is: costs = selling price − markup, then there are two ways to find out whether you as manager have control over costs. The first and worst way is to wait until the end of a month or quarter and see from the income statement whether your profits (contained in the markup) have fallen or not. This is a poor way to manage because then it is too late to correct and recoup the lost profits. True, you can try to reduce costs or raise prices for the future accounting period, but you still will not know whether you are successful until the next accounting statement appears.

What you need is a predictive estimate of your costs and markup, so that you can take corrective action in time to influence your profits favorably if you need to. The predictive estimate can be made by sampling your costs periodically, for a day or a week at a time. We resort to a sample time period because it may be too costly to trace all of the costs, except monthly in the income statement. If you are a manufacturer with many parts and products going through the plant at any one time, it is not practical to keep an individual cost record on every piece of work at all times. Instead, we can set a standard costs for a particular product and sample from time to time whether the hours of work and the dollar costs of materials going into that product meet the standard. Similarly, if you are a retailer, it is not practical to add the labor and overhead costs to every item sold out of a large inventory, but you can sample the labor and overhead costs for a day or two, in relation to sales prices, to see if you are maintaining a satisfactory profit margin. How do you do it?

You keep a record in the form of a cost sheet which shows the material cost plus the labor costs plus the normal markup, for a product if you are a manufacturer or for a typical time period or day if you are a retailer. The results would look like Table 6–2.

In the manufacturing example above, the labor operations necessary to produce a product are shown together with the materials going into it. The overhead rate is added to their costs, giving a total cost for the product. This is compared with a standard cost. Standard cost is arrived at in this way: first, measure the time it takes for a typical worker to perform each operation, and second, divide the total material costs for a product by the number of units produced. The standard cost is, therefore, the average cost expected for all units. However, in this particular sample which was measured to test the cost control, we find that the cost is running $4.60 over the standard. This variance means that the profit on that sample unit will be $4.60 less than expected or planned, due possibly to more labor hours or more materials used for that product. The manager needs to take some action, such as: (1) check the worker training to see if the hours can be lowered, (2) check the material usage to see if there was excess waste, or (3) decide that the cost standard was wrong in the first place, in which case he would have to raise the price of the unit by $4.60 or else earn that much less profit.

The retail example is very similar. The manager has kept track of a sample day to show all the labor costs incurred and all the inventory sold. He applies the normal markup (overhead and profit) to these costs and gets a total of $704.90 for the day. But he knows that he should sell $750 per day as a goal, which is figured as his total estimated sales for the month divided by the number of selling days. He fell $45.10 short of his sales target, which means he has lost $45.10 of his gross margin for that day. The manager needs to take some action, such as: (1) increase the sales promotion and sales volume, (2) raise the markup prices, (3) cut costs, or (4) reduce his profit expectation for the month. He may also conclude that his sample day was somewhat low and not typical, in which case he would sample another day to see what results he gets.

In any of these cases, of course, the objective is to review costs to see if they conform to cost controls and profit expectations. The purpose is to predict what will happen to costs and profits at the end of the month in the income statement sufficiently in advance to do something about it.

Table 6-2. Illustrative Cost Sheet of a Sample Operation.

DESCRIPTION OF COST ELEMENT	QUANTITY/HOURS	COST PER UNIT	AMOUNT	TOTAL
Manufacturing Example				
Labor				
Lathe operation	4	$15.00	$ 60.00	
Welding	1	8.00	8.00	
Grinding	2	10.00	20.00	
Assembly	1	9.00	9.00	$ 97.00
Material				
Steel sheet	1	10.00	10.00	
Steel rod	2	8.00	16.00	
Plate cover	1	15.00	15.00	
Screws	10	.10	1.00	42.00
				139.00
Overhead Rate (40%)				55.60
Total Cost				194.60
Standard Cost				190.00
Variance				− 4.60
Retail Example				
Labor				
Salesclerk A	8	5.00	40.00	
Salesclerk B	3	3.50	10.50	
Bookkeeper	1	8.00	8.00	58.50
Materials				
Women's dresses	10	10.00	100.00	
Men's suits	5	50.00	250.00	
Shirts	15	5.00	75.00	
Blouses	5	4.00	20.00	445.00
				503.50
Overhead and Profit Rate (40%)				201.40
Total Cost of Sales (with profit)				704.90
Daily Sales Target or Requirements (sales standard)				750.00
Variance				− 45.10

Allocation Decisions Regarding Overhead Costs

The overhead costs or markup percentages used in the previous examples are four to five times larger than the variance we measured. That means that a small error in the overhead rate, and what it should be, can make a large difference in our standard costs or expected profits. Moreover, we know that the overhead rate or the markup is an estimate in the first place, so how good is it? The overhead or the markup is as good as the allocation decision which made it in the first place. At best, it is the average indirect costs per unit attributed to a product or time period. Because the overhead or markup is so large, relative to the final profit margin or variance, it should be evaluated and set with great care.

Let us take two examples to see how much the costs can change based upon an allocation decision. We will use the example of an overhead rate, which is a term usually applied in manufacturing to spread the cost of the production plan and facilities over all of the products produced. In principal, the markup, which is usually a term applied to gross margin in retail or wholesale trade, is a similar spreading of all indirect costs over the total inventory sold, and its effects are much the same as in the manufacturing example.

The Simplex Valve Company produces two products, Valve A and Valve B, in a plant which costs $10,000,000. Valve A is a big cast-metal valve which uses a great deal of material and relatively little labor or factory machine time. Valve B is a small precision product which uses relatively little material but a large portion of the machine time in the factory. Suppose the factory is amortized or depreciated over 10 years, then its overhead cost is $1 million dollars per year. How shall we spread the costs of the factory between the two valves? Several Methods are illustrated in the table on page 125.

Notice in this example that the overhead cost per Valve B unit could vary from $40 to $120 depending upon the method by which the allocation decision was made. The high overhead of $120 per unit may indeed be so extreme as to price Valve B out of the market. Still the machining-time method of allocating overhead costs is perhaps the fairest method of allocation as a means of spreading and recovering factory cost because the factory capacity and cost itself is based upon the time machines are utilized.

If $120 per unit is too high to make Valve B marketable, a dif-

| | VOLUME METHOD | | MATERIAL METHOD | | MACHINE METHOD | |
	Volume (no./yr.)	Overhead Per Unit ($40)	Material Cost	Overhead % Cost (43%)	Machining Time	Overhead (% machine use)
Valve A	20,000	$ 800,000	$500,000	715,000	20,000 hrs	400,000
Valve B	5,000	200,000	200,000	285,000	30,000 hrs	600,000
		1,000,000		1,000,000		1,000,000
Overhead cost per unit						
Valve A		$40		35.75		20
Valve B		40		57.00		120

ferent basis for allocation could be used by spreading the amortization of the plant over 20 years instead of 10 years. That would cut the overhead costs for Valve B from $120 per unit to $60 per unit. If that cost is still too high, the management could decide to subsidize Valve B by making Valve A bear more of the cost.

You can see from these examples that the allocation of overhead costs is highly discretionary on the part of management. The allocation is discretionary, but not arbitrary, because the methods are limited by IRS rules and accepted accounting practices. Still, any of the examples given above, if consistently applied, would satisfy IRS or accounting practice; and you can see that there is at least a three-fold difference in the size of the overhead charge.

The point of this discussion of overhead allocation is not to make you throw up your hands in frustration, but rather to encourage you to consider the basis for allocation decisions very carefully and to try to have as solid and as fair a basis for them as practical. The allocation decisions can make some products look profitable and others not, as in the case of the two valves. The same would be true in a retail store. Suppose one department, like jewelry, had high-value items that took relatively little space and personnel, while a second boutique department had low-value items that took a great deal of space. Then a straight percentage markup over cost would penalize the jewelry department and subsidize the boutique and may not be in keeping with your marketing or management objectives involved.

The best procedure for allocation decisions is to consider the cost recovery basis for the overhead investment, which usually will be a space or utilization factor, because the need for space or capacity is what causes you to make facilities investments in the first place. If you then choose to shift the basis of the overhead charge (as from boutique to jewelry), you should do it knowingly and on the basis of marketing and management objectives which optimize sales or earnings for the firm as a whole.

SUMMARY

Cost control is a principal means of determining profits because internal costs are wholly under your control, while revenues are subject to the influence of external market forces.

Cost control begins with establishing "cost centers" or accounts to record the expenditures for groups of activities, or organizational unit, which you wish to monitor as a means of reaching your management goals.

Cost centers are set up in terms of (1) product lines, (2) major tasks or organizational units which make a discrete product, and (3) cost elements, such as direct and indirect labor, direct and indirect materials, overhead, and administrative expenses.

Indirect costs and overhead expenses are most likely to get out of hand, because these are subject to the manager's discretion, and many personal wishes for display or power may end up as overhead costs which neither benefit nor enhance the product or its sales.

Direct labor and material expense are usually subject to close checking because of the past record of costs which are clearly identifiable as input to the product.

And important check on your costs is provided by the Cost of Doing Business ratios of Dun & Bradstreet. (A particularly important ratio is the gross margin on profit). Within the cost control target, the key items are depreciation and salary payments, which show whether you are overinvested in capital items or are over-paying personnel.

If your costs are too high, the best way to look for cost reduction is by production scheduling and control. Production scheduling is simply the organization of work and putting work-tasks in a sequence so the manager can control their flow.

The objective of scheduling is to reveal bottlenecks or to illustrate the longest, critical path which must be monitored to get the work done on time and on a cost target.

The production schedule is probably the best single performance measure a manager can devise because it represents his own organization of the work that needs to be done and because it is a means for a manager to understand his own business in detail.

Production schedules are a means of control as the manager checks to see that work is done on time; if not, he then can take action to correct performance by checking on material flow, retraining the workers, or resetting the schedules.

Inventory control is an essential aspect of cost control because inventories may account for up to 40% of total investment. Moreover, any inventory has a mix of very active and very slow-moving items. The problem, then, is to know the usage rates so that the inventory of each item on hand can be kept at a minimum running out of stock.

The reorder point for any item in stock can be calculated as the usage rate multiplied by the lead time to restock the item.

The economic order quantity can be calculated by balancing off the holding costs against the costs of reordering, in order to minimize both costs.

Pricing is normally determined by adding a percentage markup to costs. If either the costs are too high or the markup is incorrectly estimated, the firm will lose profits. Hence, cost control, covering both direct and overhead costs, is essential to predict and influence profit.

A way to predict costs and profits during the month, between accounting statements, is to sample the costs and markup for a product, or a day, and compare them with a cost or sales standard of what you expect in order to achieve your profit margin. If performance is off standard, then the manager's action is to reduce costs by checking for waste, raising prices, changing the standard, or reducing profit expectations.

The overhead or markup charges added to costs are usually large relative to the profit margin, or to the variances of performance from standard. Markups should be studied carefully because they are estimates, at best, and they can greatly influence the appearance of profit or loss for a particular product, depending upon how they are allocated.

The allocation decision of overhead and indirect costs should be made first on the basis of cost-recovery of the facilities investment (or indirect costs), and second on the basis of marketing or management objectives which spread costs to different products in a manner to optimize the earnings of the whole firm.

7

Asset Measures of Performance

Small businessmen are operators. They must be to run a firm. That is, their primary concerns are creating products, finding markets, convincing customers, managing costs, making profits, managing funds, and coping with change. These are operational activities—the running of the business. We have covered how to do most of these things in Chapters 1 through 6, because these are the first things a small businessman must be able to do to survive and grow.

The very success of small business managers as operators may, however, distract them from another important aspect of their business: the financial management of their assets. We already have seen the danger, in Chapter 2, of small businessmen concentrating so heavily on sales, profits, and the income statement that they get into a cash shortage and cash crisis, often leading to failure. In the same sense, small businessmen can concentrate on operations to the point of ignoring the impact on other assets on the balance sheet. Failure to pay attention to the financial valuation of inventory, accounts receivable or fixed assets may not create a crisis, as cash can, but the results can seriously diminish the resources of the business and the personal wealth of the owner. After all, the owner's ultimate goal is to increase his personal wealth; to neglect that aspect of management is self-defeating.

Small businessmen, then, have to school and discipline themselves in the significance of financial balance in their business and in financial evaluation of their assets. The importance of financial evaluation may not be apparent, because most people will assume that financial valuations are obvious—namely historical cost. But the use of the historical costs can seriously underestimate the replacement value of assets; and when time comes to replace, the funds may not be available. This can cause the business to become obsolete and noncompetitive. Great Britain has had serious problems with aging, obsolescent small businesses which are run by the elderly, original enterpreneurs who started the business, but who failed to value their assets so that they could be replaced. This results in sick and aging businesses which cannot easily be revived due to their high costs, obsolete assets, and lack of funds.

THE PROBLEM OF VALUATION

The way to avoid the British experience is to value assets currently. The current or market value of assets is not always easy to determine for simple reasons like: (1) you do not intend to put your store and fixtures on the market because you are using them and there is no other store just like yours to serve as an appraisal value comparison or (2) all of your inventory is not sold quickly or at one time while costs of repurchasing stock may have changed. These changes in valuations of your stock or fixed assets could be as much as 10 to 15% in a year, which may be as large as your profits. Conceivably, you could be working hard to make more profit while losing it all at the same time in the value of your assets. You want to prevent that if you can, and at least know about it in any case. Otherwise you will get some rude surprises when you try to raise more money or sell out.

So the valuation of assets is important to your personal wealth and to the future resources to finance your business. Perhaps the simplest way to understand how to deal with financial valuation of assets is to use two examples for illustration, the first is inventory evaluation, the second is the valuation of fixed assets.

Inventory Valuation

Inventory is usually evaluated at cost, which seems reasonable enough because that is what you paid for the stock. Moreover, most managers assume that the oldest items in stock are the ones being sold first as they turn over and renew the stock. The result of this practice is known as the first-in-first-out (or FIFO) valuation of inventory.

The effect of using cost of stock on a FIFO basis is to create a lag between the time of purchase and the time of sale which, on an average 90-day turnover basis, is at least three months; on slow-moving items the lag can be six months to a year. Suppose now we introduce a rapid inflation, as in recent years, that may raise costs of stock 1 to 2% per month. In three months the replacement value of the stock could be 5% higher than today, in six months or one year perhaps 15 to 20% higher. On a FIFO basis, with a normal markup, your sales price could be lagging far enough behind replacement costs of the inventory to eliminate all your profit.

A partial remedy for this undervaluation of replacement costs and prices would be to price and sell the stock on a last-in-first-out (LIFO) basis. That is, the last purchase price is closest to the current market with inflation built into it, so if you price your stock items at the last purchase cost, you are close to reflecting the current valuation of your cost of goods sold.

However, if you purchase any stock items only at long intervals, or they are slow in turnover, you may still undervalue the stock on a LIFO basis. Then you probably should resort to getting regular price quotations and revalue the stock on the latest bid price and by the LIFO method.

Let us try to be more specific as to the financial effects of these two methods of valuing inventory, because they produce different results when it comes to looking at profits or at asset accumulation as performance measures.

FIFO assigns the cost of the stock received first to the sales for the period, values the inventory at the last-in cost of stock, and during inflation yields a higher value to profits. For example, if the first-in cost of stock was $5 and the last-in stock cost $7, then the effects would be:

Sales		$20
Cost of Goods Sold		
Beginning inventory	$ 5	
Purchases	10	
Total	$15	
Minus Ending Inventory	−7	
Cost of Goods Sold		8
Gross Profit Margin		$12

LIFO assigns the cost of the stock received last to the sales for the period, values the inventory at the first-in cost of stock, and during inflation yields a lower value to profits. For example:

Sales		$20
Cost of Goods Sold		
Beginning Inventory	$ 5	
Purchases	10	
Total	$15	
Minus Ending Inventory	− 5	
Cost of Goods Sold		$10
Gross Profit Margin		$10

Which method is right? They are both satisfactory as far as accepted accounting practice is concerned, as long as they are used consistently. The effect of FIFO is to overstate profits, compared to replacement value of the cost of goods sold, but to correctly value the ending inventory in terms of current replacement cost. The effect of LIFO is to correctly value the profit in terms of replacement value of cost of goods sold, but to undervalue the inventory on the balance sheet in terms of current replacement cost. Or put differently, FIFO gives you windfall profits during inflation and precipitous losses during deflation, while valuing inventory currently on the balance sheet in either case. LIFO currently and correctly values profits, but gives you undervalued inventories during inflation and overvalued inventories on the balance sheet during deflation.

Thus, the method of accounting and evaluation can have important impacts upon profits or assets as performance measures. The important thing is for you to know the basis of valuation and what is happening in the accounts. An owner or creditor would normally prefer to see both profits and assets valued according to current market values, because that provides the most reliable performance measures for profits as an indication of management effectiveness and of assets as to their real liquidation value. In accounting terms that means in practice that, if FIFO is used, the profit needs adjustment for windfall gains and losses, and if LIFO is used, the inventory needs a reserve for overvaluation or undervaluation.

The problem, then, is to arrive at a correct and current value of assets, so that they can be relied upon as measures of the wealth-accumulation of the firm. We will later compare the asset-growth performance of one company with others, and in making that comparison we would want to know the basis of inventory and asset valuation. The approach being used, then, is (1) to understand and currently value assets as measures of wealth-accumulation and (2) to compare the wealth-accumulation of one firm by using as a performance measure the asset structure of other firms.

Valuation of Fixed Assets

Fixed assets include buildings, fixtures, furniture, machinery, and equipment. These items normally have an extended useful life, anywhere from perhaps three to seven years for equipment, and up to 40 years for buildings. Fixed assets are normally recorded in the accounts at cost and then depreciated over their useful life. For example, if a machine costs $10,000 and has a useful life of five years, its straight-line depreciation would be a charge of $2,000 per year against the sales revenues or gross margin of the business, in order to charge the cost of using up that much capital to the profits of the period, and also to provide a fund for replacing the capital equipment at the end of its useful life. The IRS, of course, allows other, more rapid rates of depreciation, such as the sum-of-the-digits method, which place more of the depreciation charge against income in the early years and less in later years. These accelerated depreciation methods, of course, recognize the time value of money, that money today or in the short term is worth more money in the distant future. However, our interest here is not to become engaged in the advantages or disadvantages of various depreciation methods. The main point to be made is that when the useful life of fixed assets is spread over an extended time period, the longer the time period, the greater the likelihood that current market or replacement values will depart from the original cost shown on the books.

We have already seen how price inflation or deflation may alter the value of inventory and profits in a matter of months. The same valuation problem occurs and becomes worse for fixed assets as prices change over years. Suppose your business has a building which cost $1 million and was assumed to be useful for 20 years, but in 10 years the value of the property had doubled and in 20 years quadrupled. You would be charging off $50,000 per year against income by straight-line depreciation, and more if you use an accelerated method. But no matter what the method, your total depreciation will be $1 million but you will need $2 million to replace the building in 10 years and $4 million to replace it in 20 years. So you are under-charging depreciation costs and overstating profits during this whole life of the building, as long as you use original cost as the book value of the asset.

What is the other choice? Use an appraised market value or replacement value of the building as book value of the asset on the balance sheet. Then the asset is correctly valued in terms of current market conditions and the profit is currently charged with replace-ment cost depreciation; but the implication is also that the firm has had a windfall capital gain on its building, which it may not want to acknowledge at the present time. How an owner may wish to handle these accounting options will depend greatly on income tax consider-ations, which have to be resolved on a case-by-case basis.

Every small businessman should be aware that fixed asset values get far out of line from reality over time, particularly during a period of protracted inflation. Most firms carry their fixed assets at original cost, which means that the book value of assets on the balance sheet are seriously undervalued. This undervaluation of assets is the cause for merger and take-over bids during inflation, because assets become seriously undervalued and competitors can take over these bargain assets by a tender-offer to stockholders to buy out their shares. That is, the use of original cost minus depreciation as the basis of valuing fixed assets seriously undervalues a firm and makes it a tempting takeover target during inflation. Still, in comparing the asset distribution of your firm with others, which we will do shortly, you should recognize that original cost minus depreciation is the most common way to value fixed assets.

ASSET GROWTH

The object of running a business, at least to the owners, is to make their assets and net worth increase from year to year. How much should they increase? Normally the increase in assets will be the same as the net profit for the year that is added to the earned surplus (or owner's equity). In Chapter 1, figures were presented on the rate of earnings on assets by asset size. Those earnings can also be used as a basis for estimating what your annual growth in assets and net worth should be.

Another rough performance measure is to recognize that the average annual earnings after taxes on assets of most corporations on the stock exchanges is about 12% per year, or 10 to 15%. True some smaller growth companies in the early years achieve 25 to 50% annual growth rates. But a good overall average is about 12%. Therefore, you should expect your total assets and your net worth to increase by at least 12% per year to be achieving average performance.

ASSET BALANCE AND DISTRIBUTION

The form in which assets are held can, of course, affect your solvency and future earnings. We saw in Chapter 2 that the cash balance must be large enough to pay all bills at all times. The quick asset ratio of cash to payables should be 100% or 1 to 1. The liquid asset ratio of cash with inventory and receivables to payables should be at least 2 to 1. However, we also noted in that chapter that carrying too much cash could reduce earnings, because there would not be enough inventory or fixed assets working for the business to deliver the products or sales. These are indications that the balance and distribution of assets are an important measure of a firm's viability. Therefore, small business managers will find it helpful to compare their own assets distribution with the balance of assets which other companies find it useful to hold. This can be done by using published financial statements of comparable business firms. Sources of comparative financial statements are trade associations, the Federal Trade Commission quarterly reports, the IRS's statistics of income, and the annual financial statement studies of Robert Morris Associates.

The *Annual Statement Studies* of Robert Morris Associates are particularly useful because they cover about 400 business classifications in manufacturing, services, and wholesale and retail trade, and their reports show not only asset distribution, but also income data and financial ratios.[1] An example of two retail business classifications, drugs and farm equipment, is shown on the following page as Table 7-1. The page illustrating drugs and farm equipment was

Table 7-1. Sample page from *Annual Statement Studies*.

RETAILERS

	DRUGS SIC# 5912					FARM EQUIPMENT SIC# 5083				
	105(6/30-9/30/77)	90(10/1/77-3/31/78)				100(6/30-9/30/77)	250(10/1/77-3/31/78)			
ASSET SIZE	0-250M	250M-1MM	1-10MM	10-50MM	ALL	0-250M	250M-1MM	1-10MM	10-50MM	ALL
NUMBER OF STATEMENTS	103	58	24	10	195	20	136	180	14	350
ASSETS	%	%	%	%	%	%	%	%	%	%
Cash & Equivalents	7.2	7.3	8.0	7.0	7.3	5.4	6.1	4.2	4.4	5.0
Accts. & Notes Rec. - Trade(net)	13.3	16.7	8.5	15.8	13.8	25.1	16.8	20.2	25.4	19.4
Inventory	56.3	47.8	57.2	52.0	53.7	51.9	59.3	56.8	44.8	57.0
All Other Current	1.1	1.2	1.2	.4	1.1	.9	1.7	1.6	2.4	1.6
Total Current	77.9	73.1	74.9	75.2	76.0	83.3	83.8	82.8	77.0	83.0
Fixed Assets (net)	15.0	15.4	17.4	18.4	15.6	13.5	12.5	11.4	18.6	12.2
Intangibles (net)	2.7	1.4	.7	.4	1.9	.3	.2	.2	.9	.2
All Other Non-Current	4.4	10.1	7.1	6.0	6.5	2.9	3.5	5.7	3.4	4.6
Total	100.0	100.0	100.0	100.0	100.0	100.0	100.0	100.0	100.0	100.0
LIABILITIES										
Notes Payable-Short Term	9.7	7.2	6.8	3.0	8.3	14.3	19.4	19.4	27.7	19.5
Cur. Mat.-L/T/D	4.2	4.3	2.4	1.2	3.9	3.1	2.4	3.2	2.5	2.9
Accts. & Notes Payable - Trade	23.1	21.5	19.1	24.8	22.2	28.4	22.4	25.2	15.5	23.9
Accrued Expenses	4.3	5.1	6.8	7.2	5.0	2.6	3.7	4.2	3.5	3.9
All Other Current	3.8	2.9	4.8	2.6	3.6	1.2	5.0	4.3	2.1	4.3
Total Current	45.1	40.9	40.0	38.8	42.9	49.6	52.9	56.2	51.3	54.4
Long Term Debt	17.8	15.5	17.4	11.6	16.7	12.6	10.3	8.7	17.1	9.9
All Other Non-Current	1.5	2.5	2.6	.7	1.9	1.4	.8	1.1	.4	.9
Net Worth	35.6	41.0	40.1	48.9	38.4	36.5	36.0	34.0	31.2	34.8
Total Liabilities & Net Worth	100.0	100.0	100.0	100.0	100.0	100.0	100.0	100.0	100.0	100.0
INCOME DATA										
Net Sales	100.0	100.0	100.0	100.0	100.0	100.0	100.0	100.0	100.0	100.0
Cost Of Sales	65.9	65.0	70.4	73.3	66.6	74.6	78.0	78.4	77.4	78.0
Gross Profit	34.1	35.0	29.6	26.7	33.4	25.4	22.0	21.6	22.6	22.0
Operating Expenses	31.1	32.0	26.4	23.3	30.4	24.3	19.5	18.3	18.4	19.1
Operating Profit	3.0	2.9	3.2	3.4	3.0	1.1	2.5	3.3	4.2	2.9
All Other Expenses (net)	.6	.3	.6	.2	.5	-.9	-.3	.0	1.5	-.1
Profit Before Taxes	2.4	2.6	2.6	3.2	2.5	2.1	2.9	3.4	2.7	3.1
RATIOS										
Current	2.8	2.5	2.6	2.2	2.5	2.8	1.9	1.8	1.9	1.9
	1.9	2.0	2.1	1.9	2.0	1.8	1.5	1.4	1.5	1.5
	1.4	1.5	1.7	1.7	1.5	1.2	1.3	1.2	1.2	1.3
Quick	.8	.9	.6	1.2 (193)	.8	1.3	.7	.7	.8	.7
	.5	.5	.4	.2	.5	.7	.4	.4	.6	.4
	.2	.3	.3	.2	.2	.3	.2	.2	.4	.2

(101)

Financial ratio table (Robert Morris Associates, 1978). Values are shown as upper-quartile / median / lower-quartile. "( )" = number of statements.

Ratio	44599M	77592M	206422M	902506M	1231119M	8773M	199876M	868236M	540487M	1617372M
Sales/Receivables (days)	5 / 11 / 21	9 / 20 / 32	2 / 5 / 12	2 / 6 / 43	5 / 12 / 24	13 / 29 / 47	14 / 23 / 33	21 / 32 / 49	38 / 62 / 81	17 / 28 / 45
Sales/Receivables	73.5 / 33.1 / 17.3	39.2 / 18.4 / 11.3	152.0 / 81.0 / 31.1	146.1 / 65.2 / 8.4	70.3 / 29.4 / 15.0	27.2 / 12.4 / 7.8	25.8 / 15.6 / 10.9	17.7 / 11.5 / 7.5	9.5 / 5.9 / 4.5	21.0 / 13.2 / 8.2
Cost of Sales/Inventory (days)	73 / 91 / 118	78 / 89 / 118	78 / 89 / 118	63 / 74 / 104	73 / 91 / 118	47 / 83 / 174	83 / 135 / 192	91 / 130 / 203	99 / 126 / 166	85 / 130 / 192
Cost of Sales/Inventory	5.0 / 4.0 / 3.1	4.7 / 3.7 / 2.8	4.7 / 4.1 / 3.1	5.8 / 4.9 / 3.5	5.0 / 4.0 / 3.1	7.8 / 4.4 / 2.1	4.4 / 2.7 / 1.9	4.0 / 2.8 / 1.8	3.7 / 2.9 / 2.2	4.3 / 2.8 / 1.9
Sales/Working Capital	6.2 / 9.4 / 17.6	5.8 / 8.0 / 13.4	6.6 / 9.2 / 11.7	4.8 / 9.1 / 13.1	6.2 / 9.0 / 13.7	5.0 / 10.5 / 21.3	5.2 / 7.9 / 11.9	5.7 / 7.9 / 12.6	4.2 / 7.1 / 11.0	5.5 / 7.9 / 12.5
EBIT/Interest	(73) 7.0 / 3.0 / 1.1	(48) 8.1 / 3.1 / 1.7	(20) 7.9 / 5.3 / 2.4	(148) 7.9 / 3.3 / 1.5	7.0 / 3.3 / 1.5	(19) 8.3 / 3.4 / 1.2	(154) 7.7 / 3.4 / 1.9	(10) 7.0 / 3.6 / 1.8	3.4 / 2.6 / 1.8	7.0 / 3.4 / 1.8
Cash Flow/Cur. Mat. L/T/D	(26) 2.0 / .6 / .3	(19) 4.1 / 1.3 / .6	(13) 6.7 / 2.1 / 1.2	(64) 3.2 / 1.4 / .5	3.2 / 1.4 / .5	(59)	(98) 6.2 / 2.6 / 1.4	(10) 7.3 / 3.4 / .8	(171) 6.6 / 3.4 / 1.8	6.4 / 2.9 / 1.1
Fixed/Worth	.1 / .4 / 1.2	.2 / .3 / .8	.2 / .3 / .9	.1 / .5 / .6	.1 / .3 / .9	.1 / .3 / 1.1	.2 / .3 / .5	.1 / .3 / .5	.3 / .5 / .8	.1 / .3 / .5
Debt/Worth	.8 / 1.9 / 5.4	.9 / 1.5 / 2.8	.8 / 1.4 / 3.1	.5 / 1.1 / 1.7	.8 / 1.5 / 3.7	.8 / 1.3 / 2.8	1.1 / 2.2 / 3.6	1.3 / 2.0 / 3.9	1.7 / 2.0 / 4.3	1.2 / 2.1 / 3.6
% Profit Before Taxes/Tangible Net Worth	(92) 58.2 / 25.4 / 8.5	(57) 30.5 / 15.6 / 3.3	38.6 / 19.1 / 11.3	(183) 37.8 / 18.3 / 9.7	42.5 / 20.0 / 6.8	46.4 / 21.8 / 12.8	(179) 29.5 / 16.8 / 8.0	(345) 29.8 / 17.8 / 10.5	26.0 / 16.4 / 8.0	29.8 / 17.3 / 9.8
% Profit Before Taxes/Total Assets	(16) 16.0 / 6.9 / 1.1	10.7 / 5.8 / 1.2	12.7 / 8.3 / 4.4	14.9 / 9.9 / 4.6	14.6 / 6.8 / 1.4	(16) 18.4 / 7.2 / 1.0	11.0 / 6.0 / 2.6	11.6 / 5.2 / 2.5	7.0 / 4.9 / 2.7	11.3 / 5.6 / 2.5
Sales/Net Fixed Assets	64.8 / 36.0 / 16.6	49.7 / 24.6 / 13.0	47.0 / 22.8 / 17.5	48.3 / 18.0 / 10.0	57.6 / 26.6 / 15.5	77.9 / 39.2 / 10.2	47.9 / 29.7 / 12.6	45.7 / 23.8 / 13.2	15.4 / 9.3 / 7.5	47.4 / 24.4 / 12.6
Sales/Total Assets	4.1 / 3.5 / 2.6	3.2 / 2.7 / 2.1	3.9 / 3.4 / 2.5	3.8 / 3.1 / 2.4	3.8 / 3.2 / 2.3	3.6 / 2.1 / 1.9	2.8 / 2.1 / 1.7	2.5 / 1.9 / 1.6	2.2 / 1.6 / 1.2	2.6 / 2.0 / 1.6
% Depr., Depl., Amort./Sales	(93) .6 / .9 / 1.3	(52) .6 / .9 / 1.1	.5 / .8 / 1.1	(176) .4 / .7 / 1.2	.6 / .9 / 1.3	(15) .5 / .8 / 1.1	(130) .5 / .7 / 1.1	(12) .5 / .7 / 1.1	(320) .9 / 1.2 / 1.7	.5 / .8 / 1.2
% Lease & Rental Exp/Sales	(90) 1.7 / 2.5 / 3.7	(44) 1.6 / 2.8 / 3.6	1.6 / 2.4 / 3.5	(157) 1.7 / 2.6 / 3.6	1.7 / 2.6 / 3.6	(13) .7 / 2.0 / 3.0	(100) .6 / 1.0 / 1.5	.3 / .5 / 1.1	(206)	.4 / .8 / 1.4
% Officers' Comp/Sales	(65) 4.5 / 7.4 / 10.3	(40) 2.3 / 4.3 / 7.2	2.9 / 5.5 / 9.0	(114)	2.9 / 5.5 / 9.0	(10) 3.1 / 4.4 / 7.2	(96) 1.7 / 2.7 / 4.3	(206) 1.3 / 2.0 / 3.1	(207)	1.5 / 2.3 / 4.0
Net Sales ($)	44599M	77592M	206422M	902506M	1231119M	8773M	199876M	868236M	540487M	1617372M
Total Assets ($)	13384M	27875M	67162M	306410M	414831M	2934M	86113M	433629M	330303M	852979M

M = $thousand   MM = $million

Interpretation of Statement Studies Figures

RMA recommends that *Statement Studies* data be regarded only as general guidelines and not as absolute industry norms. There are several reasons why the data may not be fully representative of a given industry:

(1) The financial statements used in the *Statement Studies* are not selected by any random or statistically reliable method. RMA member banks voluntarily submit the raw data they have available each year, with these being the only constraints: (a) The fiscal year-ends of the companies reported may not be from April 1 through June 29, and (b) their total assets must be less than $50 million.

(2) Many companies have varied product lines; however, the *Statement Studies* categorize them by their primary product Standard Industrial Classification (SIC) number only.

(3) Some of our industry samples are rather small in relation to the total number of firms in a given industry. A relatively small sample can increase the chances that some of our composites do not fully represent an industry.

(4) There is the chance that an extreme statement can be present in a sample, causing a disproportionate influence on the industry composite. This is particularly true in a relatively small sample.

(5) Companies within the same industry may differ in their method of operations which in turn can directly influence their financial statements. Since they are included in our sample, too, these statements can significantly affect our composite calculations.

(6) Other considerations that can result in variations among different companies engaged in the same general line of business are different labor markets; geographical location; different accounting methods; quality of products handled; sources and methods of financing; and terms of sale.

For these reasons, RMA does not recommend the Statement Studies *figures be considered as absolute norms for a given industry. Rather the figures should be used only as general guidelines and in addition to the other methods of financial analysis. RMA makes no claim as to the representativeness of the figures printed in this book.*

selected because they are quite dissimilar businesses; yet you will note that the asset balance and distribution are somewhat alike. The main distinctions are that the farm equipment retailer carries more accounts receivable and has somewhat less fixed assets than the drug retailer. Their inventories are roughly of the same magnitude, the drug store being slightly higher, and the drug firms carry somewhat higher cash balances.

The point is not to say that all firms are alike, but rather that the financial needs of any business impose a kind of necessity and structure upon it which shows up in the balance of assets employed. The effect of size on asset distribution is also interesting. For example, in both drugs and farm equipment, the larger firms in the $10 to $50 million asset class generally have a somewhat smaller portion of their assets in inventory and more in fixed assets than do smaller firms. Also in farm equipment, the cash balances are less and the long-term debt is more for large firms than smaller ones (but this is not true among drug firms).

Turning to the income data, we see that for both drugs and farm equipment the operating expenses decrease with size of organization. The profits before taxes are in the range of 2.1 to 3.4% of sales in both business classifications. The higher earnings are in the midsize firms among farm equipment retailers, but among the large firms in drugs.

FINANCIAL RATIOS

The financial ratios in the Robert Morris Associates (RMA) *Annual Statement Studies* also provide important performance measures. You will note three ratios are reported for each title, and they are, respectively, the upper quartile, median, and lower quartile ratios for the business classifications. Thus, for the smallest retail drug firms in Table 7–1, the current ratio (total current assets divided by total current liabilities) is 2.8 for the upper quartile, 1.9 for the median, and 1.4 for the lower quartile. The quick ratios for small drug firms (cash and accounts receivable to total current assets) are, respectively, .8, .5, and .2 and are somewhat on the minimal side. These low current ratios are satisfactory when the inventory is highly liquid and saleable, which is generally true in the drug field. Since we have dealt with current and quick ratios earlier, let us go on to examine the meaning of the other important financial ratios in Table 7-1 and see how they affect the interpretation of the soundness or balance of the assets.

Sales/Receivables

This ratio (sales divided by accounts and notes receivable) shows the turnover of accounts receivable and how currently they are paid by customers. The median ratio for farm equipment is about 12, which means sales are 12 times accounts receivable, or that sales turnover relative to accounts receivable is once per month, or that the accounts are generally paid within 30 days. In the drug business, the sales/receivable ratio is very high with a median of 33 to 81 times per year. That is to say, most purchases are for cash and the accounts are paid on average within a matter of days, which makes the sales turnover relative to receivables very high.

Cost of Sales/Inventory

The cost of sales/inventory ratio indicates how rapidly the inventory turns over. The median ratio in both drugs and farm equipment is about 3 to 4 times per year, which means that the inventory is turning over on average every 90 to 120 days. Slower turnover rates than that indicate that the firm has to have more capital tied up in inventory and achieves lower profits due to slow sales.

Sales/Working Capital

This important ratio tells you how hard your working capital is working for you. The median ratio for drug firms shows that sales are about 9 times the working capital, which is to say that the working capital is turning over or being recycled an average of every 45 days. This is good performance compared to most businesses. You will note that the working capital turnover in farm equipment is slightly slower. The efficiency with which working capital is used, i.e., its turnover, is an important indication of earnings, because high turnover of working capital keeps the cost of capital down.

EBIT/Interest

This ratio is earnings before interest and taxes (EBIT), divided by interest charges payable to others. This ratio is of primary concern to bankers and creditors, because it shows how many times their interest charges are earned. The higher the earnings relative to interest charges, the more protection the creditor has. That is, the loan seems more secure, and thus the business borrower is more creditable, or has more credit. Creditors usually like to see earnings at least 3 times the interest charges, because earnings may fluctuate up and down with the business cycle; creditors want their interest charges to be earned and paid even under the worst case. For the drug and farm equipment companies, the median and upper quartile companies have comfortable earnings margins over interest in most cases, 3 to 5 times or better. The lower quartile presents a more risky loan situation.

Cash Flow/Current Maturities of the Long-Term Debt

This ratio is written in Table 7-1 as "Cash Flow/Cur. Mat. L/T/D." It is figured as the net profit plus depreciation and amortization expenses, divided by the current portion of the long-term debt, i.e., the long-term debt payable within one year. The idea behind the ratio is that the cash flow of a business is the source of funds to retire debt which is coming due. The cash flow should normally be about 3 times the long-term debt coming due, to provide a safety margin in case of fluctuating business conditions. Again in the farm machinery example, we see the median and upper quartile firms have a ratio of 3 to 1 or better, but the ratios are lower in the drug business.

Fixed/Worth

This ratio of net fixed assets (net of depreciation) divided by tangible net worth shows the extent to which the owner's equity has been invested in fixed plant and equipment. A low ratio indicates a relatively smaller investment in fixed assets compared to net worth, and thus the small ratio indicates a better "cushion" for creditors in case of liquidation. Generally the median firms have about 30% of the net worth tied up in fixed assets, thus leaving about 70% of the fixed assets as security or collateral for creditors.

Debt/Worth

The ratio of total liabilities to tangible net worth shows the contribution of owners to the capitalization of the firm compared to that of creditors. Again, the higher the debt ratio to net worth, the greater the contribution of the creditors and the higher the risk to creditors. A low ratio indicates that the owners are providing the preponderance of capital, and this reduces the risk to creditors. For example, the average ratio of 1.5 for drug stores indicates that creditors are providing 60% of the capital and owners 40%. The 2.0 ratio in farm equipment means that the creditors provide 67% and owners 33% of the capital. The ratio of borrowed capital to the total is also called the *leverage* of the financial structure. The drug and farm equipment businesses are both rather highly leveraged, which means they rely on a preponderance of borrowed money. This may be good for them in good times, because their profits on the borrowed money will usually be higher than the interest they have to pay; thus, the owners are making money off of other people's money. If business conditions turn bad, however, and earnings fall, then the tables turn and the owner may be stuck with high interest payments which he cannot meet out of depressed earnings. This condition, i.e., inability to meet interest or debt repayments, can lead to bankruptcy. For this reason, creditors usually like to see owners put in a higher portion of capital than do creditors. This would mean that the debt/worth ratio should preferrably be less than 1.0 to be a conservative capitalization structure. However, a glance through all business classifications in the RMA statement studies indicates that ratios of 1.0 to 2.0 are quite common.

Percentage of Profits Before Taxes/Tangible Net Worth

This is the pay-off ratio to most businessmen which shows them how much earnings they are making on their investment. That is, the ratio is their simple rate of return before taxes. Taxes may take up to 48% for larger corporations. The median profit/worth for drug companies is 20% before taxes, and 17% for farm equipment. When these are adjusted to an after-tax basis, they would be about 9 to 11% per year, which is close to the range we discussed in a previous section on growth of assets where the average was said to be roughly 12% and the range from 10 to 15%. Farm equipment retailing appears to be at the low end of the range, and drugs are about average.

Percentage of Profits Before Taxes/Total Assets

This ratio is the same earnings-on-assets measure discussed in Chapter 1 (where it was shown for all corporations by asset size) as a main performance measure of survival. Here in the RMA statement studies, this earnings-on-assets measure is shown by industry by a small number of asset groups. Generally the figures are quite comparable, running around 7 to 9% for the small and medium-sized firms (note: in Chapter 1 the measures were earnings including compensation of officers, and here the earnings are shown excluding the compensation of officers). In the farm equipment business, the earnings decrease with increased asset size; in drugs the reverse is true— earnings increase with size.

Sales/Net Fixed Assets

In this ratio the sales of a firm are divided by the net fixed assets, which would mean total fixed assets minus depreciation. The ratio measures the extent to which productive assets are used by a business. Another way to interpret the ratio is the number of times the net fixed assets turn over per year in terms of sales volume. A very high ratio usually means that the business is very labor-intensive and does not use much in the way of fixed assets, or else the fixed assets have been depreciated. Thus, older firms which have written down their assets by depreciation would have high ratios, compared to new firms with little depreciation of fixed assets. For drug and farm equipment firms, the average turnover is about 25 times per year for the sales/net fixed asset ratio, but the variations are considerable, both for the upper and lower quartiles and for size of firm. In using this ratio for comparative purposes, then, you should give careful attention to the age and size of your firm, as well as whether your fixed asset investment is typical of your field and how long you have depreciated the assets. Of course, the higher the ratio, the more efficient a business is in using its net fixed assets.

Sales/Total Assets

The ratio of sales to total assets is also a measure of the effectiveness of a firm in using its assets productively to generate sales; it is perhaps a more useful overall ratio than the sales/net fixed assets ratio because it is more stable and not subject to such great variation due to length and amount of depreciation. The sales/total asset ratio is about 3.0 for drugs and 2.0 for farm equipment firms on average, with rather moderate variations in the upper and lower quartile, as well as by size. Therefore, you should find this ratio a fairly useful comparison to see how effectively you are using your assets. Again, the higher the ratio, the more productive is use of assets.

Percentage of Depreciation, Depletion, and Amortization Expense/Sales

This is an expense ratio which measures the percent of capital charges being written off annually against sales revenue. These capital charges (or overhead costs) represent the judgment of the accountant and general manager as to how much to charge off each year. That is, they are the allocation of overhead expense to sales, and these expenses can vary considerably by the depreciation method used and the policy of the manager as to recovery of capital and tax avoidance. The ratio is figured as the sum of depreciation, depletion and amortization expense, divided by sales and multiplied by 100. In Table 7-1 this heading reads "% Depr., Dep., Amort./Sales," and you will see that the write-off of overhead costs is roughly 1% of sales for both drugs and farm equipment, with reasonably wide variation by size and quartile. If you are charging off less than the ratios in the table, you may be underestimating your allocation of capital costs to current sales. If your ratios are much higher than in the table, you may find it necessary to justify the reasonableness of your charges to the IRS.

Percentage of Lease and Rental Expense/Sales

This ratio is intended to help you judge whether you are paying too much rent for your building or equipment. The expense ratio is figured by dividing the sum of your lease and rental costs by your sales. Notice how much higher the drug store ratio is compared to the farm equipment stores, which reflects, of course, that drug stores are convenience outlets which need to be located in high-traffic shopping centers, whereas farm equipment stores are located in outlying areas where land and rentals are cheaper. The median lease and rental expense for drugs is 2.6% of sales, with 1% for the upper and lower quartile, and not much variation by size of store. If you are paying more than this for rental expense, you may be paying too much and certainly are lowering profit.

Percentage of Officers' Compensation/Sales

This expense ratio tells you whether or not you are paying yourself too much compensation. If you are paying yourself less than 3.0% of sales in the drug field, you may be paying yourself too little; and if it is more than 9.0% you are most likely paying yourself too much. The median is 5.5% which is probably a good standard for most purposes. The compensation ratios in the farm equipment field are about one-half as much as in drugs due to big ticket items and larger dollar sales volumes.

CURIOUS CHARACTERISTICS OF RATIOS

You may find, upon comparing your firm with others, that your financial ratios look a good deal better than those in the RMA tables which we have been using for illustration. If so, that is good, but do not be surprised, especially if you are not much of a bank borrower. The RMA data are collected from bank loan officers, and there is no control over the sample. Presumably most RMA data represents firms who are bank borrowers.

The common assumption about small business firms, based upon data collected from financial sources, is that small firms have weak current asset ratios, high debt, little capital, low earnings, are inefficient, poorly managed, and slow at paying bills. In the face of such discouraging statistics, one wonders why people own small businesses at all.

But maybe this impression is based upon the kinds of firms who borrow from banks and on a financial officer's interpretation of their ratios. A different interpretation comes from a recent study of the Financial Research Associates which collected data on small firms through Certified Public Accountant (CPA) firms rather than through banks. In this sample, there appeared to be a distinct group of firms who were in debt, and a large number of other small businesses which avoided debt almost completely. The result, in terms of financial ratios, was a "skewing" of a normal distribution heavily to the right. Skewness means that the actual distribution of data departs from a normal bell-shaped curve. In positive skewness to the right, the largest number of observations cluster to the left, with the most extreme values tailing off to the right of the mean. In other words, the distribution is seen as a downward concave curve rather than as bell-shaped; the median value is considerably below the mean. The small business data collected through CPAs showed a large skewness to the right in the current asset ratios, in debt ratios, and in the sales/expense ratios. What these findings mean is that small business firms may be considerably more liquid, more profitable, better managed, and less highly leveraged than commonly observed.[2]

SUMMARY

The owner of a small firm can very easily become preoccupied with the daily demands of his business, to the neglect of the financial well being of the firm. But the owner needs to put high priority on examining the firm's financial health, at least quarterly, in order to preserve and increase his own wealth. Otherwise, from a personal point of view of the owner, the business is really not worth all the trouble and risk of running it.

The simplest and quickest way to examine the financial performance of a firm is through financial ratios. These ratios enable the owner, along with his accountant, to compare the firm's performance with like businesses in the same field to diagnose any financial problems which are emerging. The ratios enable the owner to make a judgment on such issues as: (1) whether the firm has enough liquidity to meet its bills, (2) whether expense ratios to sales are reasonable, (3) whether the firm is achieving average profits, (4) whether debt can be handled, (5) whether assets and resources are effectively used in terms of turnover, and, most important of all, (6) whether the growth in equity of the firm is increasing satisfactorily. These are all key determinants of the personal wealth of the owner and of the financial health of the firm. Such issues need to be examined regularly to detect quickly areas of potential weakness which need to be corrected and areas of potential strength (particularly resources) which can be put to new or better use. Indeed, these questions are the essence of good management over the long term, and they need to be attended to regularly for continuing business success.

We have already seen, in the earnings on assets figures in Chapter 1 and in the CPA data cited above, that most small firms are better managed than are larger ones. You want your firm to be one of the better managed. The financial ratios will give you the asset measures of performance to make you a better manager.

REFERENCES

1. *Annual Statement Studies* can be purchased for $22.20 (prepaid) from Robert Morris Associates, Credit Division, Philadelphia, Pennsylvania, 19107.
2. Droms, W., Miller, C., and Lacerte, G. "A Financial Profile of Small Retailing Firms," *American Journal of Small Business,* Vol. III, Vo. 4, April, 1979, pp. 42–58.

8

Financial Measures of Performance

Another chapter on financial management? Yes, you need to look next at the company as others see it. So far, in Chapters 1, 2, 3, and 7, you have been looking at financial problems of the firm from the inside, as the manager sees it. That is, you want to be a good manager, and successful, too. To do that, you have to master the techniques of financial management and control, which is what we have covered previously. Hopefully, you will have learned to run a business successfully as measured by earnings on assets, cash flow, flow of funds, and the financial ratios. Good, you are a success!

Isn't that enough? No. Every time you seek a loan or new capital, or want to sell the business, you have to demonstrate to others that your firm is a financial success. Yes, some day you will have to think about selling the business and turning over its operations to someone else. Whoever it is, that person will want to know its valuation. Lenders and investors look at the financial status of a firm somewhat differently from the outside than you do from the inside.

From the inside you want to know what your earnings are, whether you have the cash and funds to meet your bills, and whether your financial ratios indicate an efficient use of funds. Outside lenders and investors want to know these same things, too, but they also want to know additional information. They want to know how your record stacks up against other firms, because they have alternative investments in other businesses. In particular, they are interested in your growth record over time as to sales and earnings, the change in profits from quarter to quarter, the book value, liquidation value, the capital structure of the business, how much debt or leverage you are using, the return on capital, the return on equity, and above all, the price-earnings ratio. These are all indicators of the worth of the business, and lenders or investors look upon a business from the outside, comparatively against other firms, as to how much profit the investment will yield if they operate the business and how much cash it will yield if they have to sell it. In short, they are comparison shoppers, just as you would be in their place. That means, to be a seller, you have to be aware of comparative values, too.

BOOK VALUE VERSUS PRICE PER SHARE

The easiest way to start this comparative valuation is to look at the book value of your own firm and compare it with the book value of others. The *book value* is the value of the equity as reported on the balance sheet, usually expressed as the equity per share.

Book value essentially values the firm at cost, i.e., the cost of all the assets minus the amount owed to all the creditors in the accounts equals the net worth or equity of the owners. We have already seen, of course, that there are some problems with costs. First, some of the assets may be depreciated at rates which were too high or too low relative to their worth, which means that some fixed assets may be overvalued or undervalued on the books. Secondly, inflation or deflation of prices may have greatly changed the value of the assets from their original costs. Hence, land or resources owned by the firm may be overvalued. Then, too, some companies carry intangible assets on their balance sheets, like "good will" or patent rights; and you would either want to subtract these from the book value of the firm to make a comparison or else find some tangible evidence to validate their worth.

Book value may overvalue or undervalue assets depending upon inflation rates and depreciation practices. Still it is not a bad place to start because it tells you what accountants thought the value of the assets were on a consistent basis when they recorded the transactions at cost. So book value is a track record of what the financial manager believed the worth of the firm to be; once you have a track record you can audit it to see if you agree or not.

Book values are not hard to find for publicly held corporations; that is, book value or equity per share are commonly reported in financial statistics by brokerage houses and securities statistical services, such as Standard & Poor's or Moody's. Suppose, for example, you are the owner of a small iron foundry with a net worth of $200,000 and you serve the local and regional market by making iron castings. You are in need of more funds to improve your equipment and wish to raise another $200,000 of equity money or by a bank loan. How will a prospective investor or banker view your proposal? They are looking at your firm from the outside, with only a general knowledge of your customers, your technology, and your managerial skill; so in part they will view your business comparatively as to how well other foundries are doing. You can do the same thing. You go to Standard & Poor's reports and find, let us assume, three other foundry companies listed on security exchanges that are reasonably similar to yours. The statistics reported on their equity per share and price range per share, let us suppose, are as follows:

	EQUITY PER SHARE	PRICE RANGE
Foundry Able	$22	$14–$18
Foundry Baker	37	24–32
Foundry Cable	16	9–14

These three foundries are selling on the market at anywhere from 14% to a 38% discount from their book value. That is, investors in the market value the three firms well below cost. Why? Perhaps because many foundries operate in competitive markets and have costly equipment, so their earnings are not particularly high. But even more than that, the stock market has valued almost all stock prices in every industry well below book value for many years, i.e., from about 1969 to 1980, at discounts of 20 to 30%. Part of the reason for low prices of stocks, compared to book value, has been high inflation, and low earnings for the economy as a whole. Still, this background forms part of the picture when you go in to see an investor about equity money or a banker about a loan. They have the option of investing in Foundry Able, Baker or Cable as well as in your firm, and they know the statistics as well as you do. So you go to them and say, "I have $200,000 in equity and I need another $200,000 in loans or equity money for new equipment. I have a solid sales and management record, as you can see from these financial statements."

The investor scarcely glances at your fund-raising financial package but says, "We don't like to put more money into the business than the owner has in it. Your $200,000 net worth would be valued, at best, if we had to liquidate the business to bail ourselves out, at $170,000 and, at worst, at as little as $120,000. We will look over your financial package if you would consider an investment on our part in the range from $125,000 to $150,000. That is as high as we can go, given the market value of your firm."

The point is, of course, that to raise money or sell your firm, you need to look at it comparatively as the investor or buyer will look at it. That means you will need to know both your equity per share and comparative market values per share in order to establish the bargaining range within which you try to establish the going value of your business.

EARNINGS RECORDS

The reason market values fall below book value is that the investor is really buying the future earnings of your business, not the past costs. Therefore, the earnings record and earnings prospects are all-important in seeking to value a business, sell it, or raise money for it.

Suppose now we are in the retail food business. You need to raise money for more inventory and fixtures. You feel your financial performance has been good. Your sales were up 10% from a year ago, profits up 15%, profit margins were at 1.3% (net profits divided by sales), earnings on equity was 12%, and earnings on tangible invested assets was 10%. You feel that you can present a strong case for raising money based upon this commendable performance, and you go in to make a hard pitch to an investor. The investor looks at your financial statements and pulls out a copy of *Business Week* which contains a quarterly report on corporate sales and earnings, like the sample Corporate Scoreboard shown below.

The investor then says to you, "Your performance is slightly below par, but I think with a little improvement in performance on your part we can invest some funds with you, though not as much as you are asking until you get your earnings and growth rates up over the average for your industry. Otherwise, we might as well invest in one of the other companies."

Table 8-1. Corporate Scoreboard.

COMPANY	SALES		PROFITS		MARGINS		RATIOS			10-YEAR GROWTH		MARKET VALUE SHARES O/S 4-30 $ MIL.	12 MONTHS' EARNINGS PER SHARE
	1ST QTR. 1979 $ MIL.	CHG. FROM 1978 %	1ST QTR. 1979 $ MIL.	CHG. FROM 1978 %	1ST QTR. 1979 %	1ST QTR. 1978 %	RET. INV. CAP.	RET. COM. EQY.	P-E 4-30	COM. EQY. %	E.P.S. %		
RETAILING (FOOD)													
Albertson's (11)	681.3	30	9.7	22	1.4	1.5	NA	28.8	7	16	17	260	4.76
Alterman Foods (8)	110.8	16	1.1	37	1.0	0.8	9.5	11.4	7	7	0	27	2.76
Borman's (11)	201.4	18	1.3	-13	0.7	0.9	9.7	11.9	5	-1	-12	18	1.27
Circle K (8)	107.6	20	1.8	32	1.7	1.5	NA	21.0	8	25	15	82	2.00
Cullum (6)	177.4	18	2.0	24	1.1	1.1	12.3	21.4	5	13	8	46	3.76
Dillon (6)	440.6	20	8.7	27	2.0	1.9	21.7	25.1	9	23	22	317	3.21
Fisher Foods	318.8	-12	0.6	-61	0.2	0.5	7.3	10.3	10	17	6	86	1.40
Giant Food (10)	360.4	16	7.9	57	2.2	1.6	14.5	19.3	5	11	11	84	5.09
Great Atlantic & Pacific Tea (10)	1907.6	2	-36.9	NM	NM	0.0	NA	-11.8	NM	-4	-25	187	-2.09
Jewel (11)	952.6	15	16.6	63	1.7	1.2	8.8	12.5	7	10	4	270	3.59
Kroger (11)	1927.2	15	19.7	59	1.0	0.7	12.3	17.5	6	6	7	550	6.75
Lucky Stores (11)	1326.0**	15	30.4	20	2.3	2.2	NA	27.4	9	22	12	727	1.72
National Tea	218.1	7	1.5	11	0.7	0.7	10.3	12.7	6	-9	NA	44	0.75
Petrolane (3)	295.5	13	16.6	14	5.6	5.6	15.2	22.8	9	27	18	475	4.24
Pneumo (1)	177.8	25	1.1	47	0.6	0.5	9.0	10.7	8	9	18	56	2.36
Ruddick (3)	105.2	8	1.5	9	1.4	1.4	NA	14.6	5	8	4	17	1.61
Safeway Stores	3029.8	8	23.1	-8	0.8	0.9	10.4	16.1	7	8	9	940	5.51
Southland	812.1**	25	8.1	15	1.0	1.1	10.3	16.1	10	18	15	553	2.88
Stop & Shop (11)	487.4	15	10.5	15	2.1	2.2	9.4	15.0	4	8	9	71	4.00
Supermarkets General (11)	611.3	33	7.6	55	1.2	1.1	NA	17.7	6	13	2	105	2.09
Weis Markets	148.5	18	7.3	25	4.9	4.7	20.6	20.6	8	14	14	215	4.30
Winn-Dixie Stores (6)	1183.0	13	23.5	8	2.0	2.1	NA	22.0	8	14	12	738	3.29
Industry composite	15580.5	13	163.9	20	1.5	1.2	11.3	15.5	7	11	5	5867	2.76

RETAILING (NONFOOD): Department, discount, mail order, variety, specialty stores

Company													
Alexander's (5)	161.8**	9	3.1	14	1.9	1.9	4.8	7.8	7	5	-4	36	1.11
Allied Stores (11)	728.0**	11	51.2	7	7.0	7.3	10.3	14.4	6	8	12	462	4.08
Associated Dry Goods (11)	559.1**	14	31.6	4	5.6	6.1	7.2	7.5	8	8	3	264	2.55
Caldor (11)	162.6	20	9.0	39	5.6	4.8	22.1	26.8	7	20	18	112	2.66
Carson Pirie Scott (11)	120.9**	8	5.2	7	4.3	4.4	9.2	13.6	5	7	11	59	3.50
Carter Hawley Hale Stores (11)	784.2**	35	40.3	20	5.1	5.8	NA	12.6	7	14	5	404	2.52
Cook United (11)	119.0	13	3.3	80	2.8	1.8	NA	5.2	11	6	-16	42	0.64
Dart Industries	569.3	39	34.3	26	6.0	6.7	11.8	14.6	8	17	14	1021	5.50
Dayton-Hudson (11)	1040.6**	23	60.5	26	5.8	5.7	NA	20.3	10	17	15	951	4.12
Dillard Department Stores (11)	116.5**	29	4.0	22	3.4	3.6	8.9	10.6	6	18	7	38	2.97
Eckerd (Jack) (5)	385.6	17	22.3	18	5.8	5.7	17.4	17.6	11	39	22	611	2.36
Fed-Mart (4)	255.0**	61	-2.0	NM	NM	1.1	-2.0	-13.3	NM	14	6	41	-2.91
Federated Department Stores (11)	1827.7**	12	98.9	0	5.4	6.1	12.4	13.6	8	10	9	1512	4.11
Gamble-Skogmo (11)	580.9	25	13.9	69	2.4	1.8	NA	9.8	5	7	3	112	5.47
Garfinckel, Brooks Brothers (11)	135.6**	17	7.5	12	5.5	5.7	NA	14.6	7	9	9	88	2.92
Goldblatt Brothers (11)	107.4**	5	0.6	-45	0.6	1.1	NA	-4.3	NM	2	-20	12	-0.57
Gordon Jewelry (4)	125.5	28	16.2	52	12.9	10.9	15.9	20.6	5	15	13	120	4.60
Gray Drug Stores (8)	116.1**	14	3.3	27	2.8	2.5	NA	14.9	6	8	5	40	2.75
Hartfield-Zody's (11)	100.4	10	2.9	14	2.9	2.8	11.0	20.0	5	10	-1	37	2.11
K mart (11)	3871.9	22	160.4	29	4.1	3.9	18.2	20.2	10	21	20	3191	2.74
Kay	139.0**	11	0.5	142	0.3	0.2	19.3	29.3	7	7	53	44	2.26
King's Department Stores (11)	159.7**	2	5.8	-22	3.6	4.8	13.9	18.4	6	13	12	96	2.00
Kuhn's-Big K Stores (11)	109.2	6	1.7	9	1.6	2.1	NM	-1.7	NM	16	12	10	-0.17
Lane Bryant (11)	101.2	17	3.3	9	3.2	3.5	10.8	12.0	8	8	5	86	2.23
Levitz Furniture (11)	134.2	10	5.3	64	4.0	2.7	NA	17.1	6	37	17	92	3.84
Longs Drug Stores (11)	196.7	22	7.8	22	3.9	3.9	21.2	21.2	13	21	18	299	2.23
Lowe's (11)	175.5	25	0.9	-81	0.5	3.5	14.4	18.3	10	24	21	228	1.82
Macy (R. H.) (5)	666.6**	13	40.4	11	6.1	6.2	14.0	14.8	6	9	10	378	6.46
Marshall Field (11)	278.2	30	13.8	46	4.9	4.4	NA	8.9	8	5	0	169	2.22
May Department Stores (11)	911.7	20	54.3	14	6.0	6.2	NA	15.3	7	5	10	605	4.15
Melville (11)	369.5	13	6.3	-16	1.7	2.3	24.6	26.7	8	19	17	733	3.47
Mercantile Stores (11)	316.9**	22	19.9	23	6.3	6.2	12.2	16.0	5	12	12	212	6.80
Murphy (G.C.) (11)	237.2	17	-2.3	NM	NM	1.9	NA	0.2	NM	3	3	57	0.05
Niagara Frontier Services (6)	113.2	13	2.1	10	1.8	1.9	19.1	22.2	6	19	25	47	3.95
Pay Less Drug Stores (11)	108.3	12	4.6	20	4.3	4.0	16.2	19.9	8	17	16	79	2.25
Pay'n Save (11)	193.7	13	7.4	27	3.8	3.4	13.7	16.7	8	22	22	139	3.14

NM = not meaningful
NA = not available
Reprinted from the May 21, 1979 issue of *Business Week* by special permission.

You feel like questioning the investor's judgement until you look closely at the Corporate Scoreboard yourself. Then, by making the following comparisons, you see that your performance has been below the average for your field.

	YOUR STORE	RETAIL FOOD AVERAGE	% DIFFERENCE
Sales (% change from yr ago)	10%	13%	−24
Profits (% change from yr ago)	15	20	−25
Profit margins	1.3	1.5	−13
Earnings on equity	12	15.5	−23
Return on invested capital	10	11.3	−12

Indeed, what looked like good financial performance on your part, standing alone, now appears to be nearly 25% below the standard of other companies. In fact, the investor's response has been fairly generous in giving you a chance to improve your performance. If you had to sell the firm at this point, a hard-minded buyer would only pay you about 75% of your book value because that is all it is worth based upon earning power.

Price-Earning Ratio

The price-earnings ratio for a listed security is obtained by dividing the average price per share of the stock by the earnings per share. The price-earnings ratio (P/E ratio) for retail food stores in Table 8-1 may be found in the ninth column of the table. The average P/E ratio for the food retailing industry is 7. That is, the average stock sells at 7 times earnings per share. You will note that the range runs from 4 times earnings for Stop & Shop to 10 times earnings for Fisher Foods and Southland, both of which are regional food chains with higher than average records for growth in earnings. This measure of performance suggests that, if you are running a food retailing store with average performance, the market value of the firm is seven times its annual earnings. Suppose your store earns $30,000 net after taxes and executive compensation; its average value would be $210,000, or perhaps somewhat less because an individual firm does not have as broad a market as do shares of stock.

Whenever you seek capital for your firm, or consider its sale, you should always check the current P/E ratios, because they vary considerably over the years depending upon economic conditions and interest rates. For the period 1954–1975 the median price earnings ratio of composite stocks in all industries was 14. During the 1960s, the composite price-earnings average was about 18 to 19; but by 1977–1980, the average P/E ratio had dropped by one-half to 8 or 9. The reason, of course, is that interest rates had doubled during the period and risen from about 7% to 13% or more on the prime rate. The higher cost of money was brought about by inflation. As prices rise, savers want a higher rate of interest for capital funds because prices are expected to be higher in the future at the time of repayment or payment of interest. If the basic long-term interest which savers want to induce them to save is 6%, and if prices are going up at a rate of 7% per year, then savers will demand an interest rate of 13% to cover both the true interest rate and the inflation rate.

Similarly, in the stock market a P/E ratio of 18 implies an interest rate or rate of return of 5.5% (i.e., 1 ÷ 18), while a P/E ratio of 8 is equivalent to a rate of return of 12.5%. Thus, the stock market reflects the same pattern as interest rates. Shareholders were satisfied with a return of 5.5% (plus the chance of some capital gains) in the 1960s, but price inflation went to 7% per year. Then by 1980 the shareholders wanted a 12.5% return or a P/E ratio of 8.

The P/E ratio behaves inversely to the interest rates. When interest rates go up, P/E ratios go down; when interest rates go down, P/E ratios go up. This is true because they are simply arithmetic opposites, or inverse to each other. That is, the P/E ratio is the price divided by the earnings, and the rate of return or interest rate is the earnings divided by the price. They are reciprocals of each other, and thus behave in opposite directions.

Therefore, another quick way to estimate the value of a firm is to take the current prime rate of interest at banks, or the industrial bond average, and find its reciprocal (i.e., divide it into 1). This will give the equivalent P/E ratio. Then you multiply the P/E ratio by the earnings of the firm to get its market value. For example, the current interest rate is 14% and the earnings of the firm are $50,000. The equivalent P/E ratio is 7.1 (1 divided by 14) and the value of the firm is $355,000 (7.1 x 50,000). These are, of course, rough rules of thumb; but they illustrate the principle that the value of a firm's earnings is related to the cost of capital or the interest rate in capital markets, because investors are buying future earning power at today's capital cost. To be more precise, you would want to check on specific industries by looking up current P/E ratios in an up-to-date source like Table 8–1.

10-YEAR GROWTH RECORD

Since investors are buying future earnings when they put money into a business, they are greatly concerned with its growth prospects. Indeed, this is perhaps the single more important factor in an investment decision. One way to judge the growth prospects of a firm is by looking at its track record, or growth history, in the past. The 10-year growth record in equity and earnings per share is shown in Table 8–1 for all firms in their list in columns 10 and 11.

The retail food group has, on average, an 11% per year growth in common stock equity and a 5% growth in earnings per share—the basis for the 7 times price earnings valuation in the eyes of investors. Some of the firms have higher than average growth records, for instance, Southland with an 18% growth in equity and a 15% annual increase in earnings per share, and this high performance record is what justifies the high price of 10 times earnings. Notice that most of the firms in the list which have high growth records also have high P/E ratios. Where this is not true, the firm is either undervalued or may have some financial problems, such as temporary slump in sales, a change in management, a catastrophic loss, or some other indicator of an interruption of their growth pattern. Those firms which are truly undervalued, in the sense of having high growth records, low P/E ratios, and no financial problems, are good buys for investors who want to buy stock, or for other companies who want to make corporate acquisitions. Albertson's, for example, has been the subject of some take-over proposals, because it has one of the highest growth records in the list and has an average P/E ratio. That is, it appears to have the prospects of a high future earnings record and yet its market value is at an average price for the industry.

The growth record of a firm is crucial in the eyes of investors because it is the best single indicator of the competence of management. Investors want to see a strong track record of management competence before they put money into a business. The best evidence of management competence is growth in earnings, or earnings per share. Investors essentially invest capital where the management has competence to produce a growth in earnings into the future. For this reason, continuity of management is important. Investors, who are buying future growth in earnings, want to have the same proven management running the company in the future as ran it in the past because that is their best guarantee of continued growth. A change in management is disquieting to investors, as is a sharp shift in a company's financial plan. New management or new financial ventures introduce new risks into a company's performance which cast doubt on the continuity of its earnings growth. Therefore, investors essentially want three things in putting capital into a company: (1) a strong record of growth in earnings, (2) continuity into the future of competent management who produced the past earnings growth, and (3) a financial plan which demonstrates how reinvestments by management will produce a solid and conservative extension of past performance.

THE FINANCIAL PLAN

A fund-raising package to seek additional capital will often, then, require a financial plan to accompany your usual financial statements, earnings record, and financial ratio analysis. The financial plan shows, essentially, what you propose to do in the future with your sources and uses of funds. Chapter 3 discussed in some detail the fund statement and how you use the sources and uses of funds for internal planning and control. The same information can be used, in seeking outside capital, to demonstrate how you propose to increase the growth in your earnings. Your financial plan will cover such elements as:

1. A demonstration that the assets of the business are being used in such a way as to bring the highest possible return on the money invested.
2. An evaluation of the need for new assets, how they will be used, and what products, markets, and earnings will be produced by the new assets.
3. A realistic assessment of the sources of funds to finance new asset additions.
4. A financial management plan which shows how both old and

new assets will each contribute its full share toward the profitable operation of the business.

5. A schedule of how loans will be repaid or how earnings on equity will be realized.
6. A schedule of when new capital will be needed, how much it will cost, and how the capital costs will affect earnings.
7. *Pro forma* income statements and balance sheets showing the expected impact of all of the above (items 1 through 6) on the financial statements five years into the future.

THE LOAN PACKAGE

Perhaps the simplest way to visualize the contents of a financial plan is to show it in the context of a loan package submitted to a lender as an application for a loan, as illustrated in Figure 8–1.

SOURCES OF FINANCING

Once you have a complete financial plan and financial package, you may seek out funds from a variety of sources, which are described in the following paragraphs:

1. Equity capital is the foundation of a financial structure, and most entrepreneurs have to come up with their own personal funds to get started. A new enterprise is a high-risk venture, and only you and those who have personal knowledge of you are likely to have the confidence to put up the first money needed to start a business. Therefore, the first round of equity money is likely to come from your own personal resources or from family and friends. Once you get started and have some kind of earnings, you may be able to supplement your equity capital from local sources, by including partners from among high-income people you may know. Public accountants are frequently aware of professionals and businessmen with available capital; by talking with your accountant you may be able to organize a small capital pool of limited partners from among such investors.

2. Secured working capital for a going business can often be obtained from banks to cover inventory and accounts receivable. You will need an earnings record, financial statements, and at least the first three parts of a loan package to obtain the credit. The credit will

The Loan Package

The outline of a complete loan package below illustrates the type of detailed presentation sometimes required by lenders such as banks and the Small Business Administration. However, this degree of detail is often unnecessary for businesses already known to the lender.

Many debt sources never require such complete documentation. Instead, they seek the particular information described in previous sections of this report.

The sample loan documentation on the following pages demonstrates an acceptable rendition of only the major parts of a loan package. It does not represent the complete loan package outlined below, and it adheres to the business buyout format rather than the forms for business start-up or expansion.

This particular example involves a hypothetical SBA-guaranteed bank loan, but does not include any SBA loan forms.

Sample Loan Package Outline

I. Summary

  A. Nature of business
  B. Amount and purpose of loan
  C. Repayment terms
  D. Equity share of borrower (debt/equity ratio after loan)
  E. Security or collateral (listed with market value estimates and quotes on cost of equipment to be purchased with the loan proceeds)

II. Personal information (on all corporate officers, directors, and any individuals owning 20 percent or more of the business)

  A. Education, work history, and business experience
  B. Credit references
  C. Income tax statements (last three years)
  D. Financial statement (not over 60 days old)

III. Firm information (whichever is applicable below—A, B, or C)

  A. New business
    1. Business plan (see outline of business plan on page 19)
    2. Life and casualty insurance coverage
    3. Lease agreement
    4. Partnership, corporation, or franchise papers, if applicable

  B. Business acquisition (buyout)
    1. Information on acquisition
      a. Business history (include seller's name, reasons for sale)
      b. Current balance sheet (not over 60 days old)
      c. Current profit and loss statements (preferably less than 60 days old)
      d. Business's federal income tax returns (past three to five years)
      e. Cash flow statements for last year
      f. Copy of sales agreement with breakdown of inventory, fixtures, equipment, licenses, good will, and other costs
      g. Description and dates of permits already acquired
      h. Lease agreement
    2. Business plan
    3. Life and casualty insurance
    4. Partnership, corporation, or franchise papers, if applicable

  C. Existing business expansion
    1. Information on existing business
      a. Business history
      b. Current balance sheet (not more than 60 days old)
      c. Current profit and loss statements (not more than 60 days old)
      d. Cash flow statements for last year
      e. Federal income tax returns for past three to five years
      f. Lease agreement and permit data
    2. Business plan
    3. Life and casualty insurance
    4. Partnership, corporation, or franchise papers, if applicable

IV. Projections

  A. Profit and loss projection (monthly, for one year) and explanation of projections
  B. Cash flow projection (monthly, for one year) and explanation of projections
  C. Projected balance sheet (one year after loan) and explanation of projections

Figure 8-1.   The Loan Package.

Printed with permission of the Bank of America from its *Small Business Reporter* on "Financing Small Business."

LOAN REQUEST

Amount	$60,000
Terms	Eight years with no prepayment penalty. First payment due four months after date of note.
Interest rate	Current SBA rate
Debt/equity ratio	$60,000/$20,000 3/1
Collateral	1. Security interest under California UCC-1 on all business assets. 2. Personal guarantees of Mr. and Mrs. Cho. 3. Second deed of trust on home. 4. SBA guarantee.
Guarantee fee	Borrowers to reimburse bank for SBA guarantee fee of 1 percent of amount guaranteed, or $540.
Other conditions	1. Borrowers will assign life insurance in the amount of the loan and keep it in force during the term of the loan. 2. Borrowers will maintain hazard insurance with loss payable endorsement in the amount and type required by lender. 3. Borrowers will provide annual financial statements to lender.
Purpose of loan	The loan, together with the applicants' equity, will enable Mr. and Mrs. Cho to purchase the liquor store, buy new equipment and fixtures, make improvements, and provide working capital.

The complete financial plan and specific use of loan funds is shown on p. 3.

SUMMARY OF LOAN APPLICATION

Applicant	Mr. Gene K. Cho and Mrs. Betty S. Cho (husband and wife) 555 Seaside Avenue San Francisco, CA 94112 (415) 201-0613
Business	Rainbow Liquors 5775 Ocean Avenue San Francisco, CA 94112 (415) 201-6789
Type of business	Retail liquor store
Size of business	Annual sales have been about $200,000; meets the SBA definition of small business.
Method of acquisition	Buyout
Ownership	Husband and wife partnership
Availability of funds from net worth outside of business	Mr. and Mrs. Cho are injecting $20,000 from the sale of their previous business. In addition, they will use their station wagon in the business. They will maintain $2,000 for personal emergencies. Their home will provide the collateral for the loan. The Chos have no other assets that can be contributed to the business. Thus, they meet SBA requirements on outside net worth.
EOL Program	The Chos are members of a socially and economically disadvantaged group and qualify for the EOL Program.

USE OF FUNDS

	SOURCE OF FUNDS		
	Loan	Equity	Total
Purchase of business			
Inventory	$28,000	$ 0	$28,000
Liquor license	10,000	0	10,000
Fixtures and equipment	2,500	0	2,500
Good will, covenant not to compete	0	17,500	17,500
Subtotal	$40,500	$17,500	$58,000
Closing costs	0	1,200	1,200
Deposits	0	1,300	1,300
Working capital	4,500	0	4,500
New equipment, fixtures, leasehold improvements	15,000	0	15,000
Subtotal	$19,500	$ 2,500	$22,000
TOTAL	$60,000	$20,000	$80,000

New equipment includes new refrigeration ($4,000); fixtures include new shelving and displays ($7,000); leasehold improvements include painting and floor covering ($4,000). Price quotes from suppliers and contractors are included in the documents section.

Loan repayment
The loan will be repaid from the business's cash flow. The projections of sales, expenses, and cash flow indicate that there is sufficient earning power to provide adequate loan coverage.

Cash Sources	10/1/79-9/30/80
Earnings	$20,735
Depreciation	3,000
	$23,735

Cash Uses	
Loan Principal*	$ 5,108
Owners' Draw	14,000
Income Taxes	1,000
	$20,108

*Interest portion of loan payments was included as an expense before net earnings.

The cash coverage is 1.2 ($23,735/$20,108) and is adequate to assure repayment of the loan. Owners' draw is, of course, subordinate to loan payment. As the business grows, the cash coverage will become even stronger.

Break-even analysis

The break-even analysis shows that the sales projections, upon which repayment ability is calculated, are reasonable.

$$\frac{\text{Fixed expenses and loan principle payments (\$35,143)}}{1.00 - \text{variable cost as a percentage of sales (.76)}} = \frac{\text{Break-even sales}}{\$146,429}$$

The sales level needed to break even on this basis is $146,429 or 70 percent of projection ($208,000). This provides ample leeway for meeting fixed obligations.

Analysis of purchase price

Evaluation of the purchase price using the SBA formula indicates the price is reasonable. The purchase price is analyzed in two components: the tangible assets and good will, which includes the noncompetition covenant.

The tangible assets to be purchased include:

Inventory	$28,000
Equipment and fixtures (book values)	2,500
Liquor license	10,000
	$40,500

Assessment of value for good will:

Average annual profits for the past three years ($15,283) less owner's salary ($7,000) and earning power of tangible assets (based on SBA factor of 7 percent multiplied by $40,500)= $5,448. Three years average earning power ($5,448) multiplied by three gives a value to good will of $16,344, compared to $17,500 in the sales price.

The conclusion is that the sales price is reasonable based on the SBA formula. Total actual price is $58,000, compared to $56,844 by the formula.

Figure 8-1. (*cont.*)

RESUME

Name	Gene K. Cho
Address	555 Seaside Avenue San Francisco, CA 94112
Phone	(415) 201-0613
Personal	Born: February 23, 1938 Married, two children U.S. citizen
Education	Lincoln University San Francisco, CA MBA, 1970 San Francisco State University San Francisco, CA B.A. in Business Administration, 1963
Employment and Business Experience	1973-present Dandy Wig Company Daly City, CA Owner-Manager Mr. Cho established and built this business himself. The company imported wigs from the Far East and sold them wholesale and retail. Mr. Cho established reliable supply lines and developed the distribution system for the West Coast. 1968-1973 Bank of America San Francisco, CA Data Processing Clerk

	1963-1967 East Wind Trading Company San Francisco, CA Salesman Duties included establishing and servicing sales accounts. Also was successful in developing new markets for new products imported by the company.
Personal Credit References	Bank of America Ocean Avenue Branch San Francisco, CA Savings Account: 4578-02023 Checking Account: 7641-02666 Golden East Savings and Loan 5546 Seaside Avenue San Francisco, CA Auto Loan No. 05532-05523 Home Loan No. 308-055921

PERSONAL FINANCIAL STATEMENT
As of August 1, 1979

Assets

Cash on hand and in checking accounts	$ 625
Savings accounts	22,000
U.S. government bonds	0
Accounts and notes receivable	0
Life insurance cash value	0
Other stocks and bonds	50,000
Real estate	4,500
Automobile	14,000
Other personal property	0
Other assets	0
TOTAL ASSETS	$91,125

Liabilities

Accounts payable	$ 840
Notes payable to banks	0
Notes payable to others	0
Installment account (auto)	1,820
Installment account (other)	317
Loans on life insurance	0
Mortgages on real estate	28,247
Unpaid taxes	0
Other liabilities	0
TOTAL LIABILITIES	$ 31,224

| NET WORTH | $ 59,901 |

RESUME

Name	Betty S. Cho
Address	555 Seaside Avenue San Francisco, CA 94112
Phone	(415) 201-0613
Personal	Born: October 1, 1945 Married, two children U.S. citizen
Education	San Francisco State University San Francisco, CA B.A. in Political Science, 1967
Employment and Business Experience	1972-present Orient Importing Company San Francisco, CA Part-time office assistant Duties included handling purchase orders and billings and bookkeeping. 1967-1970 San Francisco Chamber of Commerce San Francisco, CA Assistant Office Manager Duties included supervising clerical staff and preparing reports for Chamber of Commerce officials.
Personal Credit References	Bank of America Ocean Avenue Branch San Francisco, CA Savings Account: 4578-02023 Checking Account: 7641-02666 Golden East Savings and Loan 5546 Seaside Avenue San Francisco, CA Auto Loan No. 05532-05523 Home Loan No. 308-055921

Figure 8-1. *(cont.)*

BUSINESS PLAN

Name and Address of Business

Rainbow Liquors
5775 Ocean Avenue
San Francisco, CA 94112
(415) 201-6789

History of Business

The business was established in 1938 by the current owner's husband, Carl Costello. Mr. Costello died three years ago, and since then, Mrs. Costello has managed the business alone. She has not been in good health, nor has she had much interest in the business since her husband passed away. She has curtailed the hours of operation and often leaves the employees unsupervised. Sales have fallen from $235,000 to $180,000 in the past three and one-half years. Gross profit margins have been erratic, and no capital improvements have been made in years.

Mr. and Mrs. Cho have been customers of Rainbow Liquors for a number of years as they have lived in this neighborhood since 1972. Mr. Cho believes that a younger and more vigorous management can make this well-established business begin to grow and prosper again.

Plan of Operation Under New Owners

Sales Plan

1. Extend business hours (currently 10 a.m. to 7 p.m.) to 9 a.m. to 9 p.m.; extend business days (currently six days) to seven days a week.
2. Refurbish the store to make it more attractive and modern.
3. Expand the product line by adding cold sandwiches, magazines, and more wines.
4. Increase advertising, using the local weekly shopping edition and occasional neighborhood leafleting.
5. Improve point of purchase displays and do more in-store promotions.

Cost Reduction

Mr. Cho's plan to reduce costs is to:

1. Restore the gross profit margin. Cost of sales has fluctuated in the past three and one-half years, and profit margins have fallen to a current low of 13.5 percent. Compared to an industry average of 25 percent, there is great room for improvement. Strict control over inventory and pricing should make the business profitable again very quickly and restore the gross margin to an appropriate level.
2. Reduce payroll costs. The store presently employs three full-time workers as cashiers and clerks, with Mrs. Costello attending irregularly. Mr. and Mrs. Cho will both work in the store and will hire one full-time employee. They will add part-time and more full-time help as sales grow. At present, however, they can reduce payroll costs by about $17,000 a year.

Market Potential

The growth potential is considerable. Ocean Avenue is a neighborhood shopping district for the adjoining residential area of moderate-income families. It is accessible by public and private transportation. The market area for this study has been defined as one square mile. Using the census data for the nine census tracts that fall into this radius, there was a total population of 47,347 in 1970. The average annual per capita spending in liquor stores for the entire city is $75. This would yield a potential market of $3.5 million for this one-square-mile area. Clearly, there is sufficient potential for Rainbow Liquors to expand, not only to reach the $235,000 sales level the store once had, but also to exceed it.

There are seven other liquor stores in the Ocean Avenue shopping district. Only two are of a size comparable to Rainbow Liquors. The other stores are old and quite small. With the planned improvements, Rainbow Liquors can expect to draw some of the market from these stores.

Managerial
Capacity

Mr. and Mrs. Cho have substantial business and
managerial background to operate this business successfully. Mr. Cho has a BA and an MBA in business
administration and has shown he can run a prosperous business. Mrs. Cho has valuable retail skills
from her work experience and is capable of doing the
recordkeeping and bookkeeping so essential to good
management.

In addition, Mrs. Costello has agreed to stay on for a
short period to ease the transition and introduce the
Chos to suppliers and regular customers.

Figure 8-1. (*cont.*)

RAINBOW LIQUORS
PROJECTED PROFIT AND LOSS STATEMENT
Prepared August 1, 1979

	1979 Oct.	Nov.	Dec.	1980 Jan.	Feb.	Mar.	Apr.	May	June	July	Aug.	Sept.	Total	%
Gross Sales	15,000	16,000	19,000	17,000	16,000	17,000	17,000	17,000	18,000	18,000	19,000	19,000	208,000	100
Less Cost of Sales	12,000	12,480	14,250	12,750	12,000	12,750	12,750	12,750	13,500	13,500	14,250	14,250	157,230	76
Gross Profit	3,000	3,520	4,750	4,250	4,000	4,250	4,250	4,250	4,500	4,500	4,750	4,750	50,770	24
Expenses														
Salaries	600	600	600	600	600	600	600	600	600	600	600	600	7,200	3.5
Payroll Taxes	60	60	60	60	60	60	60	60	60	60	60	60	720	.3
Alarm Service	30	30	30	30	30	30	30	30	30	30	30	30	360	.1
Advertising	80	80	80	80	80	80	80	80	80	80	80	80	960	.5
Delivery	20	20	20	20	20	20	20	20	20	20	20	20	240	.0
Bad Debts	20	20	20	20	20	20	20	20	20	20	20	20	240	.0
Dues and Subscriptions	10	10	10	10	10	10	10	10	10	10	10	10	120	.0
Laundry and Linen	10	10	10	10	10	10	10	10	10	10	10	10	120	.0
Legal and Accounting	100	100	100	100	100	100	100	100	100	100	100	100	1200	.6
Office Expenses	10	10	10	10	10	10	10	10	10	10	10	10	120	.0
Repairs and Maintenance	50	50	50	50	50	50	50	50	50	50	50	50	600	.3
Supplies	35	35	35	35	35	35	35	35	35	35	35	35	420	.2
Phone	35	35	35	35	35	35	35	35	35	35	35	35	420	.2
Utilities	100	100	100	100	100	100	100	100	100	100	100	100	1200	.6
Miscellaneous	50	50	50	50	50	50	50	50	50	50	50	50	600	.3
Depreciation	250	250	250	250	250	250	250	250	250	250	250	250	3,000	1.4
Insurance	100	100	100	100	100	100	100	100	100	100	100	100	1,200	.6
Rent	300	300	300	300	300	300	300	300	300	300	300	300	3,600	1.7
Taxes and Licenses	150	150	150	150	150	150	150	150	150	150	150	150	1,800	.9
Interest	512	509	506	502	499	495	491	488	484	480	476	473	5,915	2.8
Total Expenses	2,522	2,519	2,516	2,512	2,509	2,505	2,501	2,498	2,494	2,490	2,486	2,483	30,035	14.0
Net Profit/(Loss)	478	1,001	2,234	1,738	1,491	1,745	1,749	1,752	2,006	2,010	2,264	2,267	20,735	10.0

EXPLANATION OF PROJECTED PROFIT AND LOSS STATEMENT

Gross Sales. Sales are expected to have a seasonal variation as well as a growth component. With the changes planned in operations, sales are expected to return to the level of a year ago.

Cost of Sales. Cost of sales is expected to improve gradually until it reaches a standard 75 percent.

Gross Profit. (Also called Gross Margin.) This is the difference between sales and cost of sales.

Expenses. Operating expenses are itemized below.

Salaries. The Chos plan to hire one full-time employee during their first year of operation. As sales increase, they can add staff as needed. Both Mr. and Mrs. Cho will work in the store; their wages are shown as owners' draw on the cash flow.

Payroll Taxes. Estimated at 10 percent of payroll to cover employers' share of FICA, unemployment insurance, and workers' compensation.

Alarm Service. Burglar alarm service is contracted at $30 per month.

Advertising. The Chos plan to increase the advertising budget from $50 to $80 per month.

Delivery. A modest sum is allocated for business travel.

Bad Debts. For direct write-offs of bad checks. Based on the store's historical experience.

Dues and Subscriptions. A small amount is set aside for subscriptions to trade journals and memberships in trade associations.

Laundry and Linen. Smocks for clerks and restroom towels.

Legal and Accounting. Mr. Cho will use the accountant who serviced his previous business. The rate provides for financial statements and an annual income tax return.

Office Expense. For office supplies such as stationery and postage.

Repairs and Maintenance. For conservative purposes, this estimate is slightly higher than historical averages of $40 per month. It is more likely that this expense will be reduced, because a number of capital improvements will be made at the outset.

Supplies. Mainly for paper bags; estimated slightly higher than historical average of $30 per month due to inflation.

Phone. A $35 per month budget provides for some increase due to inflation.

Utilities. Gas and electricity estimated at $100 per month based on historical experience, allowance for longer hours, and inflation.

Miscellaneous. For contingencies and miscellaneous items.

Depreciation. $17,500 of fixed assets, such as equipment, shelving, leasehold improvements; fixtures are depreciated over five years on a straight-line basis for about $3,000 per year. This rate provides for a remaining salvage value of $2,500 at the end of the five-year period.

Insurance. Fire and liability insurance at current rate.

Rent. Based on the lease agreement.

Taxes and Licenses. Includes business license tax.

Interest. Interest on requested loan of $60,000 amortized over eight years at interest rate of 10.25 percent.

Total Expenses. Sum of the above expenses.

Net Profit. (Also called Net Income.) Difference between total expenses and gross profits. Net profit is about 10 percent of sales and is comparable to the historical experience two years ago when adjusted for a reduced payroll.

Figure 8-1. *(cont.)*

167

RAINBOW LIQUORS
PROJECTED CASH FLOW

	Pre-Operating	1979 Oct.	Nov.	Dec.	1980 Jan.	Feb.	Mar.	Apr.	May	June	July	Aug.	Sept.	Total
Cash Sources														
Equity	20,000													20,000
Loan	60,000													60,000
Net Profit	0	478	1,001	2,234	1,738	1,491	1,745	1,749	1,752	2,006	2,010	2,264	2,267	20,735
Depreciation	0	250	250	250	250	250	250	250	250	250	250	250	250	3,000
Total	80,000	728	1,251	2,484	1,988	1,741	1,995	1,999	2,002	2,256	2,260	2,514	2,517	103,735
Disbursements														
Purchase of Business	58,000													58,000
Closing Costs	1,200													1,200
Improvements and Equipment	15,000													15,000
Deposits	1,300													1,300
Loan Payments (Principal)	0	406	410	413	416	420	424	427	431	434	439	442	446	5,108
Owners' Draw	0	1,000	1,000	1,200	1,200	1,200	1,200	1,200	1,200	1,200	1,200	1,200	1,200	14,000
Income Taxes	0							1,000						1,000
Total	75,500	1,406	1,410	1,613	1,616	1,620	1,624	2,627	1,631	1,634	1,639	1,642	1,646	95,608
Net Cash Flow	4,500	(678)	(159)	871	372	121	371	(628)	371	622	621	872	871	8,127
Cumulative Cash Flow	4,500	3,822	3,663	4,534	4,906	5,027	5,398	4,770	5,141	5,763	6,384	7,256	8,127	

EXPLANATION OF PROJECTED CASH FLOW

Cash Sources. Sources of cash detailed below.

Equity. The borrowers will inject $20,000 of cash into the business.

Loan. The requested loan will provide $60,000 of initial cash.

Net Profit. Net profit after expenses is a source of cash and is taken from line 26 of income and expense projection.

Depreciation. Depreciation was deducted as an expense before net profit. Since it is a noncash expense, it is added back here as a cash source.

Total Sources. The sum of items from cash sources through loan injection.

Disbursements. Detailed below.

Purchase of Business. The sales agreement calls for a purchase price of $58,000 including inventory.

Closing Costs. Escrow costs are estimated to be $1,200 and are treated as a preoperating expense.

Improvements and Equipment. A capital outlay of $15,000 is expected at the beginning for new equipment, fixtures, and improvements.

Deposits. Deposits for rent, sales taxes, and utilities are estimated at $1,300.

Loan Payments. Principal portion of loan payments, based on eight-year amortization of $60,000 loan at 10.25 percent interest.

Owners' Draw. Expected to fluctuate with state of the business and growth. Draw of $1,000 per month for Mr. and Mrs. Cho is reasonable in the early months. As earnings grow, draws can be expected to increase, subject to their subordination to debt service.

Income Taxes. Income taxes for 1979 are due in April of 1980, and $1,000 has been projected for this purpose.

Total Disbursements. The sum of items from purchase price to income taxes.

Net Cash Flow. Monthly cash flow is the difference between total cash sources and total disbursements.

Cumulative Cash Flow. Sum of the monthly cash flows cumulated month by month. The business ends with a healthy cash surplus of more than $8,000.

Figure 8-1. (*cont.*)

RAINBOW LIQUORS
PROJECTED BALANCE SHEET
Current Status (after purchase of business) vs. One Year Later

ASSETS	Oct. 1, 1979	Oct. 1, 1980
Current Assets		
Cash on Hand and in Bank	4,500	8,127
Accounts Receivable	0	0
Inventory	28,000	28,000
Total Current Assets	32,500	36,127
Fixed Assets		
Fixtures and Equipment	17,500	17,500
Less Depreciation	0	(3,000)
Net Fixed Assets	17,500	14,500
Other Assets		
Liquor License	10,000	10,000
Good Will	17,500	17,500
Deposits	1,300	1,300
Total Fixed Assets	46,300	43,300
TOTAL ASSETS	78,800	79,427

LIABILITIES	Oct. 1, 1979	Oct. 1, 1980
SBA Loan (Current)	5,108	5,657
SBA Loan (Long-term)	54,892	49,235
Total Liabilities	60,000	54,892
Equity (Beginning)	20,000	20,000
Plus Earnings (Preoperating)	(1,200)	(1,200)
(Operating)	0	20,735
Less Draws	0	(15,000)
Ending Equity (Net Worth)	18,800	24,535
TOTAL LIABILITIES AND EQUITY	78,800	79,427
Debt/Equity Ratio	3.1	2.1
Return on Equity	—	104%

EXPLANATION OF PROJECTED BALANCE SHEET

Assets. Current and fixed.

Cash on Hand and in Bank. Taken from projected cash flow statements.

Accounts Receivable. Borrowers do not plan to extend trade credit.

Inventory. Initial inventory level of $28,000 is expected to be purchased and is more than sufficient to support first year's expected sales level.

Current Assets. Sum of cash and inventory.

Fixed Assets. Detailed below.

Fixtures, Equipment, and Improvements. Includes $2,500 worth of equipment purchased with the business and $15,000 worth of new expenditures.

Depreciation. Amount taken from projected profit and loss statement.

Net Fixed Assets. Difference between original cost and depreciation of equipment, fixtures, and improvements.

Liquor License. Purchased as part of the business.

Good Will. Included as part of the business purchase price.

Deposits. For rent, utilities, and sales taxes.

Total Assets. Sum of current and fixed assets.

Liabilities. Current and long-term liabilities.

Current Liabilities. Current portion of loan requested.

Long-term Liabilities. Balance of loan less current portion.

Total Liabilities. Sum of current and long-term liabilities.

Beginning Equity. Includes $20,000 initial cash injection.

Earnings. Preoperating loss of $1,200 closing costs incurred at time of loan; at end of one year of operation, earnings are taken from projected profit and loss statement.

Draws. Owners' draws for salaries and taxes are deducted from equity.

Ending Equity. Beginning equity plus profits and less owners' draws equals ending equity.

Total Liabilities and Equity. Sum of total liabilities and ending equity equals total assets.

Debt/Equity Ratio. 3.1 at time of loan; falls to 2.1 as a result of one year's operations.

Return on Equity. Net earnings as a percentage of owner's initial equity shows a favorable 104 percent return; indicates a reasonable investment and 29 percent return after adjusting for draws taken for labor.

Figure 8-1. (*cont.*)

be secured by your inventory and receivables, and you will be expected to clear up the loan when it is due or at least annually.

3. Secured fixed asset loans can be obtained by mortgaging real property or by equipment loans from manufacturers to finance those portions of your business which are physical property. Banks, mortgage companies, and the credit companies used by equipment manufacturers are the main source of funds. You will have to use your physical assets as security or collateral. The typical term for equipment loans is about three years, and perhaps 20 years for buildings secured by mortgages.

4. Unsecured working capital is possible to obtain in small amounts from banks and short terms, like 30 to 60 days, on much the same basis as a personal note. The interest rate is likely to be one-half again as high as the prime lending rate of the bank; and your business would have to have an earnings record and a good working capital ratio (at least 2 to 1) in order to obtain such loans.

5. Growth capital for the expansion of a business is likely to be a combination of equity capital and secured loans. The equity capital would have to come from investors seeking capital gains at reasonably high risks, which means they would be local professionals or businessmen with money who know you and your performance. The classified ads of newspapers frequently list persons seeking equity investments, but you should be cautious and wary in exploring these options. While many such capital sources are real and sound, some may be seeking to take advantage of capital shortages by an owner to get a very large share of the business. Get information on their financial background before dealing, and be prepared for shrewd negotiations on your own behalf.

6. Venture capital firms and pools exist explicitly to invest in new growth businesses. These are usually experienced investors with several million dollars who are trying to pick a diverse list of new companies to back with the expectation that one or two out of a dozen may be big winners for them. Venture capitalists are hard bargainers and will normally expect to take over a majority share of ownership from you. You will have to have a very complete financial package to show them and to convince them personally of your management experience and performance.

7. Small Business Investment Companies (SBICs) are organized to provide equity capital and loans for growth situations. They obtain

some of their capital by borrowing themselves from lines of credit provided by the SBA and the Federal Financing Bank. Because they are operating in part on borrowed money, SBICs will seek collateral or more secure evidence of repayment than venture capital firms; they also will be interested in a strong ownership position in the business.

8. The SBA is a source of loans for small firms, but they regard their role as being a lender of last resort. Hence, you need to show that you have exhausted the other possible sources of capital before the SBA will consider your application. The SBA's criteria are much the same as a bank, and you will need to produce a loan package much like the one illustrated in the previous section.

DIAGNOSTIC CHECKLIST

Any investor or lender is going to ask you a lot of questions about your business, in addition to the information which is shown in the loan package. Therefore, you will want to be prepared to discuss the operation of your business in detail. What the investors or lenders are looking for in their interview with you is evidence of good management ability and practice. You can prepare yourself for such an interview and questioning by going over a diagnostic checklist in advance. Such a diagnostic checklist would include management requirements like the following:

	Rank by Attention		
	High	Medium	Low
General Management			
1. Company has business strategy and business plan.	___	___	___
2. Company and organizational goals are clearly defined and communicated.	___	___	___
3. Employee participation in formal goal setting.	___	___	___
4. Annual budget prepared with participation of operating personnel.	___	___	___
5. Monthly monitoring of expenditures versus budget and progress toward sales and profit goals.	___	___	___
6. Assigned responsibility for achieving goals and objectives.	___	___	___

General Management (*cont.*)

| | Rank by Attention | | |
	High	Medium	Low

7. Organizational structure clearly defined.
8. Chart of approvals for authorization and expenditures.

Personnel

9. Clear policy and procedures communicated to employees.
10. Formal compensation plan for all employees with annual review.
11. Area wage and salary surveys.
12. Current job descriptions for all positions.
13. Formal performance evaluation discussed with individual.

Financial Standing

14. Current financial statements and profit analysis.
15. Current budgets and profitability analysis.
16. Cash flow projections with statements of sources and uses of funds.
17. Financial ratios compared to other companies.
18. Institutional credit and equity sources of funds currently appraised of financial needs and performance.

Marketing

19. Active market research, new market and product development programs.
20. Formal evaluation of market and product performance.
21. Sales and profitability regularly analyzed by product line, customer accounts, markets, territory, and salespeople.
22. Continual review of product mix and profitability.

	Rank by Attention		
	High	Medium	Low
23. Long-term sales projections by product for use in production, facilities, manpower and procurement planning.	___	___	___
24. Short-term sales analysis for production schedules and financial management to develop a profit plan.	___	___	___
25. Clearly assigned marketing objectives.	___	___	___
26. Periodic evaluation of advertising and marketing effectiveness.	___	___	___
27. Monthly production control schedules, monitored daily.	___	___	___
28. Time and cost sheets which assign material and labor to products and cost centers.	___	___	___
29. Cost accounting system using same data as production control system.	___	___	___
30. Plant and labor productivity review process.	___	___	___
31. Profitability analysis currently by product.	___	___	___
32. Objective analysis of make or buy decisions.	___	___	___

Production

33. Reliable supply sources at competitive prices.	___	___	___
34. Standard costs developed for each significant operation.	___	___	___
35. Plant loading plan to minimize production fluctuations.	___	___	___
36. Production tasks clearly assigned and monitored.	___	___	___

Purchasing

37. Purchasing requisitions transmitted quickly to buyers with both short-term and long-term requirements.	___	___	___
38. Consolidated purchasing plans developed with buyers by commodity and supplier to facilitate maximum negotiation with suppliers.	___	___	___

Purchasing (cont.)	Rank by Attention		
	High	Medium	Low
39. Purchasing power maximized through nationwide buying contracts and blanket purchase commitments.	____	_____	____
40. Decentralized purchasing assignments to serve key locations without internal competition.	____	_____	____
41. Consolidated purchasing actions on repetitively used items by a systematic stocking program.	____	_____	____
42. Purchasing agents participate in volume plans, standardization, value analysis, make or buy, lease or buy decisions.	____	_____	____
43. Specification options worked out with buyers to give flexible choices in minimizing purchase prices.	____	_____	____
44. Purchasing assignments and authorizations clearly known.	____	_____	____

Each of these management requirements should be rated by the degree of attention given to them in terms of establishing systematic procedure and attention in monitoring them. A manager, who is able to explain knowledgeably all of the management tools (listed above) which he uses to keep on top of operations, and to describe how the firm is performing with respect to each of them, is obviously much better informed and qualified to secure new financing than is a manager who is not so prepared. In other words, you stand a much better chance of getting financing if you go in with a loan package plus the information to answer all the questions listed above in the audit or checklist than if you try to ad lib the answers. If you have made a management audit of your own and have the answers to it, you will sound like a seasoned, systematic and well organized manager. If you go in to a fund-raising interview without being prepared on all aspects of your business, you will appear to be an amateur to the lender or investor. So be prepared. Obviously the checklist could be longer and more detailed than it is, but the important point is that the loan package has to be supported by a knowledgeable, verbal portrayal of management competence.

MERGER, ACQUISITION, OR SELL-OUT

If your business is successful, you may wish to expand it by merger or acquisition. That is, you may wish to buy up other companies in your line of business to secure a stronger market and financial foothold in your field, or some other company may wish to acquire your business for the same reason.

An acquisition is the exchange of stock, or stock and cash, by one company for another, in which the purchased company continues to operate as a subsidiary of the parent (purchasing) company.

A merger is the exchange of stock, or stock and cash, by one company for another, in which the assets and liabilities of the purchased company are merged into the parent company, and the purchased company ceases to exist.

A sale is the purchase of the assets or net worth of one company by another, perhaps for stock but more frequently for cash, in which the seller pays off his creditors and turns the company over to the buyer.

All three forms of purchase of one company by another are quite similar. The main differences are the form of payment and the disposition of the purchased company. An acquisition and a sale are the most similar. An acquisition is more common among medium and large corporations with listed securities and established market values for their stock. A sale is more common among small companies without listed securities, and the sale is most often for cash or cash plus term payments over three to five years. Mergers are actually consolidations of corporations, one into the other. Mergers were most common in the period from 1870 to 1930 in the formation of the integrated steel, sugar, auto, coal, iron, and food companies. Acquisitions are more common today because the acquired firms are usually in different lines of business than the parent company and continue to operate in their own field. The motive behind merger is usually vertical integration of a production system. The motive behind acquisitions is usually diversification.

Your company becomes a candidate for acquisition as soon as your growth record exceeds your industry's average but the price earnings of your stock does not (see the section earlier in this chapter on earnings records).

Your company becomes a candidate to acquire other companies as soon as both your earnings record and P/E ratio exceed your industry's average. That is, once you have a good earnings record and a high P/E ratio, you can exchange your high-priced stock for the low-priced stock of another company to be acquired. Thus, you gain bargain-priced assets of the acquired company because your stock is highly valued. The catch is, of course, that you then have to turn that acquired company into high earnings performance, like your own, or else the investors will cease to value your stock so highly and your P/E ratio will fall. However, you can keep the merry-go-round going as long as you have a high P/E ratio of your own stock and as long as you can raise the earnings record of the acquisitions. This process was the basis of the Go-Go funds and the conglomerate acquisition movement of the 1960s. Unfortunately, the bubble burst with the recessions of 1970 and 1974 because the earnings growth of the acquired companies could not be raised.

However, the acquisition movement is burgeoning again in the 1980s because low stock prices make it cheaper to buy the assets of existing companies rather than to purchase new assets or plant capacity at inflation prices. Many stocks are still valued at mid-1970, or preinflation, prices. Indeed, the stock market in constant dollars, i.e., corrected for inflation, has been declining since 1966. But the price level of new plant, equipment, and inventory is up two to three times since then. That means you can acquire the assets of some companies by acquisition at a 50 to 67% discount. You need to be careful about obsolete plants or products lines in such acquisitions, but if you have strong product lines which can use an acquired plant efficiently, the acquisition route can be an inexpensive way to expand. Foreign companies, especially those with strong currencies like Germany, Japan, and Saudi Arabia, have been busy picking up U.S. companies at bargain rates by acquisitions.

So, if you have a successful company with a strong earnings record and P/E ratio, and if you wish to expand, consider acquisition. If you have a low P/E ratio with an average earnings record, you may wish to consider a sale.

Arriving at a Selling Price

A simple way to arrive at a selling price is to multiply recent annual earnings by the P/E ratio for your industry. This is probably the way a buyer will look at the price, because he is essentially buying future earnings.

A seller is most likely to expect to recover his costs and to be compensated for his effort in starting and running the business. The costs are easy enough to identify from the accounting record by figuring out the adjusted net worth (tangible assets minus all liabilities). However, the value of the business as a going concern is moot. A going concern has value due to its location, leases, reputation, and established customers, all of which are termed *good will*. One formula for arriving at the value of good will is shown below.

1. Estimate how much the buyer could earn elsewhere with an investment similar in amount to the tangible net worth.

2. Add a salary compensation for the owner-operator of the business.

3. Determine the annual average earnings of the business (including officer compensation) for the past three to five years.

4. Subtract the comparative earnings and owner salary (lines 1 and 2) from the average actual earnings (line 3), to determine the extra earnings power of the firm.

5. Multiply the extra earnings power (line 4) by 3 to get the value of good will.

6. Add the good will value (line 5) to the tangible new worth to arrive at a selling price.

Example of Business Valuation

	BUSINESS ABLE	BUSINESS BAKER
TANGIBLE NET WORTH	$100,000	$100,000
1. Comparative earnings of similar investment elsewhere @ 13%	13,000	13,000
2. Owner salary	20,000	20,000
3. Average actual earnings	38,000	30,000
4. Extra earnings power (line 3 — [line 1 + line 2])	5,000	— 3,000
5. Good will (line 4 x 3)	15,000	None
6. Sales price (line 1 + line 5)	115,000	100,000 or less (91,000)

SUMMARY

The ability to raise funds from investors requires that you look at financial performance measures from their perspective, which is the prospective growth in future earnings compared to other firms or alternate investments.

The simplest way to start this comparative valuation is to measure the book value per share of your firm, which represents the tangible assets net of depreciation minus liabilities. The book value of comparative firms in your industry can be found in the standard securities statistical services. The equity or book value per share of comparative firms may then be compared with their recent price range on the market to give a preliminary idea of value.

The earnings record is the most important evidence of the managemental ability you have. The higher the earnings growth over a long period, the more value your company possesses for borrowing money or raising equity capital, because investors will regard high earnings growth over an extended period in the past as evidence of potential earnings in the future.

The price-earnings (P/E) ratio is a measure of confidence which investors have in a company's ability to continue a high earnings record. That is, a high P/E ratio indicates investors are willing to pay a high price for the stock based upon present earnings, because they expect future earnings growth to be even better. A low P/E ratio indicates low investor confidence in future earnings.

A five- or ten-year growth record of earnings helps to establish the credibility of the earnings record; the longer the record, the more confidence investors will have in management and the future earnings potential.

A financial plan is a means of showing future needs for credit or equity funds, the uses to which they will be put, and the potential earnings which may result from the added investment.

The loan package is a file submitted by the owner of a business to a lender to seek additional funds. The package typically contains financial statements, capital structure, personal information on the management, a business plan, earnings history, projected uses of funds, projected profit, cash flow, and financial statements.

The sources of funds for business are usually from personal funds (or acquaintances) for the first equity capital, secured working capital from banks, and secured fixed asset mortgages from savings institutions. With a good earnings record, growth capital may be obtained in equity markets by the sale of stock or by private placement with venture capital firms or life insurance companies.

The owner of a business should prepare himself with a management audit or checklist, as well as the financial loan package, before going into an interview to seek funds. The management checklist is a means of demonstrating a systematic and seasoned approach to all management skills needed to run a business.

Mergers, acquisition, or sale of a business may occur as an owner ages or as the earnings record and P/E ratio begins to exceed industry averages. A high earnings record and P/E ratio enables a company to acquire other firms on bargain terms. A good earnings record and average P/E ratio makes a firm an acquisition candidate, particularly if it has a high cash or liquid asset position.

The selling price of a firm may be estimated from the tangible net worth, plus good will which is measured as the extra earnings over and above the owner's salary and comparative yields elsewhere. The extra earnings are often multiplied by three or four to give an estimate of the value of the business as a going concern.

The owner of a business should periodically take a shrewd look at the value of his business as determined by book value, P/E ratios, earnings growth record, and sales value for the purpose of evaluating his fund-raising ability in case he wishes to expand or sell.

9
The Business Plan and Budget

We said in the last chapter that you cannot raise money for your business without a financial plan in your loan package, and you cannot develop a credible financial plan without first having a business plan. So now we are down to basics. You need a business plan to get ahead.

A business plan shows what you are going to sell, how, to whom, with what, and what profits can be expected. In other words, the business plan is an operating document on how you are going to accomplish your goals. This differs from a financial plan, which is a money record of the results of your operating business plan. The money men, who lend to or invest in your firm, are going to want to see the dollar and cents record of your financial plan. But before you can explain finances to an outsider, you first must figure out your operating plan of what work you are going to do to satisfy your customers and achieve your goals. That is the business plan.

To develop your business plan, you need a *budget*—a schedule of costs and revenues. The budget is your control document to see that the business plan gets carried out. The budget is also the transition step to make up your financial plan, because the budgeted results become the projected income statement. So we can see then that: (1) the business plan is a schedule of work to be done to reach your goals, (2) the budget is the control document showing the costs of the business plan, and (3) the financial plan is a record of the results from the business plan in terms of income statements and balance sheets.

The structure of the business plan is determined by the knowledge you must have to make decisions which will optimize performance and earnings. The topics to be included in a business plan are:

1. The economic and competitive environment.
2. The sales and profit goals of your firm.
3. The market plan.
4. The production or operating plan.
5. Work organization and schedules.
6. Costs and budgets.
7. Financial statements.
8. Risk-return options and trade-offs.

Each of these elements will be considered separately, and directions for the execution of each will be given.

The Economic and Competitive Environment

Your business exists in the larger world of a general business situation and, within that, the more specific competitive environment of your industry. Both of these environments will affect your performance or what you can accomplish. You can look at these several environments, which affect your business plan, within the perspective of: (1) the growth rates of the U.S. economy, (2) the competitive position of the U.S. versus foreign competitors, (3) the growth rates of your industry, (4) the competitive conditions of your industry, and (5) the profit impacts upon your business of your market share and competitive position.

The general business situation is determined by the basic economic growth rates of the nation and the stage of the business cycle at any point in time. The growth rate of the U.S. was 4.4% per year from 1950 to 1970, but in the 1970s the growth rate fell to 2.1% annually. The reason was lower rates of savings and investment, higher tax burdens, and fewer technological innovations. The savings rate of the U.S. is about 15% per year, compared to 18 to 22% for Western Europe and about 30% for Japan. Only Britain has a lower savings rate than the U.S. The results of lower savings and investment have been lower labor productivity (or output per man hour) as shown in Table 9-1.

Table 9-1. Productivity Growth 1960–1970 and 1970–1978. (annual rate of growth in manufacturing output per man hour)

1960–1970		1970–1978	
Japan	10.9%	West Germany	5.3%
France	5.9	France	5.1
West Germany	5.5	Japan	4.9
Canada	4.3	Canada	3.9
United Kingdom	3.7	United States	2.6
United States	2.9	United Kingdom	2.2

Source: Bureau of Labor Statistics.

The higher productivity and savings rates in other countries have meant that the U.S. has become less competitive in international markets, particularly in steel, automobiles, television, consumer electronics, and to some extent in clothing and apparel. If you are selling products which compete with foreign imports, your first alert is to examine how competitive your price and product designs are compared to imports.

You can also make some estimate about the future growth of the U.S. economy based on an expectation that production, markets, and income will increase at an average rate of about 2% per year, based upon the performance of the 1970s.

The next estimate of your own market potential must recognize where the economy stands in the business cycle—if the economy is moving toward recession or recovery. Business cycles are defined (i.e., marked in time as to when they start and stop) by the National Bureau of Economic Research; these business cycle markers are used by the U.S. Bureau of the Census to show the performance of the economy with respect to the leading, coincident, and lagging indicators. These indicators are published monthly in the *Business Conditions Digest,* which can be found in the government document section of most public libraries. Figure 9-1 is taken from an issue of *Business Conditions Digest* and shows the recent business cycles. You will see that there were two main cycles in the 1970s, one recovery beginning in December, 1970 and ending in December, 1974; the second recovery beginning in March, 1975 and ending in March, 1980. The coincident indicators are, by definition, the business cycle. The leading indicators move in advance of the business

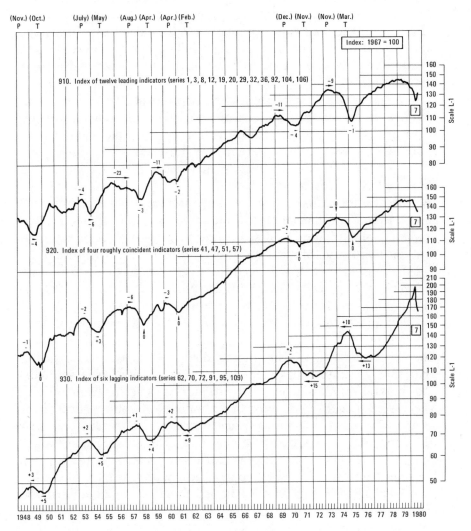

Figure 9-1. Composite Indexes.

Numbers entered on the chart indicate length of leads (−) and lags (+) in months from reference turning dates.

Source: Business Conditions Digest, U.S. Department of Commerce, Bureau of Economic Analysis.

cycle, and the lagging indicators follow it. You can get a fair idea of what to expect in terms of economic conditions by looking at the chart to see where the economy is in its recovery or recession phase, together with the movement of the leading indicators. For instance, if the leading indicators are rising, you would expect the Gross National Product (which moves more slowly) to recover to a 2% long-term growth rate and expect perhaps a 3 to 4% increase in income and sales. If the leading indicators are falling, you can expect a 3 to 4% decline in business conditions as measured by national income and product.

So much for the general economic environment. Let us turn attention next to the competitive environment. To understand your competitive position, you need information on the sales and market share of your competitors. Perhaps the most important single piece of information in your business plan is what is your own market share versus that of competitors.

General information about the performance of your competitors can be found in financial reports and business publications. For example, Table 8–1 shows sales, profit and growth rates of competitors; and you can compare your own performance with theirs. To calculate market share, you need the total sales of the industry and the sales of competitors. Such information, when it is available, is usually obtained from trade associations.

The competitive evaluation also involves an assessment of your product position relative to competitors, which we discussed in Chapters 4 and 5. The SBA, in its guides to business planning, suggests that you rate your competition by listing your own strengths and weaknesses on a product-by-product basis versus competition.[1] You would then arrive at a list of advantages of your products over competition on such factors as price, performance, durability, versatility, accuracy, speed, ease of use, size, weight, styling, appearance, and so forth. This evaluation would give you a basis for judging your sales performance versus competition in improving your market share, which is the final number (in percentage and volume) that you want to be able to estimate for the business plan.

Sales and Profit Goals of Your Firm

The evaluation of your economic environment and competitive position gives you a basis for establishing sales and profit goals for your firm. If you have numerous product advantages over your competition, and if your market share is increasing, you have a reasonable foundation for projecting a corresponding increase in sales and profit targets. If your product advantages are few or doubtful, you are sent back to square one to ask the basic question, "What business am I really in?" If you have no product or market advantages, you really are not in business—you have a money-losing hobby.

Realistic sales goals, based upon market share and competitive strength, should be projected by product, by sales territory, monthly for the first year, and annually for the next five years. Such estimates provide the basis for a five-year marketing plan and a monthly budget for the first year.

Since you know your costs and selling prices, you can then derive unit volume sales for the five-year period (monthly for the first year), operating costs, and profits.

The projection gives you profit goals for the business plan.

The operating cost estimates provide the budget for the business plan.

Now each of the broad estimates of sales, costs, and profits have to be fleshed out into the detail needed for implementation. That is the purpose of the marketing plan, production plan, budget, and financial statements which are discussed in the following sections.

The Marketing Plan

This is the key document in the business plan because the realism of the sales estimates and marketing implementation will determine how accurate and reliable your entire plan will be. Bankers and lenders will develop increasing respect for your management ability, and be more willing to lend you money, if your plans are reliable in the sense of being realized in practice.

The essentials of a marketing plan have already been covered in Chapter 5, particularly in Table 5-1 which gives an illustration of a brief marketing plan for a paint store. You will recall that the plan lists the functions and tasks to be performed in carrying out the sales activity, together with assignments as to organizations and persons, a time schedule, and the budgeted cost. Such a scheduling of activity, assignments, and costs should be made for every product and for every location, monthly during the first year and annually thereafter.

The four key decision areas for you to cover in your marketing plan are: (1) product competitiveness, (2) promotion tasks, (3) distribution methods, and (4) pricing. The coverage to be included in the marketing section of your business plan might well include the following topics:[2]

1. Product list and characteristics.
2. Advantages over competitors.
3. List of competitors.
4. Your rating of competitors.
5. Market area and territories.
6. Distribution methods and costs.
7. Principal customers, location, volume, preferences, and your share.
8. Special marketing and promotion techniques to reach customers.
9. Pricing strategy and competitive pricing.
10. Marketing trends.
11. Share of the market.
12. Sales volume by product, area, and time schedule.

Production Plan

The production plan takes the sales volume estimated in the marketing plan and schedules out how it can be produced or procured on time. The basic approach is to list all the inputs needed to produce the output and all the labor activity needed to convert the inputs. Thus, the production plan will cover the following elements:

1. List of manufacturing operations or functions.
2. Schedule of raw material purchases with source, price, and delivery times.
3. Schedule of equipment and equipment-time needed, with purchase, rental, or amortized overhead cost.
4. Schedule of labor skills, manpower loading, and pay rates.
5. Hiring or training schedule.
6. Task assignments by type of labor skills.
7. Space and facility requirements, with cost.

8. Overhead costs, including administrative, facilities, utilities, and indirect (fringe) labor costs.
9. A summary of total operating and production costs (this becomes the operating budget).

Work Organization and Schedules

All of the activities and tasks identified in the marketing and production plans have to be carried out by some persons and organizational groups and are the cost centers which need supervision. Therefore, the consolidated task and activity list from the marketing and operating plans can be assigned to individuals and organizational units to create a schedule of inputs and output for each organizational subunit in your firm. The value of such a task list and time schedule by organizational unit is that it enables you to supervise and monitor the operating plan to see that it is performed on time.

The additional benefit is that it provides clear task assignments to individuals and clear organizational structure to the firm.

Cost and Budgets

Given the time schedules and assignments by organizational unit, developed above, you can next cost out the time schedule by attributing the labor costs, machine costs, and overhead costs per hour or per unit to the assigned tasks and organizations. This enables you to break down the overall budget by cost center and to allocate detailed working budgets to individuals or organizational units. The assignment of costs to cost centers is what gives you managerial control over performance, because you can check on how much is being manufactured, and when, where, and at what cost the product is being manufactured.

Financial Statements

Financial statements are the fallout from the business plan outlined above. The revenue projection for the income statement comes from the marketing plan's sales volume and pricing. The operating and overhead expenses come from the operating budget. The difference is the net profit projection.

Given the income statement, derived from the operating business plan, a balance sheet can be projected by showing the net effect of the changes in the income statement on the present balance sheet. Similarly, cash flow and fund statements can be prepared by the methods described in Chapters 1 to 3. In short, the financial statements are straightforward derivations from the business plan. The financial statement projections are as realistic as the marketing plan and the operating budgets.

Risk-Return Options and Trade-Offs

Seen in the terms described above, the business plan is basically a simple and straightforward exercise. That is, business planning is easy in concept, yet it is a heavy chore to do. The business plan is a chore mainly because it requires a very detailed description of what you expect to do; in this sense, the business plan is hard, time-consuming work for the manager. Still, managers feel that this hard, time-consuming work of making a business plan is worth doing because: (1) it communicates tasks, assignments, and goals to the personnel in the organization and (2) it provides the manager with instruments (time schedules and budgets) with which to control the performance of the organization.

However, managers must also be wary of what happens during the somewhat mechanical process of laying out tasks, time schedules, assignments, and costs. That is, a lot of assumptions become buried in the business plan. Unless the manager is alert to the risks and uncertainties buried in the schedule and budget detail, the business plan can become an instrument of delusion. It can make everything look as if it is all right, when it really is not.

Two main uncertainties haunt the business plan. The first is whether the sales estimate is right; that is, do consumers perceive, accept and buy the products as the business plan expects them to do? The second great uncertainty is whether the costs are realistic. They may seem to be at first, but then they may go awry due to inflation, delays in receiving materials or equipment, or rising labor costs. Even when workers are trying their best and when wage rates are stable, labor costs may get out of hand due to reduced volume which raises the labor costs per unit, lowers labor productivity (as seen in Table 9-1), or slows down learning rates. Workers frequently need to learn new tasks, and the rate at which they learn may be slower than that which the engineers project as a learning curve when they set up the job. That is, jobs may really be harder to do than the production engineers think, and workers may learn more slowly than expected, both of which raise labor costs.

All of these uncertainties are part of the normal risks of business, and these affect the profits and rate of return. The manager can protect himself, to some extent, against the normal risks of business by providing for some alternatives, options, or trade-offs in the business plan. Let us take each of the main risks and examine how an alternative might be built into the business plan.

1. The marketing risk that the customers may not buy the product in the expected volume can be incorporated into the business plan by: (1) a lower sales forecast as an alternative or (2) a contingency marketing plan that has heavier promotion effort and expense. Both of these alternatives will decrease the profit projection in the business plan, but at least they will provide the manager with a range as to what his risk and return are likely to be.

2. The risk of inflation cannot really be avoided except by raising selling prices as fast as costs increase; the rapid increase in selling prices may affect the competitive position of the firm or reduce total demand by consumers. The alternative ways to incorporate the inflation risk in the business plan are to show: (1) an alternate, higher operating budget at higher costs, or (2) the impact of rapidly rising selling prices and reduced sales volume on revenue. Both of these will have an adverse effect on profit projections, but again they show the range of risk and return which may be encountered.

3. The risk of delays in material or equipment deliveries to you may be partly compensated by having alternative supply sources and purchasing contracts which provide for penalties or cancellation in the event of delays. If you have such arrangements against unfavorable contingencies, you should make them specific in the business plan so that your operating people will be alert to exercise the options and so that your financiers will realize that you have hedged the risk.

4. The risk of rising labor costs can be incorporated into a business plan by several means. One is simply to show the higher labor costs as an alternative with lower profits. A second is to expect pro-

duction engineers to develop alternative learning curves and training methods for bringing workers' skills up to standard on new jobs, which has the wholesome effect of making engineers try out their training techniques ahead of time so that they do work. A third alternative is to plan for the purchase of backup or supplemental equipment—like templates, materials-handling equipment, or automated controls—for those tasks which are likely to be so precise or complex for humans as to cause learning difficulties. The first and third of these alternatives are likely to show higher costs and lower profits; the second would not necessarily affect the financial returns except by a slight increase in engineering time.

For the most part, then, the uncertainties buried in the assumptions of a business plan can be exhumed and dealt with by alternatives, which generally affect cost, revenue, or return. However, the value of this exercise of examining the risk-return trade-offs is: (1) to make the plan more realistic in the first place and (2) to provide the manager with a measure of the range of return which he is risking and the trade-offs in cost which must be made to reduce the risks.

SUMMARY

The business plan is an essential ingredient, indeed the foundation, of the financial plan with which an entrepreneur needs to raise funds from external sources. The business plan also provides the manager with a basic control document by which to monitor the performance of an organization and each cost center. Moreover, by making explicit the risks and their alternative remedies, the manager gains a clearer idea of the trade-offs and contingencies he faces; this makes him more realistic.

The main elements of a business plan are:

1. An analysis of the economic and competitive environment.
2. A projection of sales and profit goals for the firm by products.
3. A market plan which analyzes the competitive strength of the firm and lays out the implementation tasks to sell its products.
4. A production plan that identifies all the input, materials, labor, costs, time schedules, and budget to produce the required sales volume.

5. The design of work and tasks to be done, along with their schedules by organizational units.
6. A set of detailed budgets by cost centers, based upon the time and work schedules.
7. A set of financial statements, including the income statement, balance sheet, cash flow, and fund statements, which are derived from the operating plan and budgets.
8. A listing of the uncertainties which are implicit in the business plan, alternatives to deal with them (these provide a measure of the risk-to-return relationship), and the trade-offs that are required to keep the business plan on course.

The business plan may seem to some managers to be a lot of work to document information which is already in his own head. Still, there are reasons for creating a business plan. One is to transfer the knowledge from the manager's head to the worker's head. The second is to convince financial sources that you know what you are doing so that you can raise money. The third it to convince yourself that you know what you are doing so that you can survive the risks you are taking.

REFERENCES

1. For further details, see SBA Management Aid Nos. 218 (*Business Plan for Small Manufacturers*), 150 (*Business Plan for Retailers*), and 153 (*Business Plan for Small Service Firms*).
2. For a more detailed examination of your marketing plan, see SBA Marketing Aid No. 156, *Marketing Checklist*.

10

Measures of Management Capacity

In the last chapter, we learned how to develop a business plan that organizes work and people. Previously we covered how to survive financially, control cash flow and the flow of funds, make market-product plans, measure costs and assets, and develop financial and business plans—all of these are the very essence of operating a business. Once these essentials have been mastered, presumably you know all one needs to know to run a business, right? Well, not quite. You also need to know how to manage yourself, and perhaps that is the hardest problem of all.

Human beings, even very capable and successful ones, have several limitations as managers; these are: (1) difficulty in using their own time effectively, (2) an inclination to know what has been learned rather than what needs to be learned, and (3) the inherent limits of the human mind as an information processor. In the following discussion, we will examine first how these human frailties show up as management problems. Then we will examine what can be done about them. The discussion will deal with the following topics:

1. Good management and pitfalls of failure.
2. The failure syndrome.
3. Growing with the job.
4. Problems of flexibility.
5. Measures of executive use of time.
6. Measures of information flows in an organization.
7. Size of organization in relation to executive capacity.

8. Delegation and building a professional management team.
9. Management succession.

Good Management and Pitfalls of Failure

The Royal Bank of Canada has listed what it considers to be good management for independent business.[1] They list the main keys to small business survival as:

1. Acquiring a business background.
2. Planning carefully.
3. Managing money skillfully.
4. Maintaining complete and accurate records.
5. Marketing intelligently.
6. Organizing time.
7. Handling personnel.
8. Growing with the job.

We have already covered the first six of these fairly thoroughly in previous chapters. How one handles personnel, besides being sensitive to their feelings, depends greatly upon how the manager uses his own time and how much he delegates. So the most vital factor of all is how well the manager grows with his own job. What happens when the manager fails to grow with his job? Perhaps that can best be examined by looking at what pitfalls emerge when the manager does not grow, learn, or adapt as fast as the business changes.

The Bank of America has listed what it considers to be the pitfalls of management, which are almost exactly the opposite of the good management characteristics listed by the Royal Bank of Canada.[2] The Bank of America lists these pitfalls:

1. Downgrading the need for experience.
2. Sloppy recordkeeping.
3. Reckless money management.
4. Failure to plan.
5. Misuse of time.
6. Inattention to marketing.
7. Ignoring the human factor.
8. Failure to assume the proper role.

The failure to assume the proper role means not growing with your job. The job of the small business manager changes as the business grows. In Stage One, he is the operator involved in technical product specifications—raising money, dealing commercially, accounting, and supervising employees on a person-to-person basis. That is a demanding role which takes great skill and dedication, and it is perhaps among the more creative and satisfying roles for the entrepreneur who starts the business—so satisfying that it is hard to give up. However, when the enterprise grows beyond about 50 employees, the character of the business changes dramatically: it becomes an organization. Then the role of the owner has to change to Stage Two, that of the manager. His concerns become less technical and supervisory, rather he must pay attention to organizing, staffing, directing, planning, coordinating, and controlling. That is, his role has changed from operating the business himself to making it run through other people—a whole new set of skills for the small businessman. Eventually, when the enterprise prospers and achieves stability with a large organization of perhaps 500 to 1,000 employees or more, the businessman's role changes again to Stage Three, the executive. Now he no longer directs the organization and staff so much himself. The executive's concerns are innovation, communication, motivation, strategic planning, and leadership. He is leading the leaders.

These several stages of management have led Professor Jean Robidoux of the University of Sherbrooke to identify five crises of management; these crises correspond closely with the businessman's role listed by the Bank of America.[3] The five management crises are:

1. The starting crisis.
2. The cash crisis.
3. The delegation crisis.
4. The leadership crisis.
5. The succession crisis.

We have dealt with the starting and cash crises in the first five chapters.

The delegation crisis occurs when the small businessman moves from his role in Stage One as an Operator to Stage Two as a Manager. The leadership crisis occurs when he moves from Stage Two as

a Manager to Stage Three as an Executive. The succession crisis occurs when the executive dies or retires without preparing for the continued leadership of the organization. Each of these five crises are
common failure points in an enterprise.

The Failure Syndrome

The crises of an organization are reflected in the personal characteristics of the small business manager. That is, the organizational
crises are mirror images of his strengths and weaknesses, his ability
or inability to grow with the job.

Larson and Clute have examined the financial records and experience of over 350 companies to identify the personal characteristics
which typify the failure syndrome.[4] These personal characteristics
are:

1. An exaggerated opinion of his own business competence based
   upon his knowledge and experience.
2. Has limited formal education and relies on the "school of hard
   knocks."
3. Inflexible, resists change, and lacks innovative insight.
4. Relies on his own personal taste as standards to follow.
5. Bases his decisions upon intuition and subjective judgments.
6. Oriented towards the past rather than the future.
7. Reads little literature associated with business.
8. Resists advice from qualified sources, but accepts it from the
   less qualified.

Perhaps these personal characteristics present the extreme of a
rigid small businessman making up the failure syndrome, but these
traits are understandable. They are, put positively, the exact characteristics that a person has to have to start a small business. He needs
a strong sense of his own ability, a reliance upon experience, a reso-
luteness to go ahead regardless of dissuasion or change, a reliance
upon his own judgment and taste despite skepticism of financiers,
and a stress on action versus thought or reading. Is it any wonder
that the entrepreneur continues to rely on these traits which made
him successful in starting a small business after he becomes established? The characteristics which made him an operator in Stage One

are those which he knows, and they are tested by experience and found successful.

Of course, he has to change. We know that by having observed the stages of growth of a business, its crises, and the characteristics of the failure syndrome. This brings us back to one basic difficulty with the human psyche: a person is slow to recognize change and to learn new ways when the old ones have worked. Human beings are slow learners, while business changes rapidly. It is tough to grow with the job.

Growing With the Job

What can an individual do about his or her own tendency to learn slowly and not recognize change?

The most important step is for the individual to recognize that slow learning and resistance to change are human characteristics and to guard against them. Remain self-motivated and ask at the end of the day "What's new?" or "How can we do something differently?" or "Where can I get some new ideas?" Being on the lookout for new ideas and changes is half the battle.

There are also some fairly mechanical methods for seeking to learn new ideas:

1. Ask employees and associates for suggestions or ask about what problems they have been having.
2. Remain marketing-oriented and ask customers what they want, in person or by market research.
3. Read trade and business journals that discuss the changing economic and competitive climate.
4. Follow the technology of your field to watch for new developments.
5. Attend seminars and conferences put on by your trade association or by management organizations. (The American Management Association runs a wide number of management development workshops.)
6. Go to night classes to fill in skills in any area where you have little experience or training.
7. Ask your family and friends to give you suggestions—they

know you, know your strengths and weaknesses, love you, and will try to help.

8. Seek the best professional advice you can find, especially the sharpest challengers in your own company rather than the yes-men who work for you.

All of these ordinary techniques will help you grow because they point out change to you and suggest ideas for coping. In short, you have to *want* to learn to grow with the job.

Another way to grow with your job is to periodically write—two or three times per year—a job description of what you do. Put down on paper how you spend your time, what decisions you made, problems you dealt with, changes in the competition, changes in organization size. Show this job description to your associates, family and friends. Ask them whether they think you are dealing with all the problems, or spending your time on the right things. Then, most importantly, compare your job descriptions over time with the three stages of management to see whether your role is primarily in Stage One, technical and commercial affairs of an operator, in Stage Two, the organization and control of a manager, or Stage Three, the motivation and strategic planning of a leading executive.

Also keep in mind certain checkpoints in the size of your organization. Under 50 employees you are an operator spending most of your time on the technical supervision of employees personally. From 50 to 500 employees you are mainly a manager coordinating and controlling other managers. Over 500 employees you are mainly an executive motivating and leading other executives.

In short, watch your role and adapt to the role appropriate to your organizational size and needs. All of these signals and signposts will help you grow with your job, overcome the slow-learning trait, and develop your skills and managerial capacity as the job expands.

Problems of Flexibility

If there is any one characteristic which typifies the changing role of the executive, it is flexibility. Flexibility means to learn and to adapt to change. Indeed, almost all of the traits in the failure syndrome come down to one: inflexibility. Therefore, you can also learn flexibility on the job by watching what decisions need to be made and knowing what the inflexible choice would be. Let us consider some problems of inflexibility as they show up in executive decisions. Inflexible decisions frequently take the form of:

1. Sticking with cost-based pricing when your market share is falling.
2. Keeping your existing products when competitors have come out with improvements.
3. Staying with your present equipment when more cost-efficient methods are available.
4. Using policies and procedures which employees question.
5. Hiring less competent employees than yourself, to make yourself comfortable, when more competent people are available.
6. Shunting aside staff people who criticize your decisions.
7. Extrapolating your existing technologies without making any high-risk attempts at a breakthrough.

All of the above decisions perpetuate the *status quo* which works only as long as competition and the outside world are not changing. If change occurs, these are inflexible decisions which will put you behind the times, competition, consumer needs, and your employees' interests.

How common are these inflexible dicisions? A study by Jackson et al.[5] showed that 86% of small business firms adhered rigidly to cost-based pricing without the use of break-even analysis, marginal pricing, or any demand-based pricing. Moreover, 88% of the firms used advertising without clear recognition as to which forms were most effective.

If these findings are typical, then the conclusion would be that the vast majority of small business firms are prone toward inflexibility, or merely perpetuating what they have been doing. This is a surprising finding, given the other kinds of findings reported elsewhere, such as that of the National Science Foundation that small business has a higher innovation rate than large business. Or could it be only a few small businesses are innovative? These puzzling questions can only be answered by more research.

Still, this much is clear: the only real advantages small business has over its larger competitors is flexibility. The larger firms have more resources, more technology, more people, more investment, more capacity—more of most everything except flexibility. Large firms are even more prone to keep doing the same old thing than small ones. That is where the small firm can beat them, by being more flexible.

The Wall Street Journal reported a number of instances in which small firms gained advantages over larger firms by being more flexible in coping with bad times.[6] The examples were: (1) a small apparel company buying distressed textile inventory and converting it into saleable products within two weeks, (2) a fastener company buying up nuts and bolts at low prices and funneling them into new markets, (3) a small firm cutting costs and making productivity gains from employees' suggestions, and (4) a restaurant hunting down low supply prices and passing them through to customers to beat inflation in the menu. Sure, it takes a little effort and thinking, but that is what small businesses are best at doing, and it is their main advantage over larger competitors.

Another way to stimulate innovation is to organize the generation of new ideas by having R&D teams in the firm, and by then submitting the ideas to evaluation. You can do your own evaluation of innovations or get advise and assistance. The Innovation Center at the University of Oregon, Eugene, for example will assist in such evaluations. Gerald G. Udell and Kenneth G. Baker from the Center have developed an evaluation instrument for rating new ideas which contains the following general items:

Legality	Promotion
Safety	Appearance
Environmental impact	Price
Societal impact	Protection
Potential market	Payback period
Product life cycle	Profitability
Usage learning	Marketing research
Product visibility	Research and development
Service	Stability of demand
Durability	Consumer compatibility
New competition	Product interdependence
Functional feasibility	Distribution
Production feasibility	Perceived function
Development status	Existing competition
Investment cost	Potential sales
Trend of Demand	Product line potential
Need	

The evaluation consists of rating new ideas on a positive to negative scale for each item. To obtain objectivity, of course, several persons should evaluate each idea as objectively as possible, which you and your staff may be able to do yourself or with the aid of outside help.

Measures of Manager Use of Time

If a manager cannot use his own time well, he is not likely to make good use of anyone else's time. The efficient use of time requires a sense of priority as to what is most urgent and necessary. If the manager does not have that sense of priority for himself, he will have a hard time communicating priorities to his employees because they learn from his example and from his requests.

The efficient use of time, of course, is the principal determinant of cost, because a high proportion of most business expenditures are for labor and labor time. Therefore, a poor use of time also means poor cost control and poor productivity.

The best way for a manager to measure his own use of time is to keep a log occasionally, at least several times a year, to see how and on what he uses his own time. Then he can examine the log to see whether he has indeed used his time toward the goals which he thinks have highest priority. Chances are, most executives will find themselves diverted to minor and miscellaneous chores by questions from employees, calls from customers, or complaints from any sources. These diversions may be unavoidable to some extent if the executive wants to be responsive to other people, but if they get beyond a minimal amount of time (say 10 to 15%) the executive has lost control of managing his own time. He must then find ways to delegate some of these diversions so he can concentrate on running the company. After all, other people can handle complaints, but no one else can run the company.

In keeping a log and evaluating your own use of time, you would probably keep track of specific tasks which are part of your role as a manager in your industry; these may be similar to the kinds of activities listed in the task list for the marketing plan in Chapter 5 or the business plan in Chapter 9. That is, the tasks would be unique to you because the techniques of your job and company are specific to the field or industry in which you work.

However, another way to look at a manager's job is to emphasize the common elements of management which any executive must do. That is, every manager is engaged in dealing with people, and to deal with people, one must communicate with them. So the common element of all managerial jobs is their communication mode as the executive interacts with people in goal-setting, marketing, coordinating or controlling. The measurement of communication elements is technical, and readers not interested in technicalities may wish to skip forward to page 211.

In two separate studies, Choran and Mintzberg collected information through diaries, surveys and desk observation on how managers use their time.[7] Choran studied small companies and Mintzberg somewhat larger or medium-sized ones. In small companies, managers spent 96% of their time on internal communications (35% written and 61% oral) with the remaining 4% on external oral communications. In medium-sized companies, managers spent 71% of their time on internal communications (22% written and 49% oral) and 29% on external oral communications. The number of activities or transactions handled by a manager in the small company per day, at 77, was higher then for larger companies, at 22 activities.

From these percentages of time spent by manager's communication role, we may estimate data rates as to how much information the executives are handling. The assumptions for making these estimates are shown below:

1. An 8-hour work day contains 28,800 seconds.
2. The oral or speaking communication rate, from air traffic control studies and New York Stock Exchange data studies by Miller[8] is 2 to 9 bits of information per second (assume an average of 5 bits).
3. Reading rates are 14 to 25 bits per second (assume average of 15 bits). (Miller.[8])
4. Bits of information are absorbed cognitively as "chunks" of about 5 words with 3 syllables each, or 15 bits. (Simon.[9])
5. The learning time of a receiver is proportionate to the number of chunks. (Simon.[9])
6. The fixation time of information in the memory of a human being is 5 to 7 seconds per chunk (assume an average of 7 seconds). (Brener.[10])

Then, the data rates can be estimated by multiplying the amount of time by the bits of information in each communication process. For example, the reading rate of small organization executives is estimated at 151,200 bits per day (i.e., 35% x 28,800 seconds x 15 bits per second). (See Table 10-1 below.)

Table 10-1. Estimated Data Rates for Receiving and Fixation of Information by Executives.

	SMALL ORGANIZATIONS	MEDIUM-SIZED ORGANIZATIONS
1. Written communications	151,200 bits	95,040 bits
2. Oral communications	87,840 bits	70,560 bits
3. Total information received	239,040 bits	165,600 bits
4. Data received per day in chunks (line 3 ÷ 15)	15,600 chunks	11,000 chunks
5. Fixation rate @ 7 sec per chunk	3,900 chunks	3,000 chunks
6. Potential overload (line 4 − line 5)	11,700 chunks	8,000 chunks

This simple illustration shows that the receiving rate for information is much faster than its learning or fixation rate, and therefore, a high potential for the overload of information is an ever-present possibility.

The main difference between the manager of the small company and the slightly larger ones or medium-size is that the small company manager spends more of his time operationally dealing with the internal organization, and he handles more transactions and information. That is what one would expect, of course, from the Stage One phase of a business when the head of the firm is an operator in direct contact and supervision of employees. In the medium-size firm, the manager has more communication externally, more conferences, and more ceremonial duties. Again, that is what one would expect as a manager in Stage Two works through other people and managers to integrate, coordinate and control. Therefore, the time spent on various communicative tasks will vary as the role of the manager changes with the size of the firm; his communication skills must grow with the firm. The manager's ability to grow is measurable by his growth in communication skills.

Measures of Information Flow in an Organization

The fact that managers are essentially communicators enables us to view their work in terms of the information flow which they handle, because communication is basically receiving and transmitting information. The information-handling capacity of a manager is determined by the characteristics of the human mind: the mind has enormous data storage capacity but has a slow data-processing ability. Compared to the largest and fastest computers currently in use, the human mind has about three to four times the storage capacity and perhaps one ten-thousandth of the data-processing speed. The fact that the human mind is a slow information processor limits the amount of information that a manager can handle. As the amount of information increases with larger organizational size, the manager becomes a gate or barrier. Information backs up, or forms a waiting line until the channel to the manager is cleared. Alternatively, more managers can be put on the line to increase the number of channels, but this also adds to the organizational complexity.

Human beings handle information by several processing modes described by Miller as filtering, abstracting, chunking, queuing, omission, error, and escape.[8] *Filtering* means to remove low priority or less significant information inputs; *abstracting,* to consolidate significant information; *chunking,* to put together key concepts; *multiple channel,* to duplicate information channels in organizations; *queuing,* to let a backlog of data pile up; *omission,* to let data go unused; *error,* to misunderstand data; and *escape,* to retreat by abandoning or limiting the information flow.

Miller's air traffic control study indicates that when information overloads appear, they are dealt with approximately in the the order given above, i.e., filtering, abstracting, chunking, multiple channels, queuing, omission, error, and escape. Moreover, filtering was shown in the air traffic study to reduce the data load by about 30%. Using the human mind as a data processor, then, the executives faced with the information overloads in Table 10–1 could eliminate them by using two filters, and one abstraction with chunking. That is, the executive could mentally scan the data in two near-simultaneous passes to eliminate low-informational content inputs by one-third each time, and then abstract (consolidating by one-third) and chunking (key words) the balance into more significant information. And indeed, this is what executives appear to do; they look for "exceptions" or significant data which deviate from some expected norm.

Let us assume, then, that by mental filtering and abstracting, executives in small organizations are capable of handling 15,900 chunks of information in 96% of their working day, and executives of medium-size organizations can process 11,000 chunks of information in the 71% of the day devoted to internal management. The next question is: What degree of control over how many people are they capable of supervising with their respective data-handling rates? This is a vital question, because anything beyond the capacity means that the overload data will be subject to multiple channels, queuing, omission, error, or escape. If we can find that portion of overload that is subject to omission, error, and escape, we will have a measure of the nonresponsiveness of the system. Conversely, the information-handling capacity of the organization will determine its responsiveness.

Next, we examine the degree of control over how many people an executive is capable of handling with his respective data processing capacity. This is estimated in Table 10-2.

Table 10-2. Control Rate of Channel Capacity of Executive Supervision.

	SMALL ORGANIZATIONS	MEDIUM-SIZED ORGANIZATIONS
1. Information-processing capacity	15,900 chunks	11,000 chunks
2. Supervisory task control (line 1 − 5)	3,180 person/events	2,200 person/events
3. Contacts per day	77	22
4. Person/events per contact to be cognized (line 2 − line 3)	40	100
5. Learnings fixation rate (line 4 x 7 sec)	280 seconds	700 seconds
6. Executive capacity for person/event surveillance (internal time ÷ 5)	99	29
7. Channel capacity for control	1	3.4
8. Control rate	100%	30%

The first line in Table 10-2 shows the data-handling capacity of the executive by organizational size. The second line assumes that every task which an executive seeks to know or control is characterized by data on who, what, how, where, and when—five chunks of information describing the person/event nature of the task. Therefore, an executive of a small organization is capable of knowing and controlling 3,180 person/event tasks per day (15,900 chunks divided by 5). He does this in 77 contacts per day, requiring that he absorb cognitively 40 person/event tasks per contact, which will take him 280 seconds each on the average. Since he has 27,648 seconds per day to devote to this learning and fixation process (96% x 28,800 seconds), he is capable of learning about the tasks and events of 99 persons per day (27,648 ÷ 280). That is to say, the executive of a small organization has a channel capacity to control an organization of about 100 persons and still have relatively adequate knowledge, or 100% control, of what is happening.

The executive of a medium-size organization, in contrast, has a surveillance capacity over 29 persons because of the lesser number of contacts, reading time, and total time he can devote to internal management. This means that medium-size scale organizations would need 3.4 executives (channel capacity) per 100 employees, compared to only one for a small organization. Or conversely, with one executive per 100 employees in a large organization, he has 30% control of the information about what is happening, which implies that 70% of the data is subject to queuing, omission, error, or escape. The small organization in this example is capable of a 100% response rate to individuals in terms of the quality and stability of the system, while the larger organization is capable of a 30% response rate.

Size of an Organization in Relation to Executive Capacity

Given two organizations, small and medium, we see that the informational processing capacities differ, and this may in turn account for differential response rates and quality of service performance of the organization to individual customers. Can this hypothesis be generalized to organizations of any size? Unfortunately, field research and empirical data of information-processing capacity are not available by size of organization. Yet this is a crucial question, because we would like to know what effect organizational size has upon responsiveness and quality of performance in the eyes of users.

Given two points on a curve, we can estimate the responsiveness throughout the range if we know the shape of the response curve. Let us assume that the shape of the response curve is similar to the earnings upon assets of business corporations given in Chapter 1. The rationale is that earnings upon assets represent the prime objective of businessmen. Therefore, economic organizations may be measured as capable of performance on a curve represented by their earnings on assets.

We saw in Chapter 1 that, for all corporations, earnings on assets decline logarithmically for every industry group and every size class. The earnings data can be fitted with a logarithmic regression for the average of all corporations, at the 1% confidence level, by the formula: earnings per dollar of assets $= .47 - .13 \log s$, where s is organizational size. Given that earnings on assets are assumed to be equivalent to control (for that is what executives are attempting to do), then we can use simultaneous equations to solve for the size of organizations in our example of small and medium organizations. The small organization, we have seen, is represented by an information capacity to manage an organization of 100 persons with adequate knowledge of events to establish 100% control and earn 22% on assets before taxes. Then, given $e = .47 - .14 \log s$, what would the larger organization be in terms of size?

Assume that: s = size in number of employees
                d = data handling capacity of executive in chunks
                c = percent control of data, or earnings on assets
                e = earnings on assets
   a and b = proportioning constants in regression equation
                   fitted to size and data handling information.

Then: $a \log s + b \log d = 100$ (or 22% on assets) and

$\underline{a \log s + b \log d = 30}$

yields: $50.58 \log s + 56.25 \log d = c$

finally (from $3 = .47 - .13 \log s$), the larger organization has 1,260 employees and earns a 7% return on assets.

Now we are in a position to hypothesize the relationship of the informational load by organizational size. This is accomplished by solving for the degree of control through the equation $e = .47 - .13 \log s$ (which represents the shape of the response curve), and then solving for the amount of data in the equation $50.58 \log d - 56.25 \log s = c$. The results are shown in Table 10-3 where the data load is given in events (i.e., chunks divided by 5).

Table 10-3. Data Load and Index of Control by Organizational Size.

ORGANIZATION SIZE (s)	RETURN ON ASSETS	INDEX OF KNOWLEDGE OR CONTROL (c) *	EXECUTIVE INFORMATION LOAD IN EVENTS (d)
1	47%	224	5,360
10	34	162	2,080
100	21	100	3,100
1,000	9	38	2,360
10,000	n.a.**	n.a.**	5,880
100,000	n.a.**	n.a.**	71,800
1,000,000	n.a.**	n.a.**	962,000
2,000,000	n.a.**	n.a.**	1,994,000

* Index of control assumes that adequate control, at an index of 100, is achieved with 100 employees, (see Table 10-2) and that the other control indices are determined by $e = .47 - .13 \log s$.

** Data for organizations over 1,000 are not available, because the data provided by Secretary Simon on pretax earnings on assets did not extend to large size groups of over 1,500, and the earnings regression of $e = .47 - .13 \log s$ reduces pretax earnings and hence control to negligible levels. While this assumption may seem doubtful in view of observable earnings by large corporations, the observable earnings records are post-tax, and the effective tax rate for large corporations decreases with size, as indicated below. Hence, the apparent earnings of large organizations may in fact be tax subsidies rather than comparable earnings on assets.

ORGANIZATIONAL SIZE (ASSETS OF MANUFACTURING CORPORATIONS)	EFFECTIVE FEDERAL INCOME TAX RATES
Under $50,000,000	45%
$50,000,000–$100,000,000	40
$100,000,000–$250,000,000	42
$250,000,000–$1,000,000,000	37
Over $1,000,000,000	29
All manufacturing (average)	41%

Source: FTC Financial Report, 4th Quarter, 1979.

Table 10-3 indicates that organizations are able to manage information loads more or less adequately up to about 10,000 employees in size by adding channel capacity (i.e., new organizational divisions and executives), filtering, abstracting, and chunking information. At 1,000 employees, it is third-hand and has gone through three organizational layers or filters, assuming spans of control of six or eight persons per layer. At 10,000, the information to the executive has gone through four or five organizational layers. At larger organizational sizes, the information has gone through six or more organizational filters and may be distorted by organizational aspirations and maintenance; this information may not accurately represent the original facts.

Table 10-4 estimates the probabilities of accuracy and error in executive decisions based upon the informational overloads. The information overload, or random events, is figured as random events, $r = d - (c/224 \times d)$. That is to say, the information overload is the excess of the information load over that which can be used, as measured by knowledge or control of a one-man organization which is presumably complete.

Table 10-4. Probability of Management Error and Information Overloads.

ORGANIZATION SIZE	PROBABILITY OF MANAGEMENT		INFORMATION OVERLOAD OR RANDOM EVENTS (r)
	CORRECTNESS	ERROR	
1	100%	0%	0
10	86	14	1,100 events
100	73	27	1,700
1,000	59	41	1,900
10,000	51	49	5,800
100,000	50	50	72,000
1,000,000	50	50	982,000
2,000,000	50	50	1,994,000

The probability that management decisions are correct or in error in Table 10-4 is derived from Table 10-3, as is the measure of information overloads. When executive capacity experiences overloads, information is omitted or unused with the result that random events affect the organization; in this random state of information, the executive has a 50-50 chance of being right or wrong.

Perhaps the 50% probability of error in large organizations may seem extreme, but Chester Barnard reportedly estimated that executives were right 54% of the time. Another practical test of these probabilities may be provided by the Scott Bader Commonwealth, a showcase example of responsive corporate self-governance, where the constitution of the Scott Bader Commonwealth required that the total organizational size be kept within the scope of what can be comprehended by a human mind, which is stipulated as about 350 employees. In the model given above, the Scott Bader Commonwealth could be expected to earn about 14% on assets, achieve

70% informational control, and have a 65% probability of correct management decisions.[11]

The implications of Table 10–4 are that management has the capacity to contain information overloads within bounds, by multiple channels, filtering, abstracting, and chunking up to organizational sizes of a few thousand employees. Over 10,000 employees in organizational size, the information overloads increase geometrically with size to unmanageable proportions. Then the organization is subject to the impact of random events which are unknown to management, because the data inputs are omitted and unknown. That is, management of very large organizations escapes the information problem by defining the system so narrowly as to reduce the bounds of the data inputs, say, by confining itself to accounting data only, and ignoring market information on consumer needs. This form of escape from the information problem makes the large organization nonresponsive to consumer needs and reduces the quality of human service.

Moreover, the escape of management into nonresponsive decision criteria, or into a 50–50 guessing game, has the effect in the long run of system degeneration, or entropy. That is, the organization moves from a high-information energy state, to a low or random information state.

Delegation and Building a Professional Management Team

The previous section has shown that the information-processing requirements upon a manager, and the inherent limits of the human mind as a slow data processor, mean that the channels of communication must be multiplied (or, "multiplexed" in communications jargon) as organizational size expands. As a rough rule of thumb, an organization needs three to four supervisors and three managers for every 100 employees to handle the information load generated by the organization. Now we can tie these information processing workloads into the three stages of management discussed earlier from the Bank of America booklet on pitfalls of management.

This schematic of the hierarchy of management layers is, of course, approximate and illustrative. You may run an organization and make high profits for a time with less supervision, but you run the risk that large amounts of overload information are escaping

MANAGEMENT STAGE	ORGANIZATIONAL SIZE AND INFORMATION CAPACITY
Stage One—Operator	
Under 50 employees	One operating manager and 3 or 4 supervisors
51-100 employees	One operating manager, 2 assistant managers, and 6 supervisors
Stage Two—Manager	
100-500 employees	One manager, a second line of 2-8 managers, and 6-30 supervisors
501-1,000 employees	One manager, 2 tiers of 5-10 managers, and 30-60 supervisors
Stage Three—Executive	
Over 1,000 employees	One executive 3 tiers of managers (about 10-12 per tier), and 300 supervisors

you. Then in rapidly changing business conditions, you are caught uninformed and without the data to make decisions (i.e., a 50–50 guessing game decision). The illustration indicates that the layering of management increases with organizational size. Every added layer of management adds also a filter and impedance to communication, which means that it becomes harder and harder to put communications through the organization from top to bottom. The U.S. State Department and some comparably sized corporations have as many as eight tiers of management. The loss of information and impedance in these deeply layered organizations makes them almost impermeable to data transmission. The top management can only get a semblance or fraction of its message through to the working layers at the bottom, and the operating information from the bottom becomes filtered, abstracted, and distorted before it reaches the top. Communication in these deep hierarchical organizations becomes more symbolic than factual, with a great loss in performance and organizational effectiveness as the workers at the bottom lose effective communicative contact with the top.

In Stage One, particularly with under 50 employees, the operator-manager is in direct contact on a person-to-person basis with all employees and can receive information himself by direct observation of work (which is faster than verbal communication) on individual operations.

With over 50 employees, the operator has to rely more and more on supervisors for transmitted communication by word or writing, and the information transmission slows down.

In Stage Two, from 51 to 500 employees, the manager has to rely entirely upon oral and written word transmitted through one tier of supervisors and one layer of managers. The optimum size of an organization, from an information-processing viewpoint, is probably somewhere between 500 and 1200 employees (i.e., not more than two layers of management). Statistically, we have seen in the previous section that information overloads increase geometrically after this point. A more experimental basis for this observation is provided by the Scott Bader Commonwealth in England.

Whatever the optimum size of organizations may be to handle information loads, clearly the information workload exceeds that of one operating manager somewhere in the 50 to 100 employee range. At that point, the manager must seek to delegate (multiplex) and create a formal organization with a management layer. That is, the operator must build a management team. This transition is often hard for the operator-entrepreneur to realize, and even more difficult to implement. Hofer et al. have studied a number of cases of transition from a single entrepreneur to a professional management team, and they have raised the query of whether the transition is a "mission impossible."[12] The transition is possible, they say from their cases, if the transformation includes at least five of the seven following steps:

1. The enterpreneur must want to make the change strongly enough to make major changes in his own task behavior.
2. The day-to-day decision process of the organization must change, to include delegation and consultation in a formal process including other managers.
3. The two or three key tasks which are primarily responsible for the organization's success must be institutionalized, i.e., there must be a formal process and approval authority delegated over elements of strategic planning, coordination, and control.
4. Middle-level management must be developed.
5. The firm's strategy for growth must be reevaluated and modified when necessary.
6. The firm's organization structure and policies should be modified gradually over time to reflect the new delegations, authority, and roles of additional managers.
7. The firm must develop a professional board of directors.

The failure to implement any of these transition steps greatly reduces the probability that a professional management structure will be created.

Management Succession

The creation of a professional management team is a vital step in solving the problem of management succession. Yet, if the delegation of authority to a professional management group is traumatic for the owner-manager of a small firm, the problem of management succession is even more so. In planning for succession, the owner-manager is contemplating not just delegation of authority over some functions or decisions, rather he is considering the complete relinquishment of power, the reduction of his income, the dismantling of his status and prestige, and the giving up of his life-work for the blissful boredom of retirement. Not many owners can come to the succession decision gracefully; the consequences are evident in owners hanging on long beyond their ability to lead a growing enterprise. The problem of aging owners and aging businesses has been of particular concern in Britain, where a study by the Bolton Commission has shown that most of the declining small businesses were over 40 years old with aging owners, and that the growth businesses were young firms.[13]

The first principle of succession is that the owner must really want to transfer management authority, in spite of losses of power to himself, for the sake of maintaining the profits of the firm and thus the value of his estate. The selection of a successor is beset with many perils and is probably best done by gradual evaluation, rather than picking an heir-apparent or an outside candidate. The professional management team can be strengthened by the process of generating its own successor through these means:

1. Periodic performance appraisal of all executives by an objective group, such as the board of directors.
2. Special adjustments to strong candidates which increase their scope, experience, innovativeness, and authority.
3. Job rotation of responsibilities which makes comparative evaluation of executives possible.

4. Management by objective programs which encourage executives to specify and meet their own goals annually.

5. Personal inventories which assess the strengths and weaknesses of a candidate's training, experience, and personnel relations.

6. Position descriptions which specify the role and work of one executive in relation to others.

7. Management meetings where operating and strategic problems are addressed and solved, with the owner or board able to observe the contribution of various executives.

8. Management seminars and outside training conferences to broaden the exposure and skills of the management members.

9. Expanded delegations of authority, on a gradual basis, to those executives who have delivered the highest performance, which means organizational realignment in which the owner-manager gradually yields authority to others.

10. Finally, at some point, the owner-manager must step down and allow the successor, who has survived this screening process, to take the reins. Unsolicited advice and constant meddling, however well-intentioned by the owner, will hamper the chances for success. The successor has to be in charge to be responsible and accountable.

SUMMARY

The pitfalls of small business management are: sloppy recordkeeping, poor planning, reckless money management, and poor time management, inattention to marketing, experience, and human factors, and the failure to assume the proper role.

The owner of a small business must shift from the role of operator to manager to executive if he is to grow with the firm and the job.

The failure syndrome comes down to inflexibility in dealing with the pitfalls of management. Most of all, the owner-manager must look for new ideas to adopt from employees, his staff, and customers to meet a changing business environment.

Inflexibility shows up in continuing old practices, and hence the owner-manager must regularly reexamine and revise such key business factors as cost-basis pricing, competitive product changes, cost efficiency of equipment, hiring practices, employee competence, existing procedures and technologies. Most of all, the owner-manager needs to remain open to suggestion, or even criticism, especially by able subordinates.

The only advantage the small firm has over larger ones is flexibility, finding market niches which are unfilled, or being quick to spot new methods. This means that some procedure for evaluation of innovation is important to a growing company.

The executive's use of his own time is a barometer of the efficiency of time usage and labor costs of the firm.

The executive needs to be especially aware of the dangers of an information overload, and the methods to reduce information barriers and backlogs which cost the firm dearly in delayed decisions.

Rough measures of information loads and data-processing rates of human beings can provide rule-of-thumb guides of the executive and supervisory organization needed per 100 employees.

As a firm reaches the breaking point in information loads in relation to organizational size, the executive must be ready to add staff, delegate, reorganize, and develop a professional management group.

Management succession presents traumatic decisions about relinquishing power, status, income, and work satisfaction, but it is essential to maintain the growth of the firm and value of the estate. Succession may be approached gradually by winnowing out the professional management group to find the most capable successor.

REFERENCES

1. *Good Management* (guide no. 3), available from the Royal Bank of Canada.
2. *Small Business Reporter,* Vol. 11, No. 5.
3. Robidoux, J. 24th Annual Conference of the International Council for Small Business, July 23–26 1979, Quebec, Canada.
4. Larson, C.M. and Clute, R.C. "The Failure Syndrome." *American Journal of Small Business,* Vol. IV, No. 3, October, 1979, pp. 35–43.
5. Jackson, J.J., Hawes, D.K., and Hertel, F.M. "Pricing and Advertising Practices in Small Retail Business." *American Journal of Small Business,* Vol. IV, No. 2, October, 1979, pp. 22–34.
6. *The Wall Street Journal,* March 13, 1980, p. 18.
7. Mintzberg, H. *The Nature of Managerial Work.* 1973, Harper and Row, New York, pp. 23–127, esp. 105.
8. Miller, J.G. *Living Systems.* 1978, McGraw-Hill, New York, pp. 157–161.

9. Simon, H. "How Big is a Chunk?" *Science,* Vol. 183, February, 1974, pp. 482–488.
10. Brener, J. "An Experimental Investigation of Memory Span." *Journal of Experimental Psychology,* Vol. 26, 1940, p. 467.
11. Schumacher, E.F. *Small is Beautiful.* 1973, Harper and Row, New York, p. 276.
12. Hofer, C.W. and Charan, R. "The Transitions from Entrepreneurial to Professional Management." Unpublished paper, New York University.
13. Edmunds, S.W. "Small Business in Japan, Britain, and the United States." *Los Angeles Business and Economics,* Vol. 4, No. 4, Summer/Fall 1979, pp. 15–19.

11

Measures of Government Regulatory and Paperwork Costs

Small businessmen cite the excessive cost of government regulation and paperwork as among their most serious business problems. Over the four-year period 1974–1978, the National Federation of Independent Business (NFIB), in its *Quarterly Economic Report for Small Business,* found that only inflation and taxation were cited more frequently than government regulation and paperwork as small firms' single most important problem. About one-third of the firms which took in under $200,000 in gross receipts felt government regulatory burdens to be a "major" problem, compared to about 45% in the $200,000 to $1 million range, and over 50% for those above $1 million in receipts.

Moreover, the costs of regulation and paperwork are increasing rapidly. For example, the Center for the Study of American Business reports that budget expenditures for 56 major regulatory agencies have increased 500% from $1.2 billion in 1971 to $6 billion in 1980.[1] Moreover, the compliance costs to business and the public have a multiplier of about 20 times the administrative budget of the regulatory agencies. For example, in 1979 the administrative costs of regulation were $4.8 billion and the compliance costs were $97.9 billion, for a total regulatory cost of $102.7 billion. This amounts to about $400 per man, woman, and child in the United States. If regulatory costs were distributed equally across all of the business enterprises, the cost would average about $25,000 per business firm. The effect of these regulatory and paperwork costs will be considered in the following sections:

1. Impact of government regulation on the small firm.
2. Illustrative cases of regulatory impacts on small firms.
3. Hidden costs of regulation.
4. Cost of government paperwork.
5. Origin of reporting requirements by agency.
6. Alternative approaches for reducing government costs on small business.

IMPACT OF GOVERNMENT REGULATION ON SMALL FIRMS

Small business is generally required to comply with the same government regulations as large business. Because their resources and sales volume are more limited, however, small firms bear a relatively heavier cost of government regulation. This occurs because government regulations do not distinguish the impact among different size-classes of firms. The SBA has given this example of the proportionate impact among firms by class size. Assume that compliance with a government regulation requires a capital investment of $50,000 and annual operating expenses of $5,000. Then, the effect of these outlays for firms of varying class-sizes is shown in Table 11–1 below.

Table 11–1. Cost of Compliance by Firm Class Size.

		REGULATORY COST PER DOLLAR OF OUTPUT	
FIRM SIZE	SALES	YEAR 1	AFTER YEAR 1
10 employees	$ 500,000	$0.11	$0.01
100 employees	$ 5,000,000	0.011	0.0011
1,000 employees	$ 50,000,000	0.0011	0.00011
10,000 employees	$500,000,000	0.00011	0.000011

Clearly, the small firm of 10 employees is paying a much higher percentage cost of sales for both investment and operations than are large firms. For the large firms of over 1,000 employees, the burden is neglible in terms of its effects on costs, prices, or the ability to pass the cost along to the consumer. For the small firm of 10 employees, however, the capital cost especially is large as a percentage of sales or selling price; for the small firm to try to pass on a 10% price increase due to regulatory costs could cause it to become noncompetitive and fail.

The cost of regulation raises the cost curve at the low end of the class-size scale and places noncompetitive burdens upon the small firms. This has led Professor Kafoglis[1] to argue that the uniform application of regulatory costs increases the size of firms that can compete effectively. Their outputs will have to increase in order to reduce the cost per unit of regulation; that is, they will have to move to larger scale or fail. The market share of the dominant firm will increase, while that of the smaller firms will decrease, because the small firms' cost curve will shift upward and to the right more than will the large firms'. This increase in firm size results in loss of economic efficiency, says Kafoglis, because economic efficiency is attained when competition is greatest, and when the size of the firm is as small as efficient use of technology allows. As a result, goods are not produced at the lowest costs and the highest standard of living is not obtained.

James D. McKevitt, Washington Counsel for the NFIB, states that regulation poses three problems more for small firms than large firms: (1) discovering regulation, (2) understanding regulation, and (3) paying for regulation. McKevitt provides the following hypothetical example to illustrate these problems as the small businessman might encounter them. You are a small businessman with 25 employees. As such, you are not only general manager but function as sales manager, personnel manager, and so on. You typically have a 60-hour work week. In addition to operating your business, you are expected to identify all federal regulations affecting your business from the more than 70,000 pages of the Federal Register printed annually, as well as state and local regulations, read and understand them, recognize the means by which you can comply, and then absorb the cost, with the knowledge that your per unit cost is greater than for larger competitors.[1] It has been estimated that a full-time employee and a Washington representative are needed just to discover regulatory rules.

Among the federal agencies that directly regulate small business are the Internal Revenue Service (IRS), Federal Trade Commission (FTC), Occupational Safety and Health Administration (OSHA), Equal Employment Opportunity Commission (EEOC), Wage and Hour Division of the Department of Labor, Environmental Protection Agency (EPA), Consumer Product Safety Commission (CPSC), National Labor Relations Board (NLRB), Securities and Exchange

Commission (SECO), and Labor-Management Service Administration.

Considerable costs are associated with compliance to Federal regulation. At a compliance cost of $102.7 billion for federal regulation in 1980, or over $400 per each man, woman and child in the United States, Table 11-2 shows a breakdown of the percentage cost by regulatory area.

Table 11-2. Percentage Cost of Federal Regulation by Area.

REGULATORY AREA	COST (%)
Consumer safety and health	10
Job safety and working conditions	7
Energy and the environment	13
Financial regulation	2
Industry, specific	40
Paperwork	28
Total	100%

Source: Calculated from data from the Center for Study of American Business.[1]

Table 11-2 indicates that specific industry regulations are the most numerous. However, businessmen frequently cite the regulations of OSHA, EPA, Department of Labor, and Department of Energy as being the most onerous.

Regulation effects on productivity may also have an indirect impact on job creation. It often diverts private capital which could better be used in productive expansion that creates jobs. Similarly, businesses are unwilling to undertake new enterprises—sources of new jobs—in the face of the regulatory burden. Some businesses go so far as to engage in "defensive research" to stay out of trouble with the government by avoiding regulated fields.

ILLUSTRATIVE CASES OF REGULATORY IMPACTS UPON SMALL FIRMS

The files of the NFIB, U.S. Chamber of Commerce, and the SBA contain numerous cases of small firms which come to them for help in combating the impact of government regulation upon them. From these cases a number of illustrations have been selected to show the kinds of impacts which occur.

1. The *cost* of regulation is frequently very high relative to the firm's income. The Dawson Cabinet Company in Webb City, Missouri, which operated a small family-owned wood products manufacturing firm, fired an employee who would not work. As a result, the firm was hit with complaints from the EEOC, the NLRB, the Missouri Human Rights Commission, and the Department of Labor's Wage and Hour Division. The firm was cleared of all charges, after spending four years and $50,000 in legal and administrative fees to fight the case. The owner said that he had only one regret—not to have entered the battle with more even odds, odds which could be greatly improved if the agency paid for wrongful prosecutions out of its own budget. The family business was a winner in these federal charges, but also a loser financially, mentally and physically, and the regulatory system is no more accountable as a result of these wrongful prosecutions or suits.[2]

2. The regulatory *requirements* may be so onerous as to put a firm out of business. United Security, Inc. of Wilkes Barre, Pennsylvania bid on a contract to guard a General Services Administration (GSA) building. Liz Gobla, president of the firm, said that at the time she responded to the GSA telephone solicitation to bid she did not even know what GSA meant. The General Services Administration accepted the bid and then, under the contract, required the firm to pay the prevailing wage which applied to another part of the state. As a result, Liz Gobla went out of business and lost everything.

3. Regulation may be *contradictory* and leave the small firm in the middle between several federal agencies. A supermarket was faced with a requirement by OSHA that it install grated floors in its butcher departments to reduce the danger of employees slipping. At the same time, the U.S. Department of Agriculture prohibited grated floors because they are harder to clean and increase the chances of contamination.

4. Small business may *not be informed* of regulation and still be expected to comply. A small retailer, with a large inventory of 23-channel CB radios, was prohibited from selling the radios by a Federal Communications Commission (FCC) ruling, promulgated

a year and a half earlier in the Federal Register, which banned them. The NFIB made an inquiry into the FCC's notification methods and found they consisted of filing a notice in the Federal Register and placing its announcements in the hands of its own Public Information Office, where a few representatives of trade associations in Washington picked them up. When asked about the decision's impact upon small business, the FCC could provide no information.

5. Regulation may *interfere* with the operation and decision-making of a small firm so drastically as to make it inoperable. A small contractor, whose business was so small that he had no office or secretary, was ordered by the Department of Labor to comply with 43 hiring rules. Accused of not meeting a minimum quota for female employees (he hires two laborers), and unable to afford a lengthy court battle, he signed a conciliatory agreement, which forced him to hire additional employees to help him with voluminous paperwork required by the agreement. The small contractor now must maintain written EEOC policy, appoint an EEOC officer, print a company manual including EEOC policy, record encouragement of minority and female employee promotions, record annual reviews for promotional purposes, list current minority and female craft-worker recruitment sources, produce newsletters and annual reports including EEOC policy as well as company advertising with EEOC statements, show proof that company picnics and parties were posted and open to all employees, have separate toilets and changing facilities (even though he does not have an office), submit monthly employment utilization reports, and submit quarterly reports on minority and female employee applicants, job offers, new hires, terminations, and layoffs.[3]

6. Regulation presents *time-consuming intrusions* on small business. A U.S. Department of Agriculture study shows that milk processing plants are inspected about 24 times annually on average by the 20,000 state, county, local and municipal milk jurisdictions, even though the Public Health Service recommends only two inspections per year. In one state, each milk processing plant averaged 95 inspections per year, and one plant reported that it was inspected 47 times in one month.

7. Finally, when regulatory agencies do consider the impact of their activities on small business, the *adverse impacts make very*

little differences in the agencies' final decisions. This indifference appears in the case of proposed standards for air-lead exposure levels promulgated by OSHA. The impacts of these standards on the battery industry, the largest single user of lead in the U.S., were examined in a study by OSHA. There were 143 firms in the industry, 95 of which employed fewer than 20 people. OSHA estimated that the capital cost of compliance alone would average $25 million over a 10-year period. At these costs, the study concluded that over 100 of the small battery manufacturers would be forced to close. This would eliminate one-half of the productive capacity not operated by the five major battery companies. Under the new regulations the per-unit production cost would be greater for small firms than for large ones. Because of the large differential costs and the fact that the battery prices would rise to cover the unit costs of large firms, small firms would be forced to absorb the differential in costs. The severity of the impact would force them to close.

OSHA chose to promulgate even more stringent compliance standards than those used in the studies. Its comments were as follows:

> Even if the approximately 100 small manufacturers exit the market, the standard is none the less feasible for the battery industry. Closure of 100 small businesses would have a minimal impact on the competitive structure of the industry . . . Competition from the smaller firms has little or no effect on the price of batteries . . . Closing of 100 plants employing 10 persons each would mean the loss of 1,000 jobs . . . The impact on wages would be small.[4]

Clearly, little regard was shown for small business. Nor is this an isolated case. For example, 34% of the closings of small foundries between 1968 and 1975 are attributed to EPA emission regulations.[5]

HIDDEN COSTS OF REGULATION

In the first section we looked at some of the dollar costs of regulation upon small business, and in the second section we discussed the direct impacts upon individual firms. In addition, there are also indirect and hidden costs of regulation, which have been enumerated by Weidenbaum.[6]

1. Regulation adds to inflation by increasing costs. For example, the cumulative cost per vehicle in 1977 of environmental regulation was estimated by the Bureau of Labor Statistics to be $500, or close to 8 to 10% of the car cost at that time. For business generally, the paperwork costs and costs of executive time increase the overhead of business firms.

2. The delay in decisions caused by regulation can be a heavy drain upon budgets and managers' time. These delays can run into years and greatly alter a business firm's strategy or plans. The FTC averages five years to complete a restraint-of-trade case. The Federal Power Commission took 11 years to determine how to regulate natural gas. Power plant siting used to take six years and now takes 10 to 12 years, if it can be done at all. Residential development zoning used to take about 90 days and now takes about two years. The transcontinental pipeline to move North Slope crude from the West Coast to the Midwest was discontinued by SOHIO after about two years of regulatory compliance effort (and more in prospect) because, they said, the number of years (about 8) left over in which to amortize the investment cost was not long enough to pay for the project.

3. Another hidden cost is a reduction in innovation and the introduction of new products. Interstate Commerce Commission regulation delayed the introduction of unit trains by at least 5 years and delayed the full use of "Big John" grain cars by the Southern Railroad. Food and Drug Administration regulation has dragged out new product approvals so that the United States was the 30th nation to approve the anticancer drug adriamycin, the 51st to approve the antituberculosis drug rifampin, the 64th to approve the antiallergenic drug cromolyn, and the 106th to approve the antibacterial drug trimoxazole. The costs of seeking these approvals, of course, adds to the cost of the drugs to consumers.

4. A serious hidden cost of regulation is reduced capital formation and economic growth. Regulatory costs become, in effect, a claim or tax upon new capital investment. For example, the regulatory costs for pollution control and occupational safety alone are

about 6% of total capital spending, which means a substitution effect is diverting capital to regulative rather than productive use.

5. Regulation may unintentionally reduce employment. The 1966 increase in the minimum wage is estimated to have cost teenagers 300,000 jobs in 1972. Unemployment in construction labor is substantially above the national average, partly because federally required wage rates on government-supported projects are often higher than they are in the labor market where the work is done, so contractors pay higher wages for fewer jobs.

6. A little-known effect of regulation is the diversion of manager's time from productive effort to deal with regulatory requirements. We have already seen, in the previous chapter, that executives suffer from an information overload in handling their own internal operations. The addition of regulatory time-burdens upon managers has the effect of diminishing their attention to internal affairs, increasing the information overload, and degrading the quality of their business decisions.

COST OF GOVERNMENT PAPERWORK

Government has heavy reporting requirements, independently of and in addition to its regulatory requirements. The U.S. Office of Management and Budget has found that federal agencies have 4,400 reporting forms, in addition to the IRS's 13,200 forms.[7] The Office of Management and Budget estimates that business firms and individuals spend 143 million man-hours per year filling out the 4,400 federal agency forms (other than IRS). In addition, they spend another 507 million man-hours filling out IRS forms, for a total of 650 million man-hours of working for the government filling out reports (78% of the time for IRS and 22% for other Federal agencies).

The Commission on Federal Paperwork reports that the five million small businesses spend $15–$20 billion, or an average of over $3,000 each, on federal paperwork. Small businesses are relatively harder hit by federal information requirements than larger firms, according to the report, and often lack the expertise necessary to comply.

The SBA conducted a survey to see the degree to which small businesses were able to pass on paperwork and regulatory costs in higher prices. Fifty-nine percent of the firms said they were able to pass on very little of the cost (less than one-quarter), 14% said some (about one-half), and 26% said almost all.

The Office of Management and Budget has instituted a program to try to reduce government paperwork—including the designation of an agency head responsible for the reporting burden of his agency, ceilings, impact analysis, and clearance procedures for reports—and claims to have reduced paperwork burdens by nearly 10% between 1977 and 1978.

ORIGIN OF GOVERNMENT REPORTING REQUIREMENTS

While federal agencies are the administrators of reporting require-ments, the origins lie in Congress and the executive who use legis-lation or executive orders to obtain information, some of which is, of course, necessary to federal decisions and policy-making. Some-times, too, lobby groups in the form of trade associations seek gov-ernment help in obtaining industry statistics. In short, if government paperwork is to be reduced in the long run, it will have to be done through the political process, including small business firms repre-senting their interests to Congress. If small business firms are to be knowledgeable and make intelligent choices as to what information is essential and which is insignificant and burdensome, they need some idea which agencies are demanding reports. The biggest report load, in terms of man-hours, is represented by the agencies listed below:[7]

DEPARTMENT OR AGENCY	NO. OF REPORTING HOURS, 1977 (IN THOUSANDS)
Health, Education and Welfare	50,585
Labor	20,222
Housing and Urban Development	10,948
Agriculture	9,814
Veterans' Administration	9,472
Transportation	5,589
Commerce	5,640
Energy	5,292
Defense	5,181
Treasury	4,234

(*continued*)

(*cont.*)

DEPARTMENT OR AGENCY	NO. OF REPORTING HOURS, 1977 (IN THOUSANDS)
Justice	3,482
Civil Service Commission	3,470
State	2,434
Interior	1,242
Office of Management and Budget	737
Environmental Protection	600
General Services Administration	471
Railroad Retirement	433
Small Business Administration	193
Other	1,194

ALTERNATIVE APPROACHES TO REDUCE GOVERNMENT COSTS TO SMALL BUSINESS

Clearly, government regulation and reporting requirements are powerful influences in shaping small business survival and cost structure. Government is an active partner in every small firm. Sometimes the government regulations make the small business manager move over while the government runs the firm, even out of business. Seen in this light, government regulation and paperwork are potent and expensive medicine. They adversely affect small business directly—in cost sturcture and time-consumption—and indirectly—in inflation, unemployment, loss of productivity, delays in innovation, loss of capital formation and investment. What can small business do to combat these debilitating influences? Five main measures have been considered to reduce the impact of government on small business. These are:

1. Legislative exemption, in which small firms of a specified size are exempt from laws that would impose a disproportionate burden on them. In the past, it has been very difficult to obtain approval for these exemptions. Testimony against such exemptions is often hostile and such exemptions are often struck from a bill while in committee.

2. The second approach is what Congress has coined *two-tier regulating*. This approach sets different standards for various business size-classes. Representative Andy Ireland (D-Fla.) argues in favor of this approach. He says that uniform treatment under regulation does

not always result in equal treatment. Opponents feel that this kind of legislation is unconstitutional because it violates the equal protection clause.

3. Intervenor funding involves reimbursing individuals for participating in agency rule-making. Unfortunately, as John Lewis, formerly president of the National Small Business Association, points out, "Most small businessmen are too damned busy trying to run their own shops." In fact, businessmen's responses have been small at agencies where these programs exist.

4. Agencies would be forced to reimburse small businessmen who successfully challenge their rulings in court. A survey by the NFIB showed that 85% of its members would favor such a law. However, the time constraints under which the small businessman operates may carry more weight in deciding whether to challenge an agency ruling.

5. The SBA would make loans to cover the cost of compliance. The existing programs of this kind have not been well received by small businessmen.

SUMMARY

Every small businessman has a partner whose name is Uncle Sam. The federal government, as partner, imposes about $3,000 in paperwork costs on small firms and up to $25,000 on average of regulatory costs. Sometimes the federal partner makes regulatory decisions which take over the business and cause it to fail.

The regulatory and paperwork costs represent a disproportionately heavy burden on small business, compared to large companies, because they do not have the staff or sales volume over which to spread the costs. The result is that the costs curve shifts upward for small firms, when new regulatory costs are imposed, more than for large firms, and the dominant firms then gain in market share and competitive position.

The direct impacts of regulation upon small business are upon costs, required actions, contradictory rules, interference with operations, time-consuming intrusions, and adverse small business rulings to which agencies are indifferent.

The indirect impacts of regulation and paperwork are inflation, delay, reduction of innovation, reduced capital investment, unemployment, and diversion of management's time from running the business.

The cost of government paperwork to fill out reports takes 143 million man-hours for agencies other than the IRS. The time and cost of this reporting cannot be passed along in price.

The heaviest reporting requirements, in addition to the IRS, are imposed by the Departments of: Health Education and Welfare, Labor, Housing and Urban Development, Agriculture, Veterans Administration, Transportation, Commerce, and Energy, in that order. The route to reducing reporting is political, since the reports are imposed by Congress.

The five major ways that have been used to reduce regulatory and reporting requirements have been exemption, two-tier regulation, funding participation, reimbursement of legal costs, and loans to cover compliance. Of these, exemption has been the most effective, according to small business, while two-tier regulation and reimbursement of legal costs have been helpful.

REFERENCES

1. House of Representatives, Committee on Small Business: Hearings on *Impact of Federal Regulation on Small Business.* 96th Congress, April 5-May 22, 1979, pp. 67–132.
2. U.S. Chamber of Commerce. *Washington Report,* Vol. 1, No. 40, April 28, 1980, pp. 1–13.
3. *NFIB Mandate* 425, p. 1.
4. Duncan, S.J. "Regulation: It Makes Small Business Less Competitive." *INC,* June 1980, pp. 51–54.
5. Chilton, K.W. "Small Business Survival in a Regulatory Environment." *Proceedings:* Basic Research on Small Business, NFIB, October 10–11, 1978.
6. Weidenbaum, M.L. "The Forgotten Consumer: Hidden Costs of Government Regulation." NFIB Policy Discussion Series.
7. Office of Management and Budget. "Paperwork and Red Tape." A Report to the President and Congress, June 1978, Superintendent of Documents, Washington, D.C. 20402.

12

Measures of Taxation

The government is a partner in small business, not only through regulation and reporting requirements, but also in taking a share of profits through taxation. Taxes are reported by small businessmen to be their second greatest problem after inflation, according to the NFIB's quarterly reports. Taxation is always a problem to everyone, of course, and obviously taxes are an inevitable part of having government. Still, the distribution of taxes among the population and its business institutions raises many issues of fairness and incentives. Small businessmen feel that taxation is unfair to small business relative to large, and, even more serious, taxation provides disincentives for small business to accumulate capital. These disincentives to capital accumulation limit both the startup and growth of new enterprises.

We need to examine and measure the degree to which these allegations of discrimination against small business are true or false. To do so, the following topics will be discussed:

1. The tax structure of business.
2. Measures of effective income taxation by corporate size.
3. Tax reduction methods—expensing, allocation, depreciation, and tax credits.
4. Tax shelters—retirement plans, income property, real estate, executive compensation, tax losses, capital gains.
5. Modifying business and financial plans to optimize after-tax income and wealth—or keeping what is yours.

THE TAX STRUCTURE OF BUSINESS

The tax rates on a business vary depending upon the legal form of organization, that is, whether the firm is a personal proprietorship, a partnership, or a corporation. Proprietorships and partnerships pay income taxes on business income at the same rates as for the individual income taxes. That is, for a business proprietorship, the individual fills out Schedule C (Form 1040) entitled, "Profit or Loss from Business or Profession," and then transfers the net profit or loss to the 1040 form as an element of net taxable personal income to be figured at the individual tax rates. Similarly, for a partnership the form 1065 "U.S. Partnership Return of Income" is completed and the net profit or loss is transferred to the 1040 form to be figured at individual income tax rates. The individual income tax rates are shown in Table 12-1.

Table 12-1. Individual Federal Income Tax Rates, 1979. (includes personal exemptions or zero bracket amounts)

INCOME BRACKET	INCREMENTED TAX RATE
	(%)
$ 3,400–$ 5,580	14
$ 5,500–$ 7,600	16
$ 7,600–$ 11,900	18
$ 11,900–$ 16,000	21
$ 16,000–$ 20,200	24
$ 20,200–$ 24,500	28
$ 24,600–$ 29,900	32
$ 29,900–$ 35,200	37
$ 35,200–$ 45,800	43
$ 45,800–$ 60,000	49
$ 60,000–$ 85,600	54
$ 85,600–$109,400	59
$109,400–$162,400	64
$162,400–$215,400	68
Over $215,400	70

The advantages of proprietorships and partnerships, from a tax standpoint, are: rates are lower on small business incomes, business losses can offset and reduce personal income, and personal tax deductions may, to some extent, offset business income. Also, proprietorships and partnerships are simpler in terms of legal organization costs and corporate reporting requirements.

However, the corporation income tax rates become lower than individual rates when the net taxable income gets above $50,000 or so. This can be seen by comparing the corporate income tax rates in Table 12-2 with the personal income tax rates in Table 12-1.

Table 12-2. Federal Corporate Income Tax Rates.

TAXABLE INCOME	REVENUE ACT OF 1978 (EFFECTIVE FROM 1/1/79)	TAX RATES PRIOR TO 1/1/79
	(%)	(%)
To $25,000	17	20
$25,000–$ 50,000	20	22
$50,000–$ 75,000	30	48
$75,000–$100,000	40	48
Over $100,000	46	48

Prior to 1979, the corporate income tax rate was a flat 48% except for two smaller steps of 20% and 22% on the first two increments of $25,000 in income. The Revenue Act of 1978 tried to make the corporate income tax more progressive and provide for a graduated tax from 17 to 46% as an aid to small business. In fact, the reduction in rates did not do small business much good, because this amount of corporate income taxes paid depends upon a great many other factors, such as the amount of depreciation, deductible business expenses, tax credits, and tax shelters. What really counts, then, is not the nominal tax rates shown above but the effective tax rates of what a firm really has to pay.

MEASURES OF EFFECTIVE INCOME TAXATION BY CORPORATE SIZE

The effective income taxes paid for all manufacturing, mining and trade corporations can be analyzed by size class of business from the *Quarterly Financial Reports* of the Federal Trade Commission. These are shown in Table 12-3.

Table 12-3 shows clearly that the effective tax rate paid by small firms with less than $5 million or $10 million in assets was larger than for the giant corporations of over $1 billion in assets in 1979, even after the supposed lowering of nominal income tax rates. While the nominal corporation income tax rates look progressive (i.e., increas-

Table 12-3. Effective Federal Income Tax Rates
Paid by U.S. Manufacturing, Mining, and Trade
Corporations by Size Class.

	4TH QUARTER OF			
ASSET SIZE	1976	1977	1978	1979
Under $5,000,000	47	35	36	41
$ 5,000,000–$ 10,000,000	47	46	43	48
$ 10,000,000–$ 25,000,000	48	48	47	46
$ 25,000,000–$ 50,000,000	48	46	46	45
$ 50,000,000–$ 100,000,000	45	42	43	40
$100,000,000–$ 250,000,000	47	46	42	42
$250,000,000–$1,000,000,000	40	39	42	37
Over $1,000,000,000	33	37	35	29
Average	38	38	38	34

ing with income), they are in fact regressive (i.e., decreasing with larger income size). How is that possible?

The big corporations have more funds, more choices how to spend their funds, and better accountants and lawyers to choose investments and expenditures which avoid taxes. The result is that the federal income tax system discriminates against small business, which is a very serious issue because retained earnings are the principal means for a small business to grow, especially when small firms do not have access to the capital markets to the same extent as do large firms. The tax structure is partly responsible for squeezing small businesses out of the economy and for their declining share of the national income.

Business pays state and local taxes on corporation net income as well as Federal income taxes. All but five states have corporate income taxes, and while their tax rates and methods vary, their relative burdens can be seen by the amount of revenue they derive from the corporate income tax in relation to (or per $1000 of) personal income in the state. This is shown in Table 12–4.

Most states have a fairly low or flat rate on corporate income as compared to the federal rates. However, many state income taxes on small business are also regressive, because the federal income tax is deductible from the taxable income for the state return. For example, California has a flat 9.6% tax on corporate income (with a $200

Table 12-4. Revenue of State and Local Governments from Taxes on Corporation Net Income, 1976-1977. (per $1,000 of personal income)

RANK	STATE		PERCENTAGE OF U.S. AVERAGE
1.	Michigan	$ 12.84	192.2
2.	California	10.67	159.8
3.	Minnesota	10.53	157.7
4.	Massachusetts	10.38	155.4
5.	New York	10.20	152.7
6.	Alaska	8.99	134.6
7.	Wisconsin	8.93	133.7
8.	Connecticut	8.80	131.8
9.	Pennsylvania	8.72	130.6
10.	Kansas	8.21	122.9
11.	South Carolina	7.27	108.8
12.	Kentucky	7.12	106.6
13.	Delaware	7.10	106.3
14.	Rhode Island	6.96	104.2
15.	Tennessee	6.90	103.3
16.	North Carolina	6.85	102.6
	United States Average	6.68	100.0
17.	Idaho	6.63	99.3
18.	New Hampshire	6.59	98.7
19.	Vermont	6.56	98.2
20.	Arkansas	6.46	96.7
21.	Oregon	6.25	93.6
22.	Georgia	6.20	92.8
23.	New Jersey	6.15	92.1
24.	Maine	6.13	91.8
25.	Montana	5.83	87.3
26.	North Dakota	5.80	86.8
27.	Iowa	5.13	76.8
28.	Virginia	4.99	74.7
29.	Colorado	4.84	72.5
30.	Illinois	4.66	69.8
31.	Ohio	4.60	68.9
32.	Louisiana	4.59	68.7
33.	Oklahoma	4.47	66.9

(continued)

Table 12-4. (cont.)

RANK	STATE		PERCENTAGE OF U.S. AVERAGE
34.	Hawaii	4.45	66.6
35.	Nebraska	4.44	66.5
36.	Mississippi	4.30	64.4
37.	New Mexico	4.09	61.2
38.	Alabama	4.05	60.6
39.	Maryland	4.04	60.5
40.	Arizona	3.93	58.8
41.	Florida	3.83	57.3
42.	Utah	3.78	56.6
43.	Missouri	3.71	55.5
44.	Indiana	2.61	39.1
45.	West Virginia	2.35	35.2
46.	South Dakota	.71	10.6
47.	Nevada	.00	.0
48.	Texas	.00	.0
49.	Washington	.00	.0
50.	Wyoming	.00	.0
51.	District of Columbia	.00	.0

Source: U.S. Department of Commerce, Bureau of the Census.

minimum), but the effective state tax rate amounts to 7.97% on the smallest firms and declines to 5.18% on those with over $100,00 in income. The regressive nature of the state income tax is illustrated in Table 12-5.

Table 12-5. Effective State Tax Rates.

INCOME LEVEL	FEDERAL NOMINAL TAX RATE	STATUTORY STATE TAX RATE	EFFECTIVE STATE TAX RATE
	(%)	(%)	(%)
$ 0–$ 25,000	17	9.6	7.97
$25,000–$ 50,000	20	9.6	7.68
$50,000–$ 75,000	30	9.6	6.72
$75,000–$100,000	40	9.6	5.76
Over $100,000	46	9.6	5.18

The flat (or near-flat) tax rate produces a bias in favor of the large business. A more equitable means of state corporate taxation would be to use a tax rate progressive enough to offset the federal tax. However, if California, for example, were to adopt such a tax structure based on Federal nominal rates, the net loss in state revenues for the 1980–1981 fiscal year could amount to $295 million.

TAX REDUCTION METHODS

Small firms need to become as sharp as large firms in avoiding unnecessary taxes in order to lower their effective tax rates. The main methods of reducing taxes are expensing, allocation, depreciation, and tax credits.

Expensing means to treat expenditures as current expenses rather than capitalizing them as assets. The IRS allows you, within limits, to make a choice on which way to treat expenditures for such items as carrying charges and taxes on unimproved property, development and improvements of real property, R&D expense, development of fuels or mineral property, publisher's circulation expense, and some types of short-lived equipment.[1] The IRS allows this latitude of choice on the part of business, because they figure they will get the taxes sooner or later. If you write off the expenditures as current expenses, you reduce the current year's income tax, but you have to pay more next year and later if the expenditure was a productive one in producing income (which presumably it is or, as a good businessman, you would not have made it). If you elect to capitalize the expenditure and treat it as an investment in an asset, you pay less now and you stretch the tax payments out over the future as the income-producing asset yields new revenue (less depreciation). That is, the choice of expensing or capitalizing an expenditure is a no-lose schedule for the IRS; all they want to know is when they get paid.

However, for the businessman the choice is more significant because his decision on how to treat the expenditure can make a difference in the amount of taxes due. As a general rule, the small businessman should consider treating all expenditures as current expenses which (1) produce little direct increase in revenue or (2) do not appreciate in value. That is, write off everything you can which does not have income potential. Conversely, everything which has large income potential or appreciates in value over time should be capitalized. The reason is that by capitalization you stretch the depreciation charges for the asset into the future to offset the income generated by it, and you take advantage of the lower capital gains tax if you sell an appreciated asset. The Revenue Act of 1978 lowered the top capital gains tax rate from 49% to 28%, so that anything which can be sold for a capital gain will normally be taxed at a lesser rate than current income.

Allocation is the means by which you spread overhead costs over time, i.e., how much to charge off in any one year. Again, the IRS provides latitude as the number of years over which you write off assets as well as the rate at which you write them off. The straight-line depreciation method spreads the capital cost evenly over the years. Faster depreciation methods allowed by the IRS are the sum-of-the-digits or the double-declining balance methods. These methods place more of the depreciation charges in the early years and less later. The faster depreciation methods result in lower income taxes for you in the early years, which is important if you are in an industry with rapidly changing technology, rapid obsolescence, and high rates of profit. The slower depreciation methods are suitable for industries with slow-changing technology and low profit rates.

Other allocation problems include how much to charge the company for your own compensation as chief executive. That is, what is the allocation of the firm's earnings between executive compensation and profit? The IRS will disallow unreasonable compensation on the grounds that it is unreasonably reducing profits and business income taxes. What is reasonable? A rough approximation is that the average chief executive compensation for a business with under $2 million in sales is about $45,000, and over $10 million in sales about $100,000 (in 1980). However, the range of compensation around these averages can be quite wide. For example, the compensation might be 10 to 15% higher than the average for high-profit companies (over 25% after-tax return on capital) or 10% lower for low-profit companies (less than 12% return). Also, the range of compensation may be another 25% lower or 50% higher for extraordinary services of the chief executive officer, such as actually performing two executive jobs, or having a creative and innovative talent with a demonstrably higher market value. However, the more that executive compensation deviates from the general averages, the more justification IRS will require to stand the test of "reasonableness."

Tax credits are incentives offered by the U.S. tax laws to encourage business decisions which are regarded as having a social purpose, for example, increasing employment or increasing productivity through investment. The job credit is based upon the wages paid and reported under the Federal Unemployment Tax Act (FUTA), and generally amounts to about 50% of the new employment created by the business during the year. The investment tax credit is more complicated and generally applies to equipment with a useful life of seven years or more. The investment credit amounts to 10% of the qualifying investment, subject to some limits (like not to exceed the tax liability). There are also energy tax credits, work incentive, and self-employment tax credits.[2]

Small businessmen should study these tax reduction options in order to get their effective tax rate down to the low levels which larger businesses do.

Tax Shelters

The previous section has dealt with various forms of tax *deductions* available to business. In addition, small businessmen should be aware of *tax shelters* which are various forms of investments made deliberately to avoid taxes. The main tax shelters are in retirement plans, income property, real estate, executive compensation plans, tax losses, and capital gains. Other forms of shelter are farming syndicates, oil and gas exploration, producing and holding motion picture films, or leasing personal or tangible property (other than buildings). The tax laws and regulations governing these tax shelters are complex enough so that the advice of an accountant or tax attorney is highly desirable. A simplified explanation of several of these tax shelters may cause a small businessman to explore them further.

Retirement plans allow a business owner or executive to deduct a portion of their retirement contribution from income, thus permitting a tax-free accumulation of a retirement fund, which will later upon retirement be taxed as income at the lower rates of your retirement income.

Executive compensation plans often include stock options, which allow an executive the right to purchase a specified number of shares, at today's price, at some time in the future. If an executive has the option to buy 10,000 shares of company stock at the current price of $20 per share, then in 10 years, with the growth in earnings raising the stock value to $40 per share, the executive can purchase the stock at $20, sell it at $40, and make a $200,000 profit, taxable at the capital gains rate of 28%. The purpose of the stock option, of course, is to motivate the executive to increase the earnings and value of the shares.

Real estate and income property can provide substantial tax shelters through large development and depreciation deductions which are allowable. By charging off equipment, furnishings, and buildings at the most rapid depreciation rates, a property investment can often be made to produce accounting losses, or *negative cash flow,* at the same time that the capital value of the property is increasing. The losses can be taken as deductions from current income, and the capital gain can be realized in the future upon sale of the property at the favorable capital gains tax rate.

Tax losses are sometimes utilized by one business to offset income in another. Suppose you operate a profitable chain of variety stores, and you learn of another variety chain that has been losing money due to poor management. You may find a tax advantage in buying the chain with accumulated tax losses, and then using those losses to offset the profits in your own chain. Of course, this makes sense only if you know you have the management capacity to straighten out the problems of the chain losing money and rehabilitate it to a profitable venture.

Indeed, the cardinal rule of tax shelters is never to invest in them for the shelter alone but only if they make economic sense in contributing to your own business.

Modifying Business Financial Plans for Tax Purposes

Big businesses get their effective income tax rates down to around 30% or less, while small businesses commonly pay 40 to 48% in income taxes. The way to get taxes down is to utilize all the allowable deductions and tax shelters which make sense for your business. This means observing some do's and don'ts in financial and tax planning.

1. Do invest in equipment which will produce an income and upon which you can take investment tax credits.

2. Don't invest in equipment which you do not need or which will not increase your earnings just for the sake of tax credits.
3. Do invest in real income property if you have excess capital and can use part of the space yourself.
4. Don't invest in real property if you are short of capital and if you have no use for part of the space, because you will divert your resources.
5. Do invest in farming syndicates, oil exploration, or moving picture production if it is part of your main line of business because it will provide extra tax deductions.
6. Don't invest in these tax shelters if they are not in your line of business, because they may not contribute to your earnings, merely to your deductions, and you are not likely to know enough about these sidelines to make as good business choices as you can in your own business.
7. Don't try to take a tax shelter deduction for more than the amount of cash or property which you actually have at risk or stand to lose. That is, the IRS imposes an "at risk limitation" on tax shelters which you should recognize.

How then, in light of these do's and don'ts, is it best to proceed?

The best procedure in tax planning is to do exactly as you would do to run the best business you know how to run. That is, prepare careful business and financial plans as shown in Chapters 8 and 9 to produce the best earnings which you possibly can in your present enterprise. Having done that, then go back over all of the items in the financial statements and ask the question, "Are there any choices that I have which will produce just as much income but reduce my income taxes?" For example, should any of the business expenditures be capitalized rather than expensed for tax purposes, or vice versa? Are any of the investments eligible for the investment tax credit, or could you make an alternative investment which would accomplish the same purpose and get the tax credit? Has your increase in employment been sufficient to get the job credit, or could you increase your employment, in lieu of a labor-saving investment, to get a larger job credit than an investment credit? Can the executive retirement deduction be increased, rather than increasing executive salaries, to benefit both the executives and the company from a tax standpoint? Has your business and capital resources grown to a size where you should consider buying rather than leasing commercial property?

In other words, tax planning consists of combing through the financial statements to see what alternative forms of expenditures, investment, or tax treatment you can make to reduce your income taxes. That is not only legal, it is the only sensible way to increase your after-tax income, and to keep what is yours. If the government did not want you to utilize tax deductions, they would not have put them into the law. The tax deductions are there as incentives to encourage certain kinds of business decisions which are regarded as socially desirable, like developing property, investing in productive equipment, or increasing employment. You can think of yourself as being patriotic by fulfilling public purposes, as well as saving yourself tax dollars, by looking for all of the allowable tax reductions which the law authorizes. Besides, it is the only means by which a small business can retain enough earnings to compete with the big businesses that are experts at tax reduction.

SUMMARY

Taxes reduce the ability of a business to use retained earnings to build up their capital funds; this is a serious barrier to small business which has limited access to capital markets. For this reason, small businessmen regard taxes as a problem second only to inflation.

While the corporation income tax rates are nominally progressive, the effective income tax actually paid places a heavier burden on small rather than large businesses because the big companies have more funds, more options on the use of funds, and better accountants and attorneys to keep their taxes down. As a result, even after the 1978 tax bill which tried to make the corporate tax more progressive, the effective income tax rate is still regressive—i.e., hitting small business harder. For example, in 1979, the effective income tax paid by smaller firms was 41 to 49% while the largest corporations (over $1 billion in assets) only paid 29%.

State income taxes generally are at low or flat rates which, taken together with the deductibility of the federal tax, makes the state income tax regressive as well.

The relatively heavy burden of income taxes on small business makes it essential for the small businessman to do tax planning along with his financial planning, in order to take every allowable tax reduction which is available to him. The main tax reductions are in expensing versus capitalization, depreciation, allocations of overhead and compensation, and tax credits. In addition, tax shelters, can be found in retirement and executive compensation plans, real estate, resource development, income property, tax losses, and holding appreciating assets for capital gains. The only important rule is never to make a tax move which does not make sense as a business decision to improve your income-producing capacity.

The main means to take advantage of tax options is to comb through the financial plans (as described in Chapters 8 and 9) and look for sound business choices that will reduce your tax liability. In that way, you will increase your after-tax earnings and keep what is yours. In a sense, that is what this book has been about—a means to help you start a business, survive, develop products, marketing, business and financial plans, and finally to examine your tax options so that you can optimize your income and wealth to keep what you have earned. Good luck! Besides this book, you will need all the help you can get. You are up against the big boys who have more after-tax resources than you have. But you have flexibility and ingenuity on your side. With help and determination, you can win.

REFERENCES

1. See IRS Tax Guide for Small Business 334.
2. The details on all of these tax credits can be found in the above publication.

Index